FIGHTING MEN

A Chronicle of Three Black Civil War Soldiers

by John Zubritsky

BRANDEN PUBLISHING COMPANY
Boston

Library of Congress Cataloging-in-Publication Data

Zubritsky, John.
Fighting men : a chronicle of three black Civil War soldiers / by John Zubritsky.
p. cm.
ISBN 0-8283-1963-4
1. United States--History--Civil War, 1861-1865--Fiction.
2. Afro-American soldiers--Fiction.
3. Afro-American men--Fiction.
I. Title.
PS3576.U2245F54 1994
813'.54--dc20 93-44852
CIP

Entire text was produced with *Pages and Windows* for WordPerfect 5.1 (DOS).

Branden Publishing Company
17 Station Street
Box 843 Brookline Village
Boston, MA 02147

DEDICATION

Then distress fell on the nation,
  And the flag was drooping low;
Should the dust pollute your ban-
    ner?
  No! the nation shouted, No!
So when War, in savage triumph,
  Spread abroad his funeral
    pall--
Then you called the colored soldiers,
  And they answered to your call.

And like hounds unleashed and
    eager
  For the life blood of the prey,
Sprung they forth and bore them
    bravely
  In the thickest of the fray.
And where'er the fight was hot-
    test,
  Where the bullets fastest fell,
There they pressed unblanched
    and fearless
At the very mouth of hell.

From "The Colored Soldiers"
    by Paul Laurence Dunbar

To all the African-American men who fought and died in the Civil War, this novel is respectfully dedicated.

CHAPTER ONE
JULY 1863

ELIJAH DORSEY
Belmont Plantation, near Ellicott Mills, Maryland

First I see just a little dot in the sky way over the trees. And I see the dot circlin' round and round and comin' closer. And I know he's a hawk. I quit hoein' and just watch him ridin' on the wind. Ridin free--goin' where he want ta go, doin' what he want ta do.

I shut ma eyes. Try ta feel what it be like in the sky circlin' round and round like that. Only a soft wind blowin' over me; sun warm on ma back. Lookin' down on Mr. Hammond Dorsey's tabacca fields like they ain't nothin' ta me. Like I can just turn and fly way from 'em forever.

"Lijah," Momma call.

Ma eyes open, and I see the hawk swoop down and ketch somethin' in his claws. Then he swing up just enough ta clear the trees on the other side of the creek.

"Lijah," she call again.

But I don't pay her no mind. I gotta watch him till I can't see him no more. I got this queer tight feelin' down in ma gut. And I keep watchin' till ain't nothin' ta see, but the feelin' keep gettin' tighter and tighter.

Maybe Hawk's gone. But I'm still here...doin' what I done since the sun come up this mornin'. What I done yesteday and every day far back as I can remember--workin' Mr. Hammond Dorsey's tabacca. With the flies and bees buzzin' round ma face. Gnats flyin' in ma eyes and nose. Dust stickin' on ma sweatin' body, linin' ma mouth, chokin' me.

Ma back, ma shoulders achin' so I just can't do no more. I throw down the hoe, stand up straight, stretch till I feel the knots untyin' in ma back. Just rest ma back and stare up through the gray blanket of haze 'tween me and the sun.

"Lijah, you best start choppin' them weeds."

I turn ma head and see Momma. She wearin' old raggedy end of some dress handed down by the Dorseys to they house servants and finally ta Momma. So faded and patched now you can't tell the color.

"Old Taylor ketch you restin', he goin' ta whip you."

"Momma, what past them trees yonder?"

She get a look on her face I ain't seen before. Her voice sound soft and faraway, "I don't know. I ain't never bin over them trees. I ain't never bin nowheres but this here plantation. I born here same as ma momma, same as you. And I bin plantin' the Dorseys' tabacca...and hoein' and cuttin' and strippin' it since I bin a chile. So don't go on like a fool askin' me what's over them trees. Might just as well ask me what's on the moon."

She jerk her head at a white man makin' his way through the tabacca. "Old Taylor comin'. You goin' ta ketch it for sure."

Hot in the cabin t'night. Air heavy with the smell of greens and fatback. I step outside where folks talkin' kinda low and tired-like, half-slappin' at mosquitos. Where kids runnin' round chasin' lightnin' bugs till they tired enough ta sleep. But I ain't got no interest in bein' with them. I stroll up the "street" and head for the field where I was all day. Set down by a big old stump so I can look up at where I saw that hawk.

I set starin' and starin' at the dark line of trees. Like I want them ta tell me about the world. About some place called Balmore where they free black folks who can hide a runaway and help him get someplace safe. But nobody I know, no field hands ever bin there. And from what Momma say, ain't likely I'm ever goin'.

And I get that tight feelin' again. So tight I can't hardly breathe, and I know it ain't just cause so hot t'night.

I get up, walk round.

Don't know why I ain't never thought about bein' off the plantation before. It never bother me I don't know no place but here. T'night, though, it do.

I walk and walk, and a word come in ma head. A word a white man say one day. A white man who came out in the fields, and he said, "Brothers, you must be free. God says you must be free."

Then Old Taylor and some men I never seen before come and run him off. Taylor say don't pay him no mind. He's crazy. Taylor say Mr. Dorsey treat us better'n if we was free niggers.

Funny, bein' here, thinkin' about all that t'night.

Set down again, lean back, close ma eyes. Maybe I sleep, maybe not. But I feel a body next ta me. A voice whisper, "Lijah, why you here by yourself? Everybody's gone ta bed."

Open ma eyes and see Momma. Don't say nothin' cause words hard ta get right in ma head. Finally ask, "Momma, you ever want ta be free?"

It's so quiet I think I hear stars movin'. Her arm go round me. She rest her head on ma shoulder. Answer in a voice make me feel like cryin', "Only a hawk really free."

FLETCHER HOWARD

Fells Point, Baltimore, Maryland

The Union navy need ships. Ta blockade the secesh, chase their warships off the sea, haul soldiers down South. The shipbuilders on Fells Point doin' their best ta give the navy ships. All kinds of ships--side-wheelers, stern-wheelers, barks, frigates, cutters, man 'o wars--bein' built right here.

Air always full of the smell of fresh cut oak and pine, of tar heatin' in caulkin' pots, and of sweatin' men. And seem like the sound of sawin' and chiselin' and hammerin' and cussin' never stop. Not at night, not even on Sunday.

So many hulls bein' worked on here, don't seem like room for 'em all in the harbor or even in Ches'peake Bay.

The noise, the smell, the work don't bother me, Fletcher Howard, free-born black man and paid-up member in the Black Ship-Caulkers' Association. I'm happy workin' twelve hours a day, seven days a week, cause I'm makin' more money 'n I ever make before. And a good thing too since everythin' cost so much on account of the war.

This mornin', like I do every mornin', I sling ma tools on ma shoulder and leave ma house just past where the Philadelphia and Wilmington and Baltimore Railroad tracks cross Dillon Street. Walk a mile straight west till I reach Lucerne Street. Go north ta Canton Avenue, and head west again till I reach Wolfe. Then I turn left on Wolfe and go south till I see William and George Gardner's Ship-Yard on the corner of Lancaster and Wolfe. This mornin', I see more'n I want ta see. I see trouble.

A bunch of dirty-lookin' Micks blockin' a wagon tryin' ta deliver oakum. Driver givin' 'em hard looks and tellin' 'em, "You boys best be gettin' outta me way. I got a delivery here."

One of 'em, a broken-nose, red-head I seen before, yell at him, "Boy-o, ya ain't deliverin' nothin' here, not till I say so. And I ain't sayin' so till the last nigger's outta there."

"Boys," driver say, "your quarrel ain't with me; it's with Mr. Gardner. So, go argue with him and let me do me job."

"Sure we've done that already," Red Head say. "And didn't he tell us ta go ta hell. That it ain't none of our business who he hires ta do his caulkin'. That he'll hire niggers or Chinamen or apes outta the jungle if it suits him--ain't that what he said, boys?"

They agree.

"So, I'm repeatin', boy-o, yer not deliverin' nothin' to Mr. George Gardner, Jr's ship-yard till he fires every last nigger and replaces 'em with good, honest white men--right, boys?"

Ta show how right, they start rockin' the wagon like they goin' ta turn it over.

Driver hold up his hands. "Listen, boys, I'm a workin' stiff same as you. And I ain't got no more love for niggers 'n you. So, let me wagon alone, and I'll haul ass outta here so fast ya won't see nothin' but dust."

"Yer doin' the right thing," they shout, and in a few minutes he's headin' west on Lancaster Street. Watchin', I think on how it usta be. How thirteen years ago, when I started caulkin', no white man would do this "nigger work." Then we sign a agreement with the ship-wrights sayin' we work t'gether on the ships, or don't none of us work. And the war brung so much ship-buildin' we can't hardly keep up. So, now the Micks want ta be caulkers cause it pay a whole lot more'n night-soil collectin' and stevedorin'-- about all they really good for. And they slowly forcin' us outta the trade.

"Hey boys, c'mere and take a look at what I found."

I feel hands grab ma shoulders and turn me round. I see a Mick, face all splotchy red from whisky he bin drinkin'.

Don't say nothin'...too many comin' for me ta start somethin'.

Red Head come over, spread his feet apart, stick his face so close I can see his dirty green teeth, smell what he drunk this mornin'...and last night too.

"And where da ya think yer goin', nigger boy?"

"Work, same as every mornin'."

"Not this mornin' ya ain't, boy-o." His hand grab ma tool bag. "And ya won't be needin' these caulkin' tools anymore."

"Get your dirty Mick hands off me," I say and swing ma bag round hard as I can. It ketch him right in his balls. He fold up and I start runnin' for yonder ship-yard gate. Woulda made it too if I didn't trip on a broken pavin' block and go sprawlin' in the street.

They on me like flies on horse shit. Haul me up on ma feet. One grab holda ma hair and jerk ma head back. Red Head so mad all the veins in his head poundin'. "Ya black bastard, I can have ya arrested for what ya just done. But I'm a kind man, so I'll let ya apologize."

Before he even finish, his knee come up in ma nuts so hard, feel like everythin' inside me broke. Tears in ma eyes, I double over, and his knee ketch me in ma nose. Blood go flyin' everywheres.

"I didn't hear ya," Red Head say, and one holdin' ma hair yank so hard I stand up in spite a the pain.

I figger they kill me anyways, so I spit in his face. Ain't nobody ever goin ta say I apologize ta Micks.

"Ya rotten, fucken nigger bastard. Yer gettin' a lesson now ye'll never forget."

One, two, three his punches slam in ma belly. I double over again. One behind jerk me back up, and Red Head hit me so hard in ma face, I hear knuckles crack. "Jesus Christ, I broke ma fucken hand on his hard nigger head," he yell. Like that a signal, one holdin' me let go, and I fall on the pavin' blocks. All of 'em get in a circle round me and kick at ma ribs, ma face, ma hands holdin' ma balls, ma arms, ma legs, ma ass till I think I be dead soon.

Finally from someplace on other side of the pain, I hear Red Head, "That's enough. He won't show his fucken face on Fells Point no more." He grab ma throat, choke me hard as he can. "Cause if he does, I'll cut his nigger throat wit' a rusty knife."

They walk back over the ship-yard gate, laughin' the whole time. When I can, I get up and limp real slow back home.

"So, what do we do now?" ma wife ask. "Winter comin' on and you got no work."

I look around the small whitewashed room, at the pine table and chairs thrown out by white folks we fixed and painted. At the curtains Rebeccah made from scraps white ladies give her. At the gaps in the walls we gotta chink up before it's cold outside. At the rickety ladder goin' up to the loft where we sleep with our chil'ren. At the Bible that's bin in ma family since ma grandfather was a young man.

"What're you talkin' about, no work. Tomarra, I'm goin' ta the ship-yard same as everyday. Show them Micks, Fletcher Howard ain't afraid. They can't take ma job away."

She look me hard in the eye. "And didn't they swear ta kill you if you come back?"

"You don't understand. I got a responsibility to ma brothers in the Association. I gotta fight for 'em, for what we built these last fifteen years. I can't just turn tail and hide in ma house while a bunch of cheap-whisky-drinkin' Irish take over work black men bin doin' since Frederick Douglass himself work in that same ship-yard."

"What about your responsibility ta me...ta them?" She point up ta young black faces pearin' down from the loft. "Suppose you go back tomarra and fight them Micks. And they kill you. Then--what me and the chil'ren do? I can't make enough money ta pay rent and feed us all. What're we suppose ta do--beg in the streets?"

Deep in her eyes I see love and worry and fear all mixed t'gether. I hate seein' her go through this. I hate havin' ta choose 'tween takin' care of her and our chil'ren and standin' up for what I know's right. I hate them Micks so much I could kill every damn one of 'em.

"Woman, you ain't gotta tell me that." I walk over by the Bible. I'm so mad I don't feel the pain in ma ribs, ma belly, ma balls. "Always same goddamn thin', ain't it?"

I open the Bible, point ta names on the first page. "Ma family ain't bin slaves for seventy-five years. Ever since Old General Howard himself free ma grandfather after the Revolutionary War. But it don't mean nothin'. Cause we can only work where white folks say we can. Can only live where white folks let us. Can only be paid what white folks want ta pay us. And we can't vote. Can't even own the shacks we live in. Got ta pay rent to a white man so five of us can live like pigs."

"We gotta have same rights as white folks, or we're no better'n slaves." I pick up the Bible, ready ta fling it against the wall.

"Don't you dare," she say.

I put it back down. "If this war only about freein' slaves, then it's a bigger joke 'n I even think. Cause at the end, a whole lot of black folks down South goin' ta find out freedom without rights don't mean a damn thing."

AUGUSTUS T. ALEXANDER
Office of the Secretary of War, Washington, D.C.

The man sitting behind the desk is short. All I can see is the top of his head, sorta shiny from the gaslight over us. He is reading the letter I sent President Lincoln last January, reading the words I can still see clearly in my mind:

Toronto, Canada West
Jan. 7th /63

Sir,

Having seen that it is intended to garrison the U.S. forts with colored troops, I beg leave to apply to you for an appointment as surgeon to some of the colored regiments, or as physician to some of the depots of 'freedmen.' I was compelled to leave my native country, and come to this one on account of prejudice against color, for the purpose of obtaining a knowledge of my profession; and having accomplished that object, at one of the principal educational institutions of this Province, I am now prepared to practice it, and would like to be in a position where I can be of use to my race.

If you will take the matter into favorable consideration, I can give satisfactory reference as to character and qualification from some of the most distinguished members of the profession in the city where I have been in practice for about six years.

I Remain Sir,
Yours Very Respectfully,

Augustus T. Alexander
Bachelor of Medicine, Trinity College

Finished, the Secretary of War studies me for some time before he asks, "You wrote this letter to President Lincoln back in January?"

"Yes, Mr. Stanton, right after he issued the Emancipation Proclamation."

"Then what happened?"

"Well, sir, in March I sent my credentials to the Army Medical Board, but they turned me down. They thought because I was in Canada, I was a British subject. Then, I wrote to Surgeon General Hammond in April telling him I was born in Virginia and offered to provide proof I was."

Stanton takes off his glasses, blows on them, gives them a few wipes with a large white handkerchief he pulled out of a drawer.

"What was General Hammond's reply?"

He told me if I wanted to appeal the board's decision, I needed to come to Washington. I could not do it by letter."

I feel myself getting mad again. Mad as I was that day in Toronto when I read Hammond's letter the first time. Mad as when I realized I was being, politely but firmly, put in my place. Mad as when I made up my mind I would come to Washington and fight.

"So, you took General Hammond at his word and came here?"

"Yes sir, at great personal expense and inconvenience. But I meant what I said in my letter to President Lincoln. I want to be of service to my race, whether with a colored regiment or in a camp."

Stanton gives me a puzzled look over top of his glasses. "Your appeal must have been successful. I have a copy of Special Orders 109 assigning you to the Camp for Colored Persons under a Captain Farrar."

I forget myself for a minute and lean over Stanton's desk, "Well sir, the trouble is the board was so impressed with my letters of recommendation that it commissioned me...a brevet major. And when I reported to the camp, Captain Farrar looked at me and said he could not have an assistant surgeon who outranked him."

Stanton gets up and walks over to a big window and stands there staring out of it for some time. So long, I start worrying he is trying to find the words to tell me to go back to Canada.

"Major Alexander, you have my solemn word you will be the chief surgeon of the next colored regiment the army recruits."

CHAPTER TWO
AUGUST 1863

Special Orders
No. 293

HEAD-QUARTERS,
MIDDLE DEPARTMENT
EIGHTH ARMY CORPS.
Baltimore, August 15th, 1863

This order extends the authority granted in Special Order No. 202, dated June 27th, 1863, to wit:

1. Free-born colored men may be accepted for enlistment immediately. Penalties for interference on the part of former masters or employers are set out in Appendix A.

2. Bondsmen may be enlisted only if their masters consent. Further, such masters must be judged loyal to the Union.

3. Masters so judged will be entitled to compensation from a commission to be established for that purpose.

4. If thirty days from the issuance of this order, recruiting goals have not been met, I hereby authorize that bondsmen whose masters have not sworn the oath of loyalty may be enlisted without said masters' consent.

By Command of Major Gen. Schenck;

Samuel B. Lawrence,
Asst. Adjt. Genl.

ELIJAH DORSEY
Belmont Plantation

I'm workin' on fences day recruitin' men come. They five white and two black ones. They all dressed in blue uniforms but the colored men's kinda big. But them two got a look on their face like I never seen before on no black man's face. All the hands stop workin' cause they never seen nothin' like them two in blue uniforms.

"Who told ya ta stop?" Old Taylor ask. Then he see the recruitin' men. I never seen nobody surprised as him.

"What the hell are they supposed ta be?" he ask.

"Soldiers in the United States Army," the fattest of the white men say. I kinda felt sorry for his horse carryin' that much weight.

"Soldiers? They look more like the dressed up monkey I seen one time in Balmer. Fellow playin' a hurdy-gurdy had him on a leash collectin' money from the crowd." Taylor, he start laughin'. "Maybe you oughta have one for them, too."

I see the black men's jaws tighten up and they look like they ready ta kill Old Taylor. One of the white men see it too and shake his head.

"I can assure you," say the fat one, "these men <u>are</u> soldiers in the Union army. And as soon as the Fourth Regiment, U.S. Colored Infantry is full, they will be off fighting the Rebels right beside their white brothers."

Taylor shake his head. "I don't believe that--not in a million years."

Maybe Old Taylor don't believe it, but I do. Black men fightin' gainst the rebels same as whites. I see maself in one of them uniforms. Soon as I think that the tight feelin' I bin carryin' in ma gut start loosenin'. And I start feelin' I can be free...like the hawk.

"It may interest you to know, sir, I am empowered to recruit not only free coloreds, but slaves as well."

The fat man hold up a paper for Taylor to read. Course he don't know, Taylor can't read no better'n me.

Taylor he don't even look at it. "I don't care nothin' for you, your paper, or Mr. Abraham Lincoln either. You and them...them goddamned monkeys get off Mr. Dorsey's property, or I'll personally shoot all of you."

Then, Taylor look at us. "And don't you get any fool ideas in them black heads. You belong to Mr. Hammond Dorsey, and you ain't goin' nowheres less he say so."

"Not necessarily true, my friend," say the fat man. "If I don't reach my recruiting goals in 30 days, I can come back and enlist them all...without your Mr. Dorsey's consent."

I feel like he sayin' them words right ta me. So I ask him, "If a black man like me join this here regiment, he be free?"

"The process of manumission...freeing...wouldbegin as soon as he enlisted," the fat man say and give me kinda a wink.

Taylor's face get all tight. He look ready ta kill somebody. "Mister, you just try comin' back here and takin' any of these boys without Mr. Dorsey's say-so. You just try it and see what happens to you."

The fat man he stare straight back at Old Taylor. "The name is Birney, Colonel William Birney, United States Army. And I will be back, if I need any of them. And neither you nor Mr. Dorsey will be able to stop me. But for now, I bid you a good-day, sir." He dig his spurs into his horse, and the others follow.

One black man, the one who want to hit Old Taylor, look back at me. I know I goin' ta see him again.

Taylor lean way outta his saddle, say loud enough for everybody ta hear, "Lijah, you and the others forget any ideas you got about runnin' away. Only place you goin' is back to the south field. Now move."

Walkin' down that hot dusty road I still see them two black men in blue uniforms. Make me think about how I look in a blue uniform. Make me think how I'm gettin' free.

Late that night I tell Momma I'm runnin' away.

"Lijah, how you goin' ta find that white man? You ain't never bin off this here plantation? You goin' ta get lost or worse patrollers ketch you. Then, anythin' can happen."

I know what she really sayin'...she don't want me ta go. I put ma arm round her. "Momma, Colonel Birney gotta be in Balmore, and everybody know you just follow the creek over yonder to the Patapsco River and the river go right there."

She look up at me, and I see she cryin'. "Son, knowin' how ain't the same as gettin' there." She put her arms round me, squeeze me real tight. "It just ain't that easy. You can get hurt...or shot. And since your Daddy sold before the war, you all I got in this here world."

I kiss her forehead. "Momma, I knowed what you sayin' true, but I gotta go and join the army cause that's only way I ever be free. Time the war over, I come back and take you with me. I swear it."

She hug me harder. "Lijah, I love you, and I pray Jesus keep you safe, and everythin' work out the way you say."

ELIJAH DORSEY
Camlin's Slave Pen, Baltimore, Maryland

Momma was right. I get over Balmore, no trouble. But time I do, patrollers ketch me, and put me in this here slave pen. I don't give no trouble, so they don't shackle me like they done William Sims and Charles Foote and a whole bunch of others. Them men can't do nothin' all cept set on benches and stare at the high brick wall and three rows of stinkin' jail cells that close us in.

Just like over Belmont, every day here the same. Mornin' time, a white man cut on the hydrant and I help fill big wooden tubs with water for the day. Then, the women wash clothes and I hang up lines for the dryin'. Maybe sometimes, I play with the little boy what was birthed here. His momma, Betsey Ward, bin here 'most two years. Somctimes, I take water to the men in shackles. Can't hardly move they got so much iron on their ankles. But mostly, I just walk round and round the brick courtyard--twenty steps over, forty down, twenty back, forty up. Over and over till I'm hungry enough ta eat, or either tired enough ta nap over in the corner.

Night time, I'm locked in a cell with two men and a boy about twelve. The straw stink from bein' pissed on and it crawlin' with bugs. Ain't never really tired enough ta sleep, so I just lay awake thinkin' how I ain't no better off here than I was over Belmont. Maybe worse off cause I miss Momma and the other folks I knowed all ma life.

Nappin' in the corner this afternoon, and I hear a commotion. Somebody yellin' real loud. Sound like Old Jones, the white man what run this pen, and he real mad about somethin'. He yell so loud women stop washin' clothes. Sims and the other shackled mens starin'. I gotta see what the fuss all about.

First, I don't see nothin' cept Jones and the scabby-face one he call Slim. Then, I seen Colonel Birney just standin' and waitin' while Jones yellin' and wavin' his arms in the air.

Finally, I guess Colonel Birney have enough cause he say, "I repeat, Mr. Jones, I do have the authority. Paragraph 10 of Special Order 202 issued by General Robert Schenck, commander of the Middle Department and 8th Army Corps, says 'Colonel William Birney is authorized to proceed to Camlin's Slave pen in Pratt Street and enlist the slaves of Gen'l Stuart and other Rebels and Rebel sympathizers incarcerated there in the service of the United States--and liberate all others confined there.'"

I'm sure I'm dreamin'. So, I pinch ma arm hard till I feel the pain. No, I ain't dreamin'.

"And I repeat, Colonel, none of General Stuart's slaves are here. They're all in City Jail. So you and them Union-suited baboons go over there, and let an honest man go about his business." And Jones he smile like he just told off Abe Lincoln hisself.

Birney, he don't even raise his voice. "The order says that I can enlist the slaves of 'other Rebels and Rebel Sympathizers incarcerated there.'" He point at me. "Does your master support the rebels?"

"Yes sir," I say.

He point to Henry Toodles standin' next ta me, "Does yours?"

"Yes sir."

Colonel ask every one, even the little boy, same question. And he get the same answer.

"You see, Mr. Jones, all of these good folks are the property of secessionists, and this order gives me all the authority I need. Now, please stand aside, or I will let these, what did you call them...baboons in blue...have the untold satisfaction of shooting you."

Jones he look at Colonel Birney; then, he look at the two soldiers; then, he step aside.

FLETCHER HOWARD

Pratt Street, near Camlin's Slave Pen

Stevadorin' ain't the kind of work I like. Hard on the arms and legs and extra hard on the back. But the only work I can get now. Now that the Micks takin' over ship-caulkin'.

Every mornin' no later than six o'clock, I'm down here on Pratt Street or even over on Light Street lookin' for a ship ta load or unload. Don't usually take long ta find one cause the army seem ta need everythin' from locomotives to blankets.

This mornin' start out same like any other. Foreman give us black men the heavy machinery ta unload, and he give whites the easy stuff. Only four of us ta carry off all the heavy wooden crates. After a couple hours, I'm so tired, I can't hold on the crate, and ma end crash on the deck.

Foreman come runnin' over. "What the hell's the matter with you, boy? I oughta kick yer nigger ass for bein' so damned clumsy."

It bin workin' on me since them Micks beat me and stole ma job. Bin eatin' away at ma insides, so I can't think about nothin' else. All of a sudden, I can't stop it pourin' out ma mouth. "I ain't clumsy, I'm just tired. You got four black men bustin' their balls, and a bunch of white boys just playin' like they workin'. How come? And how come they get more money and don't never get the hard work?"

It's all out now. And for a minute, so quiet you can hear seagulls squawkin' at each other.

For a part of the minute, he stare at me like I got snakes crawlin' out ma ears. Don't even look like he breathin'. Then, the great dirty hole he call a mouth open up. "Who the fuck ya think yer talkin' to, nigger? I don't have ta explain anythin' ta you or any other black-faced baboon. So, get the fuck back ta work or get the fuck off this wharf."

He turn his back and start walkin' away. I know I shouldn't say no more. I bin trained since a chile not to. But I got to--cause I may never get another chance.

"I can't accept that," I say quietly. "We work harder and get less pay. And that ain't fair."

"Oh, it ain't? Well, boy-o, let me tell you this--nothin' ta do with niggers has ta be fair."

"I think you wrong. I think this war about makin' things fair for black folks," I say loud so the big crowd of black and white men standin' round us can hear. Some black ones nod their heads, say "Amen, brother."

Foreman stick his face up next ta mine, show his dirty green teeth. "If these was normal times, I'd have yer black ass in jail. But they ain't. So the best I can do is see ya don't work on this or any wharf in Balmer again. Now, get the fuck outta here."

So now I sit here cross the street from where I worked. Tryin' ta think what ta do next. How can I tell Rebeccah, I ain't got a job again, and ain't likely ta get one soon?

Then, I hear a big commotion over by the slave pen. Some loafers from the corner start runnin' that way, but I ain't interested. I seen them poor runaways before, and hear how they wail and cry time their masters come for 'em. No, I got ma own problems, so I just set starin' at the ships.

But I hear more and more folks runnin'. Then more shoutin', but it ain't sad like I heard before. So now, I got ta see what's happenin'.

Over at the slave pen, a big crowd of black folks's standin' and cheerin'. Can't see anythin' so I ask a brother, "What's happenin'?"

"Some white man from the army come and free everybody inside."

We wait till heavy old door start swingin' open. Nobody ain't sayin' a word, just waitin', holdin' their breathes.

Then a fat white man in a blue army uniform come out. Next come some black men in uniforms. Last come about 20 or 30 brothers and sisters, smilin' and wavin' and laughin' and cryin'. Then I see they got no chains, no manacles on.

"Praise God Almighty," somebody call out, "they free."

The crowd open and let 'em pass, cheerin' and hollerin' like you never heard before. Louder and louder till you can't hear yourself think.

And it don't stop when they start on down Pratt Street and turn on Light. Crowd follow after so the whole thing look like a parade with the fat white soldier leadin' it.

Since I got nothin' ta do, I follow 'em too. Whole time, I keep thinkin', You fools think your troubles all over. But just you wait. They just beginnin'.

The parade stop over near Fort McHenry at a place called Birney Barracks. Ain't nothin' special, just some brand new wooden buildings around a dusty, weed-filled lot. Then, the fat soldier--somebody call him Colonel Birney--tell the women ta go inside one of the buildings. He say, "You men come and listen to me for a minute. I got something important to tell you."

I go over with 'em so I can hear.

He say, "Colored men, I freed you from that terrible slave pen because I believe that no one has the right to hold another human being in bondage. I believe that you have as much right to be free as any white men has."

They like the sound of that.

"But you will not be free long, not while the scourge of slavery remains. Not while the rebels hold many, many of your brothers and sisters in cruel, inhuman bondage. Not while, in this very state of Maryland, the evil system prospers."

Two or three say, "Uh huh," and I know this Colonel Birney got the gift. He could be a preacher for sure.

"No, gentlemen, the only way you and your women and your children will ever be truly free is when the beast of slavery is destroyed forever. And the only way to destroy it is to crush the secesh rebels and free every last slave in the Confederacy."

Black heads noddin', black voices sayin' "Tha's right."

"And you, my friends, can help. I have been authorized by the Secretary of War to recruit a second colored regiment from Maryland. A regiment of black soldiers to fight alongside the brave men of the 4th U.S. Colored Troops, alongside the brave white soldiers who have fought and died for <u>you</u> for over two years. Now, I am asking you to step forward...enlist in the 7th U.S. Colored Regiment. Freedom will be yours only if you are willing to fight for it."

He stop and they press round him, wavin' hands and beggin' ta go fight the rebs. I ain't so sure they know what they gettin' into. I turn and start walkin' away.

"What about you?" a voice behind me ask.

"Why I should join, I'm free now." I answer over ma shoulder.

"This war is about more than just freeing slaves. It's about education, employment, voting--in short, it's about equality... for you, for the slaves, for everyone."

I turn round. I ain't really surprised ta see Colonel Birney. "I ain't heard nobody else say that except Frederick Douglass."

"Not yet you haven't, but you will. Remember a year ago, President Lincoln was still insisting this war was to save the Union. It only took the victory at Antietam to change his mind. And once you black men give him some more victories, you will see how quickly he'll listen to your demands for full equality."

Ain't no doubt, Colonel Birney got the gift. I'm almost ready ta go off and fight, but I think about Rebeccah and ma chil'ren. "I can't just go off and join the army. I got a wife and chil'ren ta keep."

"The army pays a private ten dollars a month, plus three dollars for uniforms. It's not much, but it'll help keep their body and souls together until the war's over. Then, think what a bright future you'll all have."

What can I do? He seem ta know everythin' in ma heart, and he say all the right things. "O.K.," I say, "I will join your new regiment."

"You will never regret it," my friend.

MAJOR AUGUSTUS T. ALEXANDER
Birney Barracks Baltimore, Maryland

Mr. Stanton was good as his word. He made me a chief surgeon, but so far the 7th Regiment, U.S. Colored Troops, is only a handful of recruits. However, Colonel Birney returned from Camlin's Slave Pen, and maybe he found some healthy men there, although I doubt it. Folks kept cooped up in slave pens are usually ailing.

"Major Alexander, we got some more recruits for you."

"How many, Lieutenant Califf?"

"Twenty-seven and all eager to join the army and fight the secesh. And all they need now is your usual fine medical examination."

The sarcasm was unmistakable, and Lieutenant Mark A. Califf intended it that way. Never openly hostile nor disrespectful, he and the other officers make it very clear they have no use for me. A black enlisted man is one thing--it's perfectly "natural" for white men to boss darkies...even in the army. But a black officer...and a major at that...why it's unthinkable. Why it's...it's...anabomination. No, I never actually heard anyone say anything like that, but I could tell those thoughts were in their minds when I first came here. In fact, are still in their minds.

"Then, I better not keep them waiting. On your way out, tell Sergeant Anderson to send the first one in."

For a moment he stares at me, no doubt weighing whether he has been given a direct order or merely a request. Deciding it must have been an order, he draws out the "y-e-s s-i-r" to show his displeasure, then leaves.

"What's your name?"

"Lijah."

"Elijah what?"

"Just Lijah."

"Sorry, who was your master and where were you born?"

"Mr. Hammond Dorsey, and I was born on Belmont Plantation."

"All right, from now on you are Elijah Dorsey. Do You understand?"

He nods energetically.

"Open your mouth, please."

His jaw stays clamped shut. His eyes tell me not to force the issue.

"Elijah, I have to look at your teeth. The army won't take you if you don't let me see them."

Reluctantly, the jaws open a little. I gesture with my hand. Then, they slowly open all the way.

I am pleased to see that he has all of them and they are in reasonably good condition.

"Now, Elijah, please remove your shirt."

Again, I am pleased to see he has no scars, lesions or skin ulcers. His back is broad and straight. His muscle tone is excellent. Apparently Mr. Hammond Dorsey was not a cruel master.

"Now, drop your trousers."

A quick check reveals a powerful set of legs and no evidence of hernia or venereal disease.

"You appear to be in very good health, Mr. Elijah Dorsey. Please take this piece of paper to the sergeant in the other room. He will tell you what to do next."

A few moments later, the next one enters the examining room.

"What is your name, who was your master, and where were you born, please?"

"Fletcher Howard and I never call no man master."

Outside, it is a warm Maryland afternoon. The summer heat is temporarily gone. The sky is blue and clear; the way it was in Toronto. Even though it is not quite seven o'clock, the sun is already settling low on the horizon throwing long shadows across Colonel Birney's "parade ground". All in all not the worst day to be sworn into the army.

The new recruits are lined up at the wrong end and are squinting at the flag waving half-heartedly in the weak breeze. They are wearing odds and ends of clothing that are little more than rags, but the rags do not shame the recruits as much as the white folks who once owned or employed them.

The adjutant calls them to attention. "I do solemnly swear to defend the Constitution of the United States," Colonel Birney begins.

There is so much hope on the black faces and enthusiasm in the voices that I feel a lump in my own throat. And I pray silently that they, we, will not be betrayed. That the Union we are being asked to fight and die for will not abandon us when the war is over.

CHAPTER THREE
SEPTEMBER 1863

FLETCHER HOWARD
Near Union Bridge, Maryland

"Where do you think you're goin' with them niggers?"

Old Creager, he look over the private who ask that question. Then, Creager he spit a long brown stream that don't all make it past the end of his beard. "I'm takin' 'em to Union Bridge ta git the train for Balmer."

"No, you ain't. Major Cole sent me to take you back to Frederick. Colonel Maulsby wants to talk to you."

Creager spit out some more tabacca juice, then kinda squint at the private, who's tryin' real hard to look older than he is. "And just what the hell does your Colonel Maulsby want ta talk about?"

"I don't know. But I know you better come with me."

Creager take a folded up piece of paper outta his pocket and wave it in the air. "Look, sonny, you go back and tell your Major Cole and your Colonel Maulsby too that ole J.P. Creager's got an order signed by General Schenck himself authorizing him to recruit in these parts. He aims to do just <u>that</u>. And nobody better try and stop him."

Creager dig his spurs in the side of his horse and wave his hand for me and the twenty black men we recruited from Carroll Manor ta follow. The private he just set there on his horse watchin' us. Then, he turn back toward Frederick City. And I get a feelin' we ain't seen the last of him.

"I sure told that kid off, didn't I?" Old Creager say.

"Maybe, but I think you goin' ta need that order from the general before this day's over."

He start laughin', "You mean this?"

He open up the piece of paper, show it ta me. "This ain't nothin' but a letter from ma wife tellin' me the baby's got the croup."

In Union Bridge, they're waitin' for us. Eight mounted soldiers, one of 'em the private, who point out Creager to a major with a face full of red whiskers and the hardest lookin' eyes ever I seen. Old Creager ain't bluffin' him so easy.

The major don't waste no time. "Let me see your recruiting authorization from General Schenck."

Creager look at the major, then at the private, then at the major again. "I don't have the order from the general with me, but I do have a letter from Colonel Birney that says about the same thing."

The major glare at the private, who seen somethin' on the ground and won't look up at nobody.

"And just who the hell is this Colonel Birney?"

Creager puff himself up like a tom cat ready ta fight. "Colonel William F. Birney is the Superintendent of Colored Recruiting for the entire state of Maryland. That's who he is."

"Indeed...then may I read his letter of authorization?"

Creager unbutton his shirt pocket, take out a dirty, folded up piece of paper and start to open it up. The major snap, "Never mind, I can do that."

He read it, then look Creager right in the eye. "You had better come back to Frederick City with me. Colonel Maulsby will want to talk to you further about this business."

"You got a writ to arrest me?" Creager ask, his face gettin' real tight-lookin'. "Cause, if you don't, I'm not goin' nowheres except ta Balmer with these men. That letter makes it real clear I'm an agent of the United States Army bein' paid to recruit for a new colored regiment. And you, an officer in the same army, got no business interferrin'."

For a minute or two, I think Creager goin' ta bluff his way out again.

"It just so happens, you nigger-lovin' sonofabitch, I do. And it charges you with inciting slaves to leave their rightful owners. That's a very serious crime in this state."

He slip his pistol out the holster. "Now, are you coming peacefully, or do I have to shoot you for resisting arrest?"

The color drain outta Creager's face. I feel everythin' knot up inside me. Before I really know it, I hear me sayin', "Why you arrestin' him? He only doin' his job, gettin' more soldiers for the Union army. And what do you care if these black men be free or not? Ain't you heard this war now about endin' slavery? Ain't President Lincoln himself said so?"

Creager's mouth open like he goin' ta say somethin', but nothin' come out. Major Cole he just stare at me, not sayin' a word.

"And since Creager only doin' what President Lincoln want him to, you oughta let him alone."

I see the pistol come at ma head. See it but can't move fast enough. It ketch me just over ma left ear so hard, I see hot little lights where Creager and the major was. Feel warm blood tricklin' down ma neck.

"You listen to me, you black bastard." I shake ma head, everythin' kinda blurry. "Old Abe didn't free nobody in the state of Maryland. And until he does, a man's property is still a man's property. So, I'm arresting your white friend for inciting, and you for resisting arrest. And if you open your mouth again or make any funny moves, you're a dead nigger."

Sept. 19th 1863

Dear Col. Birnie,
Under the circumstances I thought best to write to you again not haveing heard from you either as to my dispatch or letter. As I informed you earlier, I am held on $1,000 bail, which I have not bin able to raise since everybody here calls me nigger lover, etc. On Monday I sent for an attorney who frankly told

me that he was proslavery & was opposed to taking negros into the army. He examined your letter to me and said you would have to come here to verify its authenticity. He wants to charge me $50 to get me out on Habeus Corpus, but I don't have any money. Can you send me some? That soldier you sent with me, Fletcher Howard, got pistol whipped by the Major Cole who arrested me. Howard told him he had no business arresting me. I hear they got him over in a cell with the boys we were bringing you for the 7th. They might be giving him a real bad time over there, so please send enough money to get him out too. Better yet, why don't you come? I believe they will listen to you.

J.P. Creager
Written at Frederick City, Md.

FLETCHER HOWARD
Frederick City, Maryland

Time Colonel Birney get here, they take us up before the judge. First time I bin outta that cell since we bin arrested. Ma head still hurtin' from the beatin' they give me the first night for bein' a "uppity nigger." Ma ribs still sore from Major Cole's kicks when I can't stand up for no more of his punches in ma guts. The colonel don't hardly recognize me ma face so swelled up.

The judge me and Creager and the colonel standin' in front of look like he just got outta the bed. I can see his night shirt stickin' out round his collar. And he don't look too happy about bein' here this time of night.

First question he ask, "William Birney, huh, are you related to that no good Abolitionist, James G. Birney?"

The Colonel say he is and proud of it too. Then, the judge ask if Birney tell Creager he can steal property away from rightful owners. Birney say, "No man has the right to own another man."

"And I say that this so-called recruiting agent of yours was stealing slaves legally owned by citizens of this state and that under the laws of Maryland, he is guilty of a crime...and so are you."

The colonel got his back up now. He pull out his copy of General Schenck's order. "Your honor, this is a copy of General Order No. 329. Are you familiar with it?"

The judge's glare say he ain't.

"Well, this document gives me and my agents the authority to recruit free black men and those owned by masters who have not sworn the oath of loyalty to the Union."

"Let me see that."

The colonel hand him the order, and the judge he study it some time. "I don't believe this. Major Cole, did you know about this order?"

"Yes, but I never actually read it."

"Well, you'd better listen real close, then go wake up Colonel Maulsby and tell him what you heard."

Major Cole's face got the look on it like he ain't goin' ta appreciate what he about ta hear, but they ain't a damned thing he can do about it.

I know I always goin' ta remember that judge with the frock coat coverin' his nightshirt readin' out loud while the smoky light from one lamp throw shadows all around the little courtroom in Frederick City. I know I'm always goin' ta remember the words,

"If thirty days from the issuance of this order, recruiting goals have not been met, I hereby authorize that bondsmen, whose masters have not sworn the oath of loyalty, may be enlisted without said masters' consent.

/signed/ Robert C. Schenck, General
Commander, Middle Department"

I'll never forget how I feel time Colonel Birney say <u>no</u> to the judge's question, "And have your recruiting goals been reached?"

Or when the judge say, "I have no choice, Major Cole, but to release the agent, J.P. Creager, the soldier Fletcher Howard, and the darkies they were escorting to Baltimore. Unless, you have a record somewhere their masters took the oath of loyalty."

The major don't look so fierce as he did time he was kicking ma private parts or ma ribs. "You know we don't."

"Case dismissed," the judge say, soundin' more tired than sorry. "Now, let's all go back to bed."

CHAPTER FOUR
OCTOBER 1863

Special Orders
No. 1206

HEAD-QUARTERS
MIDDLE DEPARTMENT,
EIGHTH ARMY CORPS
Baltimore, Oct. 7, 1863

On October 20, 1863, the Seventh Regiment, United States Colored Troops will proceed to Brown's Wharf. There it will board the steamer, John Tracy, for shipment to Camp Stanton, Md. for training.

By Command of Maj. Gen. Schenck;

Elias Livingston,
Asst. Adjt. Gen'l.

ELIJAH DORSEY
Camp Stanton, near Benedict, Maryland

Time we march to the wharf, look like half the white folks in Balmore waitin' for us. They line up on both sides of the street and yell, "Back to the plantation, niggers," and "The Confederates got plenty of hot lead for you goddamned monkey soldiers." And some boys run up and spit on us. I like to shoot a couple, but Lieutenant White he say, "Eyes straight ahead, men. They're nothing but secesh trash."

Some sweet white ladies they stick out their tongues at us. Hard not to laugh they look so stupid. But nobody throw nothin' at us, so we get to the wharf without any real trouble.

The colonel he want us on the John Tracy soon as we get there. But the steamer ain't ready, so we set round for two, maybe three hours. Some play cards. Most just stand in small bunches talkin' about what the war goin' ta be like time we done trainin'. One or two brag on how many secesh they goin' ta kill, or either what they goin' ta do time they see old master or overseer. Most of us don't pay no mind ta that kinda talk.

Finally, the John Tracy get up steam. The crew throw off the lines, and she start backin' away from the wharf. Everybody start cheerin' and poundin' backs and cheerin' some more. And we keep it up till we head out to the harbor.

Then, everythin' get real quiet. Don't nobody say nothin'. Like maybe they thinkin', same as me, about their Mommas or maybe about their wifes and chil'ren. Maybe wonderin', same as me, they ever goin' ta see 'em again. They ever goin' ta see anybody or anythin' they know again.

Don't really know what I expect the army camp ta look like. Maybe full of smart-lookin' soldiers marchin' and bands playin' and flags wavin'. But standin' on the John Tracy this evenin' lookin' through the rain, what I see ain't impressin' me none. Benedict just a bunch of small houses and a white wood church. Another small buildin' that may be a store. Couple rickety lookin' wharfs stickin' out in the Patuxent River. Over on ma right, a good piece away from Benedict, I can see rows of tents. Everythin' I see look cold, wet and muddy. I got this feelin' that must be Camp Stanton. And I also got this feelin' like ma guts sinkin' down in that mud.

FLETCHER HOWARD
Camp Stanton

Rain finally stop this mornin'. Make me feel good so I don't mind I bin wet since I got here. And ma blue wool uniform smell like an old hound dog too long in the rain. No, the sun shinin' this mornin' and I don't mind soakin' ma hardtack in the coffee so I can eat it. And I don't mind Lieutenant White fallin' us out for drill soon as we finish. And I don't mind dressin' right and wheelin' right by columns and doin' right flanks and left flanks, and all the other movements we bin learnin' since Birney Barracks.

But I'm lyin' if I say I don't mind the mud. It's the red clay kind of mud that stick on your shoes till you a couple inches taller and each foot feel like it weigh about fifty pounds more.

We drill in that mud almost four hours; then, Sergeant Ash come for Lieutenant White. The lieutenant say we can be at rest till he come back.

"What you think tha's about?" this fella name Elijah Dorsey ask.

"Prolly we ain't drillin' enough."

"Yeh, prolly somethin' like that."

So we set round waitin'. Then we see the lieutenant comin'. He got this big smile on like he goin' ta tell us somethin' important.

"Fletcher, you and Elijah and...let me see...Brentford...you three come with me. The rest of you go with Sergeant Ash and get ready for school."

We get lots of funny looks as the rest of A Company march away. But don't none of 'em say anythin'.

"Boys, we're going on a little rescue patrol," White say. "Seems like one of the local secesh stopped two free black men on their way to join our regiment. The colonel wants us to shake them loose."

He don't ask if we want ta go. He tell us we goin'. In the army the officers, all whites, give the orders and the privates, all blacks, obey. That ain't no different from back in Balmore where whites done the orderin', and we done the workin'.

Still, White ain't the worst of 'em. Them two surgeons, Lieutenant Morgan and Lieutenant Grange, they always cussin' and accusin' us of malingerin', so nobody like goin' on sick call less he almost dead.

"That must be The Pines over there." Lieutenant White point to a two story old brick house settin' back off the road.

I ain't no authority on plantations, but this one got a look I don't like. A look that maybe say the soil ain't no good, and it's bin a long time since they were a big cash crop here. I got this feelin' this rescue ain't goin' ta be so easy as the lieutenant thinks. Specially since him and me the only ones got weapons. And I ain't loaded mine.

"Let's keep real close together," White say time we turn off the road. "We don't want to alarm Colonel Sullivan."

I look over us--four blacks, two unarmed, and a white lieutenant just old enough to shave. I don't think this Colonel Sullivan goin' ta be "alarmed."

While we stopped, I decide ta load ma Enfield. I slide the muzzle-loader off ma shoulder. Pour some black powder down the barrel. Slide a minie ball down too. Ram both in tight. Bite the paper on a percussion cap. Slip it in place. Pat the stock after the weapon back on ma shoulder. Still feel shaky inside, though.

Up close the house worse than I think. Nothin' but weeds in the lawn. Shutters need a coat of paint. Porch too. No, this Colonel Sullivan ain't goin' ta be no easy man to deal with.

"Just what the hell do you want?" a voice say time the lieutenant half way cross the porch.

"I'm Lieutenant White of the 7th U.S. Colored Infantry, and I was sent to investigate a report that you are holding two free black men who were on their way to join our regiment."

I'm standin' on the broken-up brick steps, but I see Sullivan step out the doorway aimin' a double-barrel at White. I see he prolly a handsome man once. But his face all red now, like Murphy's, from drinkin' cheap whisky. And his mean, red little eyes say he ain't a man ta fool with.

"The hell you are." He point the double-barrel at White. "You and them goddamned niggers got ta the count of ten ta get off my property."

"I have been authorized by Colonel William Birney of the United States Army to search this property. Please stand aside."

I hear the click of a trigger pulled back.

"And I'm telling you for the last time get off my property or I start shooting."

"You shoot, and I do too," I say, pointin' ma Enfield at Sullivan.

He look at me, at White, at me again. The double-barrel swing away from the lieutenant. "You'll find the two you want tied up in a drying shed out behind the house a piece."

"Thank you, Colonel Sullivan. We will release them and be off your property in no time."

"I appreciate that," Sullivan say, smilin' and showin' yella, tabacca-stained teeth.

I ketch somethin' in that smile, or maybe in them rat eyes. Somethin' that worry me on the way over ta the dryin' shed.

We find 'em all right. Stripped to the waist and tied ta posts so they gotta sit on the ground in that freezin', drafty shed.

"Praise the Lord, y'all here," the two say time we cut 'em loose. "We never think we be free again."

Lieutenant White see the fresh cuts on their feet, on their backs from where Sullivan whipped 'em. He see some of the cuts go almost ta the bone. "How can anybody do this to another human being?" His voice quiet and tight and he look real pale.

"We ain't human beings," Lijah say. "Old Taylor, overseer at Belmont, tell us some big white judge say we <u>property</u>. Guess this how Colonel Sullivan treat property."

Lieutenant White look far off. Like he hear somethin' rest of us can't hear. Then in a voice older, angrier than I ever hear before he say, "Not any more he won't. We're going to teach him a lesson. One he will never forget. We're going to free everyone we can find on this plantation and take them with us."

I seen slave quarters before, but I never seen nothin' worse'n the "cabins" on The Pines. They nothin' more'n little wooden boxes settin' at crazy angles: never bin painted, no windows, no real doors, big cracks in the walls so the wind, the cold, the mosquitos can get in. Folks sleep one on top the other--eight or nine in each "cabin." Just a old clay-daubed fireplace for heat and ta do the cookin' on. And no tables or chairs. Guess they set on the floor and eat.

They see us, the chil'ren, and they run tell everybody, "The Yankee soldiers here." Folks tumble out, stand in little groups, look us over real close.

"My friends, no...my brothers...I am here to set you free."

Don't none of 'em say anythin'.

"Didn't you hear me?" the lieutenant ask. "I said you're free. Get your things and come with us."

One toothless old man ask, "The colonel say we can go?"

"It's not up to Colonel Sullivan. It's up to me and the United States Army. And we say you're free. Now get your things and come with us."

The old man look at a old woman. "What we can lose?" she ask and go inside a cabin. She come out with a small bundle tied up in a rag. She walk over ta the lieutenant. "I'm ready."

The rest they go and do the same.

"And just where the hell do you think you're going with my property?"

We're just comin' on the cattle barn, time Sullivan step round the corner. That damned double-barrel raised up. This time, a short, strong-lookin' young man with him. He also got a double-barrel.

"They aren't yours any more," the lieutenant say. "Where I come from, folks treat dogs better than you did these people."

"Soldier, this is Maryland, not Massachusetts, and what I do to my hands...on my land is strictly my own affair."

The lieutenant walk straight for Sullivan even with the two double-barrels pointin' at him. "No, that's where you're wrong. The people of the North are fighting this war to put an end to...."

"Don't take another step," Sullivan warn.

I raise ma Enfield, aim at the young man, figure he may be a son. "You shoot the lieutenant, you dead too, young man."

"And so are you, nigger," a voice behind me say.

I don't have time ta find out who it is cause, just then, the lieutenant go for his pistol.

"I'm not afraid of you, Sullivan. I know you won't shoot me in front of witnesses."

I don't think the lieutenant ever bin wronger in his life. Before his hand touch his pistol, Sullivan open fire and both barrels ketch White in the chest. He kinda jerk back on his heels, hang there for just a second, then pitch over backwards.

I squeeze the trigger like he tell me, and the young man spin round and drop down on one knee. Somethin' like a red hot poker slam across the back of ma head. Then, they nothin' left inside me but pain.

ELIJAH DORSEY

Ain't nothin' but smoke and dust for a couple minutes. I see black folks runnin' every which way, 'fraid the colonel goin' ta shoot 'em too. But he ain't payin' 'em no mind. He rush over ta the young man Fletcher hit in the shoulder, yellin' "Son, son, you all right?" And bend over him, hold up his head. The other one, he come runnin' over too. I see I got just one chance, so I run for the lieutenant's pistol, pick it up, and aim it straight at Sullivan's head.

"Don't none of you move," I say and cock back the hammer so they know I ain't foolin'. Can't either Sullivan or his other son do nothin' cause their guns layin' in the dirt. It come in ma head, Shoot him, shoot the sonofabitch slave owner. The world be just that much better off with one less of his kind.

For maybe a second, I actually think I goin' ta do it, but then I know I can't. Don't really know why. Maybe this just ain't the right time, the right place for settlin' that kind of debt. Look over at the lieutenant, but his eyes seein' only God. Brentford he the same. Fletcher got a big red gash back of his head, but he carryin' on enough for three men. I bend down, not takin' ma eye or the pistol off Sullivan--and drag Fletcher up ta his feet.

"This man and me goin' back ta Camp Stanton. And I kill the first one who try and stop us."

"What the hell..." the guard at the entrance ta Camp Stanton so surprised seein' me half-carryin', half-draggin' Fletcher over his way he don't even challenge me.

"Don't stand there with your mouth open, fool, gimme a hand before I drop this here wounded man in the dirt."

The guard he grab Fletcher, and I feel ma knees want ta go, but I make 'em hold me up anyway. "Take him over the infirmary, I gotta tell Colonel Birney what happen."

The guard he just shake his head, "Can't do that. I leave here, and the army shoot me."

"Jesus Christ, you gotta help me. I brung this man almost three miles, but I can't tote him no more. And the captain gotta be told a pack of secesh over The Pines murder Lieutenant White and Private Brentford Sims. And he gotta get some men over there and ketch them murderin' dogs."

Ma knees give way, and I hear him yellin', "Corporal of the guard, corporal of the guard," time I hit the dirt.

Captain Leary say, "Ease back the throttle, soldier," and the launch, Cecil, slide real quiet up ta Sullivan's landing. I can't see the house cause so much river mist this early in the mornin'. All I can think is we shoulda bin here last night. But Colonel Birney he gone off ta Balmore and Captain Dennett gone with him. They left Lieutenant Lockwood, the adjutant, in charge, and he ain't sure what ta do. Finally, he send somebody over the 9th regiment to ask Captain Leary, and now we here.

"Quickly off the launch and take up your positions around the house," he say very quietly soon as we tie up. And we don't make any noise on the dock or either movin' up the bank for the house. We move like we blue and black ghosts made outta river mist.

Time everybody in place, Captain Leary fire his pistol once in the air, call out, "Colonel Sullivan, you and your sons are under military arrest. Please come out with your hands up."

Ma finger on the trigger givin' it just a little pressure. Kinda holdin' ma breath too waitin' for them secesh to show themselfs.

Nothin' happen. I get this feelin' nothin' goin' ta either. Somethin' about the windows say nobody here.

The captain fire again, repeat what he just say. I hear first mornin' birds squakin' like they ain't so happy with all the noise. But still nobody come outta the house.

"You leave me no alternative, colonel. Since you won't come out, we're coming in after you."

Dark blue figures scrunch down low kinda hidin' in the mist and headin' for the porch. Other ones aim up at the windows and the door. There ain't no sound louder'n us breathin' while we waitin' for Captain Leary's signal.

"Let's get them," he say, and we all run for the veranda. Then rifle butts beat down the door and we inside. Heavy feet pound down the hall, through the front parlors, up the front and back stairs. Breathin' don't seem necessary, like I got all the air inside me I ever goin' ta need. Like the blood racin' round in me keep me goin' forever.

A big old wooden door ain't strong enough to stop me. Kick it in. Gray first light comin' in the window showin' me nobody here, nobody bin here. Still I jab ma bayonet in the feather bed--once, twice, three times. Look in all the corners, in the dark old wardrobe standin' there mindin' its own business. But ain't nothin' belongin' ta anybody in that room.

"Fall in," I hear.

Outside, Captain Leary tell us, "There's nobody in the house. They may be hiding somewhere else on the plantation. Spread out and search all the outbuildings."

Now ma feet don't hardly feel like they touchin' the ground as I head for the dryin' shed where we found them two black men tied up. I pull that old rickety door open and stare in. I can't really see nothin' cause ain't no light inside. But, I can just make out somethin' hangin' in the middle, and I know without really seein' what it is. And I'm so cold, feel like no fire ever make me warm again.

"What are you staring at?" some officer from the 9th ask.

"Lieutenant White's body, sir."

"How can you tell? I can't see a damned thing it's so dark in there."

Somebody brung a lantern, and the smoky yellow light show us both I were right. Wha's left of Lieutenant White hangin' up like he just another stalk of tabacca.

"My God," the officer from the 9th say, "look at what they've done to the poor man's body."

Just look, I think, look on how they shoot him after he dead, look on how they smash his face in with gun butts, look how they hang him by the neck like they tryin' ta make sure he dead in the next world same as he dead in this one.

I don't feel cold no more.

"Cut him down...gently...gently,"Captain Leary say. Then he turn to me, "Take some men back to the house and burn it to the ground."

He don't hafta give that order twice. We run for the house. Inside, our gun butts smash every piece of furniture, every window. Like it the house's fault Sullivan done this terrible thin', like the house's fault he ain't here. Like we hurt the house enough, it tell us where he gone.

But, it don't. And we run from room to room, puttin' torches to sofas and tables and rugs piled up so they burn better. And soon, the whole place wrapped up in this bright orange fire and the only thing we hear's the house groanin' like it askin' us "why?"

Standin' there watchin' it burn, I feel cold again. And I can't hardly breathe right. And I start shakin'. But, I can't stop watchin' and thinkin', This just the first payment on what we owe Sullivan's kind.

CHAPTER FIVE
NOVEMBER 1863

COLONEL JAMES SHAW, JR.
Camp Stanton, near Benedict, Maryland

"As the new commander of the 7th Regiment, U.S. Colored Troops, I want to assure each and every one of you that I share your commitment to the cause of freedom for all black people still held in bondage in this state of Maryland as well as in those former states which now call themselves the Confederacy. Furthermore, I promise to continue the fine work begun by Colonel Birney and the other officers to make this the best damned regiment in all the Union armies."

MAJOR AUGUSTUS T. ALEXANDER

From the deck of the John Tracy, I can see them standing on the dock. Two lieutenants, their blue wool coats buttoned up tight against the chilly drizzle. Their eyes watching the lines being tied up and the gangplank being lowered. At this point they haven't seen me; they don't know what's in store for them.

"Good morning, gentlemen, I appreciate you coming out in this weather to meet me."

Their eyes take in my face and the insignia of my rank.

"I trust our relationship will be a cordial one." I extend my hand. It hangs in the air waiting for company. The shorter, sandy-haired one extends his partway, glances at the face of the taller, dark-haired one, then withdraws it.

"You're Major Alexander?" the taller asks.

The note of challenge in his voice is hard to miss.

"And you are?"

"Lieutenant Joel Morgan."

"Henry Grange," the other adds.

Why don't I just get back on the steamer, I think. Examining new recruits in Baltimore was a lot less complicated than this is going to be. But the idea is gone almost as quickly as it came. I was sent here to do a job, and by God I mean to do it. These two don't have to like me or my race, but I'm going to make damned sure they respect me as a officer.

Summoning up all the dignity and authority I have inside me, I say, "Shall we visit the infirmary first?"

A little surprised, Morgan's, "Yes sir," sounds almost civil.

I push back the flap of the first infirmary tent, step inside. It takes a few moments for my eyes to adjust to the dark. Then, I make out four black men lying on cots.

"Why isn't there any light in here?" I ask.

"Measles," Morgan answers, "these are the worst cases."

I touch the forehead of the closest man. I feel the cold sweat of a very high fever. I put my hand on his chest and feel him shivering under the thin blanket.

"Get me a lantern, a candle, any kind of light. I want to examine these men."

The light shows me a cast iron stove with no fire in it. I touch it and know there hasn't bin one in a long time. I see a slop jar over-running. I see scraps of food, filthy tin plates and cups.

"Lieutenant Morgan, I want a fire in that stove immediately. Then I want this place cleaned up."

Morgan just glares at me.

"That's an order, Lieutenant Morgan."

He doesn't move a muscle.

"Very well, let's go see the Colonel and find out from him whether a lieutenant can disobey a direct order from a major."

"Fine with me, let's go."

I had forgotten that Colonel Birney was no longer commanding officer. Standing in front of Colonel Shaw, I don't know what to expect.

"You say, Major Alexander, that you gave Lieutenant Morgan a direct order and he refused to obey it?"

"Yes sir, I found four sick men in a filthy, unheated tent, and I ordered Lieutenant Morgan to have it cleaned up and a fire made at once."

"And you refused to do this, Lieutenant?"

Morgan's voice is low, but there's no missing the intensity, the conviction when he replies, "Sir, I believe in freedom for the colored as much as any white man in the Union armies, as much as Abe Lincoln himself. I wouldn't be in this regiment if I didn't, but that don't mean I'm going to take orders from him or anybody like him. It's a question of self respect, sir."

Shaw's forehead wrinkles; his eyes fix on mine, as if trying to stare into my brain. And what are you looking for in here, Colonel, some small sign that I will be the one to back down? You would like that, wouldn't you, Colonel? It would make things easier for you, wouldn't it? But, don't you see, Colonel, after what Morgan just said, I can't? Because if I do, I will disgrace my race, myself, and even this rank.

Shaw finally takes his eyes off me, clears his throat, and begins, carefully choosing his words. "Both of you can appreciate that this is not only a unique, but a very difficult situation. I am not personally aware of any other instance where a colored officer outranks white ones. However, it seems that was the intention of the War Department as Major Alexander's orders name him the Chief Surgeon of this regiment. It would also seem, Lieutenant Morgan, you have no choice but to obey any direct order that Major Alexander gives you."

Morgan glares at me, at Shaw.

I sense that Shaw isn't finished, that I'm not going to like the rest.

"As I said, this is a most unusual situation. And I don't think we can really settle this thing without clarification from the War Department. So, until I can send a telegram and get an answer, I propose this division of responsibilities. The colored men now in the infirmary are under Dr. Alexander's care. Any new cases will be the responsibility of Drs. Morgan and Grange. This arrangement to continue until such time as I receive a reply. That's fair, isn't it?"

Morgan's smirk shows just how fair he thinks it is. Satisfied, Shaw picks up some papers from his desk signaling that the interview is over.

I suppose if I were a better person, I would admire how neatly Colonel Shaw got himself out of that difficult situation. But I do not. Instead, I want to know where he learned what the word fair means. From watching his rich mother ordering black servants around?

"Is there something else?" Shaw asks, with the slightest hint of irritation in his voice.

"No sir," I hear a token black officer reply before executing an about face and leaving. Outside, from behind me, I hear, "We showed that nigger," and laughter.

COLONEL JAMES SHAW, JR.

William A. Hammond, Surgeon General
War Department
Washington, D.C.

Nov. 22nd, 1863

REQUEST IMMEDIATE CLARIFICATION RE: RANK AND AUTHORITY OF MAJOR AUGUSTUS T. ALEXANDER (STOP)

/signed/ James Shaw, Jr. Col., 7th USCI

James Shaw, Jr.,
Col., 7th USCI
Camp Stanton, Md.

Nov. 24th, 1863

Colonel:

NO CLARIFICATION NECESSARY (STOP)
MAJOR ALEXANDER CHIEF SURGEON 7TH U.S. COLORED REGIMENT (STOP)

EDWIN STANTON,
Secretary of War

MAJOR AUGUSTUS T. ALEXANDER

Colonel Shaw calls me and Lieutenant Morgan and Lieutenant Grange in his tent. He read the telegram he sent Surgeon General Hammond and the telegram he got from Secretary Stanton.

"This settles the matter as far as I'm concerned," he says. "Major Augustus is in charge of the infirmary, and you two will take orders from him. That's what the Secretary wants, and that's the way it will be." Then softer, more friendly like, he adds, "There's going to be a lot for the three of you to do in the months ahead. It will be much better for you, and for the men, if you get along."

I glance over at Morgan. The look on his face tell me he isn't ready to do any such thing.

"Colonel Shaw," he says, "request permission to speak to you privately."

"Certainly. Major, you and Lieutenant Grange are dismissed."

Outside, I hang close to the tent. I can't make out everything Morgan and Shaw saying, but I get the drift, all right.

"Got nothing against him...the principle of the thing...just don't seem right...my family originally from Kentucky."

"Agree...but hands tied...can't go against the Secretary's wishes."

"Permission to write to Secretary."

"Granted."

CHAPTER SIX
DECEMBER 1863

BALTIMORE SUN

December 15, 1863

A Shameful Occurrence

We have been reliably informed that a most shameful incident occurred recently near Upper Marlboro in Prince George's County. A detachment of colored soldiers was sent from Camp Stanton, near Benedict in Charles County, to investigate a rumor that a Colonel Sullivan, master of The Pines and alleged murderer of a young lieutenant attached to the 7th U.S. Colored Troops, one Eben White, was seen in the vicinity of this peaceful county seat.

Said detachment upon reaching Mount Pleasant, home of Robert Sasscer, Esq., demanded entry to search for Colonel Sullivan. When Mr. Sasscer refused, unless a proper search warrant was obtained, the colored soldiers rampaged, plundering his home and driving off many of his loyal servants. This same melancholy spectacle was repeated at the homes of Messers Shelby Clark and Thomas Clagett, Jr.

Obtaining no satisfaction at any of these residences, the soldiers repaired to Upper Marlboro itself and shortly after 5 o' clock P.M. seized control of the court house and the jail. The next morning, before returning to their steamer, they released a number of dangerous criminals confined in the jail. Mr. Shelby Clark, acting upon his authority as Provost Marshall of Prince George's County, most strenuously protested this usurpation of the civil authority.

It is our considered opinion that incidents, such as this, do much harm to the Union cause and must perforce cast great doubt upon the wisdom of arming the negroes.

FLETCHER HOWARD
Upper Marlboro, Maryland

We get off the Cecil at Hill's landing cause that's far as it can go up the Patuxent River. Then we march through this town called Upper Marlboro. Town they call it--but ain't nothin' more'n a bunch of little houses and a big old brick court house. Whole thing could be lost in Balmore--and not missed either.

The local black folk ain't never seen nothin' like us. Their mouths open with surprise and their eyes stay on us the whole time we marchin' past. Their backs straighten and their faces show real pride...in us, in themselves. They see what black folks can be--what they can be--if they free.

"Open this door," Lieutenant Brown say, "in the name of the United States Army."

It swing on open and a black man with a heavy lined face and just a fringe of white hair framin' it give us the once-over with tired-lookin' eyes.

"Tell your master I want to see him at once," the lieutenant say, soundin' like he really mean business.

Nothin' on the face change. The eyes don't even blink. His the kind of face seen most everythin' and nothin' any young white man, barely old enough ta shave, say goin' ta impress him.

"Didn't you hear me? I said tell your master I want to see him at once--on official army business."

Just a little nod, then he gone for a few minutes. Time he come back, he say, "Mister Sasscer send his regrets. He is engaged for the rest of the evening, and can't see you. He bids you good night."

The door start swingin' shut. Lieutenant Brown throw his weight again' it so hard he almost knock the black man down.

"You tell Mr. Robert H. Sasscer that he has one minute to come to door, or I'll send some men to drag him here."

Now the black man don't know what ta do. He look at the lieutenant, he look down the hall, but his feet act like they stuck to the floor.

"No one will have to drag me anywhere," a voice say from the top of the stairs. Then this tall man with a headful of white hair start down, takin' each step real slow, like he don't ever hurry for nobody. Time he standin' in front of Lieutenant Brown, he ask real hard-like, "By what authority do you barge into my home and make such threats against me?"

The lieutenant answer just as cold and hard, "By authority of my commanding officer, Colonel James Shaw, who has received word that you or one of your friends may be harboring an escaped fugitive, one John T. Sullivan, formerly master of The Pines near Benedict, Maryland."

"I know no one by that name."

"I think you do. I have it on good authority that his wife is related to your wife. Both are Chews, I'm told."

Sasscer so mad it make the skin red under all his white hair and a big vein in his forehead stick out, throbbin' like it goin' ta bust.

"Sir, I have nothing more to say to you. And, if you do not have a search warrant, I must ask you to remove yourself and these...uh...soldiers from my home. Otherwise I will charge you all with trespass before the Provost Marshal of this county."

The lieutenant don't even stop ta think. He shoot right back, "Apparently I didn't make myself clear. I'm not here on a social visit. I'm searching for a man who killed an officer of the United States Army during the performance of his duty. I don't need a search warrant or any piece of paper from some god-damned secesh-loving official of this county. Now get out of my way, or I'll arrest you for giving aid and comfort to an enemy of the United States."

Sasscer go kinda pale, and his voice sound just a little shaky time he step back and say, "Very well, but I shall protest this outrage to...to...the Secretary of War himself."

The lieutenant bow and say sarcastic-like, "You do that. I'm sure he will find your comments most enlightening."

Don't take us long ta go through the house. Ain't a very big one. Tell the truth, I seen better in Balmore. After the house, we go through the barns and the quarters. The black folks say they ain't seen no strange white men round here, and they got no reason ta lie.

Half a hour later, we come back ta the house and Lieutenant Brown tell Sasscer, "It appears you were telling the truth. Sullivan is not here. Sorry to have inconvenienced you. Good night and a Merry Christmas to you, sir."

We leave and go over Mr. Shelby Clark's place and do the same thing. Then, over ta Mr. Thomas Clagett's. We don't find no sign of Colonel Sullivan or his sons. Round 5 o'clock we march back to Hill's landin'.

"Can't go back tonight," the Cecil's captain say, "we're taking on water. Not too much, but I don't want to chance a night run."

The lieutenant shrug, "Can't be helped, I guess. We'll have to spend the night here on the boat."

"I don't think that's a good idea, lieutenant. With the extra weight of ten men, she just might swamp."

Lieutenant's quiet for a few minutes. "Then, we have no choice. We'll have to stay somewhere in the town. Whether, the folks there like it or not."

Back in Upper Marlboro, Lieutenant Brown tell us, "We obviously can't stay at the Marlboro Hotel." He look at us, and we know what he mean.

"No private home will take us in either. So, it appears our best chance may be the court house. Nobody'll be there tonight, and we can be gone early enough tomorrow so that we don't interfere with official business too much."

On the way over, this old black man step in the road, wavin' his arms. Lieutenant Brown ask him wha's wrong. He say we oughta take a look in the jail.

"Why?" the lieutenant ask.

"Somebody in there who know about that Colonel Sullivan you lookin' for."

"Are you sure?"

But the black man won't say no more. He just keep lookin' round like he scared somebody ketch him talkin' ta us.

Down in the basement of the court house, we find the jail and the fat, red-faced jailer, just like he bin waitin' for us.

"Where you think you're going?" he ask.

"To have a look inside," Brown say.

"Not without the permission from the Provost Marshal you ain't."

"And who is that?"

The jailer look kinda surprised, "Why Mr. Shelby Clark, of course."

I think the lieutenant goin' ta hit him. "Listen you, I'm hungry and tired. My men are too. We've wasted enough time today talking to Mr. Clark, and we don't intend to waste anymore. Either you open this door right now, or my men will break it down. Is that clear?"

The jailer hand over a big iron ring of keys. "Mr. Clark's goin' ta hear about this. Then, we'll see if you can come in here and do like you please." Soon as the keys outta his hand, he gone, mutterin' ta himself.

So dark inside, we don't see nothin', but the air so bad, we know somethin' wrong. "Bring a lantern down here," the lieutenant say.

The yellow light show a room about ten foot square. Must be twelve, thirteen women with their chil'ren in it. They blink like they bin in the dark a long time. The floor cover with straw, and we can see they bin relievin' themselfs. Some of the chil'ren look sick.

"Who are you and what are you doing in here?" Brown ask.

They don't say nothin', just stare with big scared eyes.

"We're Union soldiers. You can trust us; we won't hurt you." He push me out in front. "See, a black man, they're all black men, but me."

One woman stand up, touch ma arm, ma hand. Nod her head like she believe what she see. "Help 'em," she say, pointin' to a wooden door on the side wall.

It take us a while ta break off the heavy iron lock. But on the other side, we find another room about the same size as this one, only filled with men. The stink so bad in here, for a minute, I think Lieutenant Brown goin' ta vomit. His face get pale and sweaty, and I see he fightin' with his stomach.

The lantern show a heavy, u-shaped piece of iron bin pounded down in the brick floor. Eleven men chained hands and feets ta that iron staple. Lieutenant bend down and look real close at one man's wrists. "What are these scars from?"

"This here manacle put on hot; then, the blacksmith pound it closed with a hammer on a anvil."

"Was that done to the rest of you, too?"

"Yes sir," they say and hold up their wrists.

The lieutenant look kinda puzzled. "What did you do--kill somebody, rob your masters?"

"No sir, nothin' like that. We just try ta join the army time the recruiters come through. Masters, they don't like that, put us in here."

"And the women and children?"

"They was ketched tryin' ta run away ta Washington City."

I can see Lieutenant Brown angry. I can hear he hardly controllin' himself time he say, "Joseph, you and Aaron go get the blacksmith. Bring him here at gunpoint, if necessary, but bring him here."

The blacksmith got the first set of manacles off time Mr. Shelby Clark and the jailer come.

"Chaney, stop that immediately," he say to the blacksmith.

"Don't pay any attention to Mr. Clark," Lieutenant Brown say real quiet-like, "continue what you were doing."

"See here, lieutenant, you have no authority to enter this jail and release these men."

"No authority, huh?"

The lieutenant look at the black men. "Do you still wish to enlist in the United States Army?"

"Yes sir," they all say.

"Then, under the provisions of General Order 329, I hereby enlist you in the 7th Regiment, United States Colored Infantry, and state that your former masters are entitled to compensation and may file for same with the War Department."

Blacksmith don't know what to do. He look at Clark; he look at the lieutenant.

"Don't just stand there, man, release them," lieutenant snap. "I won't administer the oath to any man wearing irons."

Blacksmith act like he froze.

"Do it, or I'll charge you with interfering with an officer of the United States while in performance of his lawful duties."

Blacksmith shrug and start bangin' away at the chains.

Clark look round at the faces and say, "You can't take him," pointin' to fella in the corner. "He didn't try to enlist."

"Then why is he here?"

"I...uh...I'm not really sure."

"You're not really sure? Well then, maybe the jailer can tell me."

Jailer one them one men who can be a sonofabitch to black folks, but always suckin' up to rich or powerful whites. Now, he don't what to do--suck up to the lieutenant or Shelby. Tryin' to chose make him sweat worse'n I ever seen.

"Ma master put me here time he hidin' in these parts," the man say.

"And who is your master?"

"Colonel Sullivan, sir."

Lieutenant give Clark a real hard look. "So, you never heard of anybody by that name, huh?"

Mr. Shelby Clark let out a little air; his shoulders sag some. "What's the use. Yes, Sullivan came here after the...uh...trouble in October. Arranged passage for himself and his family to

Richmond. This boy tried to run away, so Sullivan asked me to keep him until he could send money to ship him south."

Then, Clark kinda straighten himself. "I give you my word as a gentleman that neither Sullivan or any member of his family has been in this area since early November."

Lieutenant don't say anythin' for a couple minutes. "Fletcher, tell the women and children to get ready. They're coming with us."

"You can't do that. They aren't enlisting."

Lieutenant stare Clark right in the eye. "No, but they're human beings, and they deserve better than this damned filthy hole. If you so much as lift a finger to try and stop me, I'll arrest you for helping a dangerous criminal escape from military justice."

For the first time, I feel like huggin' a white man.

A couple days later, Colonel Birney come from Baltimore with a newspaper sayin' how we break in Shelby's house and how we let all the dangerous prisoners outta the jail. Lieutenant Brown and us tell him what really happen, and he say, "I didn't think there was any truth in these charges; but, mark my words, a real storm is brewing. Shelby and Sasscer are powerful men in this state, and they will do their damndest to get back at you."

Then, he study each face for a couple minutes, pull out a match, strike it, and set fire to the newspaper. "Never cared much for the Baltimore Sun, always gets the story wrong," he say smilin'.

ELIJAH DORSEY

Camp Stanton, Md.

Kristmus day, 1863

Deer Momma,

This the 1st Kristmus we ain't bin with each other. And i gotta tell you how sad i feel, how much i miss you today. We din't have much back at Belmont, but we t'gether. This year we ain't even got that.

Everythin' else O.K. I like the army just fine. All the men in charge, oficers they called, white, but they treet us better'n old taylor or even mr. dorsey hisself.

You kno what a day like in the Army? The man blowin' the bugel wake us befor come sun up so we can cook us somethin' ta eet, mostly hardtack and cofee. Hardtack like a kraker what turn ta stone. If you don't soak it, you can't eet it, it so hard.

Then we march, drill the oficers call it, till noon, 'less it rainin', then we have skool. We learn reedin' and ritin' in skool. One of the oficers, loutenint Califf, he the teacher, he say i learn the fastest in the hole regiment. He say maybe i got the gift of words. I hope somebody over Belmont reed it ta you so you kno how good i rite.

Time the drillin' over, we go shoot our Enfields till we ready ta eet agin. Then we cook us a mess of bakin so we can soak the hardtack in the grees. Then go ta skool for maybe 3, 4 hours. Then we drill sum more till time for supper. If it rainin' or snowin', we stay in skool till supper.

Like i say, army just fine by me, but i see what some men meen about no colored oficers. Fletcher Howard, he from over balmore, say colored men already kno how ta do what they tole. We oughta be in charge of ourselfs, or after the war goin' ta be same as before, whites doin' the bossin' and us doin' the workin'.

Worse thing tho, we ain't bin payed yet. The men with wifes and chillrens say they got reel trouble at home. They say they don't kno how they families can live till spring, they don't get some monee soon. Ain't so bad for me since only monee I ever had was time mr. dorsey let us sell korn we grow. Remember?

Sorry, momma, i gotta go now. I hope you get this letter.

Your son lijah

CHAPTER SEVEN
JANUARY 1864

Special Orders
No. 474

WAR DEPARTMENT,
ADJUTANT GENERAL'S OFFICE,
Washington,
January 2nd, 1864

(Extract)

4. Effective January 1st instant, Colonel William Birney promoted to Brigadier General, brevet, U.S. Colored Infantry.

By order of the Secretary of War;

E.D. TOWNSEND,
Assistant Adjutant General.

MAJOR AUGUSTUS T. ALEXANDER
Camp Stanton, Maryland

"You sent for me, Colonel?"

"Yes, Major, please sit down."

I wonder if Morgan or Grange have been here crying about how hard I've been working them. Don't know what they expect as much measles as we've got in this camp.

"Do you remember when I told you I had written to the Reverend Augustus Woodbury in Providence for some things for the men, things the army doesn't issue?"

I'm relieved this isn't about more complaints from Morgan and Grange. Maybe, they're finally getting used to me being in charge. But who is Reverend Woodbury?

"I can tell by your face you don't. Can't say I blame you it was back in November that I wrote to him."

November...November...must've been right after he became commander. What would he have written to a preacher about?

"The mittens and things the men needed?"

Yes, it comes back to me now. "Mittens and towels and sewing kits--wasn't it, sir?"

He nods.

"Well, they're here. Not everything I asked for, of course, but Woodbury and his congregation were most generous: collected 500 books, 655 towels and 238 sewing kits. And I want you to see they are distributed among the men."

He seems so pleased with himself I kind of hate to ask, "but sir, isn't that more properly the job of the quartermaster or the chaplain? My assistants and I are up to our necks in measles, and...and...."

"You may well be correct about whose responsibility it is, <u>but</u> the fact remains I want <u>you</u> to do it."

No use arguing. Next thing he'll say is, "That's an order," and I'll have to do it. There just don't seem to be any way to talk to this man without him getting testy. And sooner or later, I must talk to him about the men's diet. They're eating too much salted beef and hardtack and not enough fresh vegetables. Already seeing some scurvy.

<u>Maybe some time when he's in a better mood</u>, I think, <u>whenever that is</u>. I start to get up off the camp stool.

"Since you mentioned the measles, I think you might find this report interesting. The Surgeon General's office has been keeping track of the number of white and colored soldiers getting sick; and, so far, your kind are four times as likely to catch a contagious disease as whites."

Seems like this is the opening I've been waiting for. Take a deep breath, "I think, sir, the problem may be diet."

He looks puzzled. But before he can object, I rush in with, "A lot of these men are not...uh...accustomed to so much beef and hard wheat. I think the beef is especially bad for them.

Since they aren't used to it, it gives them diarrhea. And they need more greens. I'm starting to see some scurvy."

He takes some papers out of a leather case, looks through them, then picks one. "You are no doubt aware what the standard army rations, approved by Congress in August 1861, are?"

It's more a taunt than a question, but I know the regulation well enough to rattle off, "20 ounces daily of fresh or salt beef (however, 12 ounces of pork or bacon may be substituted), 18 ounces of bread or flour (20 ounces of corn meal may be substituted), and suitable portions of beans or rice or potatoes, mixed vegetables, coffee or tea, sugar, salt, pepper, molasses, vinegar and candles."

He doesn't say anything when I'm finished, stares at me a minute like he's not sure whether I said the list so fast to mock him or not.

"So you see, major, the army has provided quite adequately for the men's dietary needs."

"May I point out, sir," I say a little surprised at my tone. "The regulation allows for the substitution of pork and cornmeal so what I'm requesting would not be against its letter or spirit, and the change would, I think, be beneficial to the men."

Silence for what seems like a very long time. Time to notice the lines across his forehead deepen, the ones around his mouth do likewise. Time to hope I had at least opened his mind to the possibility I was right.

"Major," he says as if he were scolding a naughty child, "I eat the beef and wheat diet, all the officers in this regiment, all the officers and enlisted men in every white Union regiment do too. And it doesn't bother them. Then, why should it be a problem for the colored troops?"

He paused like he needed a second to organize his next point, but I had a answer, and it spilled out without me having to think. "It's a problem, sir, because they aren't used to it. A lot of these men were slaves and ate a slave's diet--pork, greens, cornbread. Their masters were smart enough to feed them what made them the healthiest. That way they got the most work and the least sickness. Now the army feeds them what they aren't used to. This lowers their resistance, so they catch everything that comes in the camp."

He doesn't say anything, just looks kind of far away, like he really is thinking over what I said. Then, very carefully he says, "Suppose, just suppose, you're right. What would be the best way to find out?"

Now, it's my turn to look sort of puzzled.

"By conducting an experiment, that's how. You have my permission to tell Quartermaster Purinton to issue only pork or bacon and cornmeal to A, B and C companies. D, E and F will get the regular beef and hardtack or bread. In a month, we will see if there is any difference in the general health of the two sets of companies. Is that fair?"

"Yes sir, very fair."

ELIJAH DORSEY

Everybody hear the bugle blowin' assembly. I'm settin' in ma tent polishin' ma boots time I hear it. Bin so cold and blowy, we ain't done no drillin' for almost a week. But, "When the bugle blow, the soldier gotta go," tha's bin pounded in ma head since I get here. So, I'm goin'.

Over the parade ground, I see Colonel Shaw, all the other officers and General Birney. "Somethin' big happenin'," I say ta Fletcher Howard, "or else what Old Birney doin' here?"

Fletcher right away get a attitude. He screw up his face like I'm some kind of dumb nigger for sayin' that.

"Of course, it somethin' big. Ain't there been rumors for the last month we're goin' south?"

Now we standin' about four rows back from the reviewin' stand. Birney and Shaw talk kinda quiet, but keep their eyes on the crowd formin' in front of 'em. Time everybody here, Lieutenant Lockwood, the adjutant, hold up his hand. Everybody get real quiet. "General Birney has an important announcement to make."

Birney step forward. He wrapped up in his wool coat and got his hat pulled so low, hard to see his face.

"Officers and men of the Seventh, on a cold January day like this, I have some good news for you. Sometime next month, you will be leaving this pleasant place."

He stop so everybody can laugh.

"And proceed by steamer to Beaufort, South Carolina."

I start cheerin'. Fletcher he start cheerin'. Everybody in the regiment start cheerin'. It ain't just leavin' this cold, wet camp make us so happy. But also we're goin' where the secesh are. We're goin' ta the fightin', ta where we can do what we bin trainin' for--help whip the secesh and free all our black brothers and sisters who still slaves. God almighty, I'm happy.

Time the cheerin' stop, Birney say, "I'm going to ask Chaplain Gregg to lead us in a short prayer."

Chaplain Gregg, he one of them white-haired, white-bearded men white folks think look like God, step in front of Birney. "Let us bow our heads," Gregg say. "Most merciful Father, look down with favor on the 7th Regiment, U.S. Colored Infantry. Bless and protect its officers and men in the difficult days which lie ahead. Look after their loved ones and keep them safe from harm and want. Finally, dear Father, bless the Cause for which these officers and men are so willing to lay down their lives as so many others have already. Amen."

Don't nobody move, don't nobody make any noise. So quiet I can hear a steamer over on the river. And seem like the chaplain's words, "so willing to lay down their lives as so many others have already," are still hangin' in the frozen air. Seem like the first time I understand I might <u>really</u> die. I shiver, not from the cold outside, but from the hard cold truth inside--I might really die.

FLETCHER HOWARD

Baltimore
Jan. 21, 1864

Dear Fletcher,

I don't like botherin' you with the troubles we havin' at home, but I got no choice. Bin very cold and I ain't bin workin' much. So some days me and the chil'ren just stay in the bed because we got no wood for the fire and nothin' to eat. Also the baby ailin' because it's so cold, and I got no milk for her and no money for medicine.

Time you went in the Army, you said you would send us money. But the only money's come from your father. Without him, I think we all die. I know it ain't your fault. You ain't bin paid yet, but we must have some money soon.

Your loving wife,
Rebeccah

Kind of a warm evening for January. Sun shinin' and not much wind. We're gettin' paid, and everybody's bin talkin' about nothin' else since yesteday. Last night, Captain Devlin said the pay would go back ta September. He also said we're gettin' $10 a month but the Army takin' $3 out for uniforms. We ask him how much white soldiers pay for their uniforms, and he don't answer us. He don't need to. We know--nothin'.

"Ain't fair, Captain," I say.

He say, "Maybe not but the army's hands are tied. Congress passed a law in 1862 which set the pay for you colored soldiers."

"I hear," say Solomon Greene who got a sister livin' in Boston, "the 54th Massachusetts refusing their pay till it made the same as white soldiers'."

"That's true and Congressman Stevens, with Secretary Stanton's blessing, has introduced a bill to do that, but until it's passed--your pay is $10 a month and I strongly advise you to accept it."

"I got a good mind not ta take ma pay tomorrow," Greene say back in our tent. "If them Massachusetts boys can do it, so can we." He look straight at me.

"I don't like it no more'n you, Solomon, but Rebeccah's havin' a real hard time. She say she ain't bin workin' and the baby's sick. She gotta have some money."

He look real disgusted. "What about you, field hand? What you goin' ta do?"

Elijah answer, "I'd like ta have me some money ta buy some cakes and pies from the sutler, but I don't hafta. I agree with what you say about it ain't fair we being paid less'n white soldiers."

"Don't that beat everythin'? The free-born talkin' like a nigger, and the runaway slave talkin' like a free man oughta."

That did it. "Who you callin' a nigger, you big-mouthed sonofabitch?" I grab him round the throat. "Easy for you and the runaway slave to have high principles--you ain't got folks writin' you letters sayin' they starvin' and sick and cold."

I shove Rebeccah's letter in his face. "See what she say about no milk and no medicine? About not workin'? About the baby ailin'? You think it easy bein' here and ma family sufferin'? Sometimes a married man gotta think about somebody else 'cept himself."

Elijah jump up, but I already let Greene go. I ain't mad at him. I'm mad at this goddamn army that lied ta us. I'm mad cause I gotta choose between ma family and ma brothers here. It ain't fair makin' a man do that. It goddamned ain't fair.

Outside it's so cold and clear, I can see all the stars in the sky. They look so close I swear I can almost reach up and grab a handful. I stand and think and think about tomarra--what I'm goin' ta do? Stand with ma brothers...and maybe Rebeccah and the kids die? Take ma pay and feel like shit inside for lettin' everybody else down?

Ma father usta say, "Trust the Lord, He will show you the way."

I ask Him, "What should I do, Lord? What should I do?" And I wait and wait, lookin' at the stars that don't give a damn about me or Rebeccah or anyone else on the earth, but no answer come.

And I stand like that till the cold seep in all ma bones and make me shiver all over. And I don't care if God didn't give a answer. I didn't think He would. I don't know God care so much about us as some folks say.

Kinda warm and sunny today. Some of the ice on the parade ground meltin', makin' it justa little muddy. The whole regiment line up in companies. On the platform where the reviewin' officers usually stand, Lieutenant Lockwood settin' at a small table with a strong box in front of him. Standin' next ta him, Sergeant-Major Jones with what prolly the company rosters in his hands. Two armed soldiers standin' a few feet on either side of the Lieutenant and the Sergeant-Major.

"A company, single file, and report to the adjutant when your name is called," Captain Devlin say.

Elijah Dorsey first man in line. Every black man lookin' at him, waitin' ta see what he do; every one prolly thinkin' he do the same as Dorsey. And I feel kinda sorry for him. Can't be easy bein' first t'day.

"Dorsey, Elijah," Jones call out, and Elijah step off real smart, like he proud bein' a soldier, like he know he doin' the right thing.

While he walk ta the platform, mount the steps and stop in front of the table, I go through it all again in ma head. But I can't see how I can let Rebeccah and ma kids starve even if I gotta let ma brothers down.

Elijah snap a salute, then say loud enough for the whole regiment ta hear, "Private Elijah Dorsey reportin' for his pay, and refuse ta accept."

And nobody make a sound or even move a muscle while he make a about-face and march ta the rear of the line. While Lieutenant Lockwood and Captain Devlin frown. While Lieutenant Coats look kinda pleased.

Next ones all do the same as Elijah and finally ma turn. I sweatin' harder'n any time in ma life.

"Howard, Fletcher...report for pay," Jones call out.

I step off--left, right, left, right--all the time thinkin' What'm I goin' ta do? What'm I goin' ta do? Everything tight inside. Everybody lookin' at me, even Lockwood.

In front of the table. Stop. Come ta attention. Snap a salute. "Private Fletcher Howard reportin' for his pay...and ...refuse ta accept."

Camp Stanton, Md.
Jan. 26th, 1864

Dear Rebeccah,

This the hardest letter I hope I ever have to write to you. I know how much you need money, and I want to send you some. Time I got in the pay line, I think I'm goin to take my pay cause you and the kids need food and wood for the fire. But, time I see a runaway slave refuse his, I think I know I can't take mine either. You see, Rebeccah, the Army payin us black men $10 a month and keepin $3 for our uniforms, but the white soldiers paid $10 and $3 for uniforms. I know that's always the way it's bin in Balmore, but the Army got to be different. If it ain't, then after the war ain't goin' ta be different either. And if it ain't, every black man in this Army risking his life for nothin.

Because this war can't be just about freedom for the slaves. You and me know freedom without same rights as white folks don't mean a damned thing. We been pushed around and cheated all our lives. So now, I got to stand with ma brothers and make the Army treat us black soldiers same as whites. That mean I won't ever again take nigger wages for doing the same work as a white man. I'm sorry me doin the right thing goin to make you and the chil'ren suffer so much. I only wish they were some way that didn't hurt you so much.

Your loving husband,
Fletcher

CHAPTER EIGHT
FEBRUARY 1864

MAJOR AUGUSTUS T. ALEXANDER
Camp Stanton, Maryland

The Honorable Abraham Lincoln,
President of these United States

Feb. 14, 1864

"Sir, We the undersigned, Medical Officers in the Regiments of Colored Troops, under command of Brig. Gen Wm. Birney at this camp, have the honor most respectfully to ask your attention to the following Statement.

"When we made applications for positions in the Colored Service, the understanding was universal that all Commissioned Officers were to be white men. Judge of our Surprise and disappointment, when upon joining our respective regiments we found that the Senior Surgeon of the command was a negro.

"We claim to be behind no one, in a desire for the elevation and improvement of the Colored race, in this country, and we are willing to sacrifice much, in so grand a cause, as our present positions may testify. But we cannot in any cause, willingly compromise what we consider a proper self respect. Nor do we deem that the interests of either the country or of the Colored race, can demand this of us. Such degradation, we believe to be involved, in our voluntarily continuing in the Service, as Subordinates to a colored officer. We therefore most respectfully, yet earnestly, request, that this unexpected, unusual, and most unpleasant relationship in which we have been placed, may in some way be terminated."

Most Respectfully Your Obt. Servants,
J.B. McPherson E.M. Pease
Chas. C. Topliff Joel Morgan
M.O. Carter Henry Grange

"Well, major," Colonel Shaw says after I've finished reading the letter aloud.

All I can think is those dirty, racist bastards. Crying to President Lincoln because they've got to take orders from me. Degradation is it? Those lying sons of bitches don't know what the word means.

Of course, I can't say anything like that, not to this white officer, not when his eyes are glaring at me like his are. No, at a time like this, I've got to play it the way Momma taught me when I was a boy. And it won't be hard to act innocent. I really didn't know anything about the letter.

"This is a very serious matter, major," he says before I get a chance to open my mouth. "Your little quarrel with Morgan and Grange is now the concern of not only of me, but also of the Secretary of War and the President himself."

So now it's my fault they wrote the letter? For once, I don't really know what to say. However after a moment's thought, "Begging the Colonel's pardon, but I am not the one who involved the President or the Secretary of War in this," seems as good a beginning as any.

Shaw has a habit of sucking air through his clenched teeth when he's angry. Right now, the sucking noise is the loudest I ever heard.

"I'm well aware who wrote the letter. I'm the one who got that copy, and I'm the one who had the courtesy to show it to you. But, it still remains a fact, Major Alexander, I asked you to show tact and discretion in your relationship with Lieutenants Morgan and Grange."

Once when I was a boy, I went skating on a frozen pond. The ice wasn't as thick as I thought. I could hear it cracking in back of me, but I wouldn't stop. I just kept going till it broke under me. I was lucky I was close to the shore, and nothing worse happened than I got very wet and cold.

I hear the ice cracking when I say, "Believe me, I tried very hard to do just that, and I thought it was working. But, I see now they were just play-acting with me--pretending to get along, all the time waiting for a chance to stab me in the back."

Red-faced enough to have apoplexy, he pounds on his desk. "Major Alexander, that's enough."

It's so quiet for a time I can hear my own blood pounding against my temples.

Then, Shaw says, "Major Alexander, you have made a very serious accusation against Lieutenants Morgan and Grange. I think they should be present in order to answer you."

I have the feeling inside this won't go well for me.

"Corporal Wilson," he shouts. And instantly his runner is in the tent. "Go find Lieutenants Morgan and Grange. Tell them I want them here on the double. On the double, you hear?"

I don't know how long it took them to get here. It was too long to be standing only three feet from a man doing his best to ignore you. Too long to be balancing on thin ice.

The tent flap is pulled open and they enter. "Lieutenants Joel Morgan and Henry Grange reporting as ordered." They salute together.

"All right, Major Alexander, tell them what you told me."

My head aches from the back of my neck clear around to my eyes. My mouth is dry, and my tongue feels too big for it. "I...I...said...thatsince our last meeting, I have tried very hard to have a good relationship with my assistants and was...uh...surprised they had written a letter of complaint to President Lincoln."

"You're surprised," Morse laughed. "You've been lording it over us for the last two months, making us feel like dirt. And you're surprised we did what any self-respecting man would do."

He glares at me till I feel my soul hurting deep inside me. "Colonel, it's like we told you, like we said in that letter. It's unnatural and downright degrading for him to be giving orders to us...or...any other white Christian."

"Colonel, it's like we told you," echoed in my head. Shaw knew they were writing the letter. Knew and no doubt approved. I feel the ice give way, and the cold water close over me as I plunge down, down.

"Then, what you are saying, Lieutenant Morgan, is that you and Lieutenant Grange will not work under Major Alexander, nor follow any of his orders, direct or implied."

"That's right, colonel."

"Sir," I grasp at a straw, "that's insubordination and punishable under the military code."

"You may be right, major, but not by me. I'm sending this whole business up to the Secretary of War. Maybe he knows what to do."

Only last summer, I sat here in Secretary Stanton's outer office waiting to see him about becoming a army surgeon. It was hot and the windows were open. I heard a army band playing somewhere in back of the White House. I felt the wonderful energy that must surely carry the North to victory, and I prayed to God the secretary would let me have a part in it. Seems so long ago now.

As Momma used to say, a lot of water flowed under the bridge since then. A awful lot of water and it carrying away my dreams with it.

"The secretary will see you now," the thin young man in the black suit says. I see he's wearing those Burnsides that are all the rage among white men since Antietam. He opens the door and lets me in to Stanton's private office.

So quiet and rich-looking inside, it's easy to forget what a poor and ugly world it is outside. I stop in front of his big oak desk, and he lays his pen down. "Ah, Major Alexander, good to see you even under these unfortunate circumstances."

He reaches out his hand, and I shake it. "Please sit down," he says, showing me which chair.

"So, you and your assistants are at loggerheads?"

With everything inside me tied up tight, it seems to take all my energy just to nod my head. I didn't want to come here, but Shaw said, "The secretary's wish is the same as a direct order from a superior officer." And anyway, I already know what Stanton's going to do. He's going to transfer me to a contraband camp, maybe over in Alexandria, then make Morgan chief surgeon. Treating poor, sick runaway slaves isn't the same as treating soldiers. Half of me says, "Resign, go back to Canada. This isn't your war anyway." The other half wants me to stay, says this war is something that never happened before, and I've got to be a part of it.

"You know, major, I can't say I'm completely surprised this happened. When I appointed you chief surgeon, I thought it was risky. Still, I am a little astonished by how strongly Morgan has reacted. I'm sure he's the ring-leader in this, aren't you?"

He asks the question in such a friend-to-friend way...for a moment...I feel like that's what we are. It's just the two of us sitting here, talking about this and that the way friends do. But, one quick look at his business-like face knocks that idea out of my head.

"Moreover, since he used words like <u>degradation</u> and threatened to resign his commission, I must assume he is speaking from some deep personal conviction and not just from some sour-grapes impulse."

<u>I</u> am not so sure about that. He may have volunteered for the 7th mostly because he thought he'd have a better chance being a chief surgeon. Didn't figure on a colored doctor getting here first.

"Now, there are several things I can do." Stanton drops his voice and that friendly tone is back. "I can leave you chief surgeon and warn Morgan that any further insubordination will be dealt with severely. That will make you very happy and him very unhappy. So unhappy, he and the others may carry through with the threat to resign. Then, Surgeon General

Hammond will be angry because he has assured me it would be difficult to replace that many surgeons right now. On the other hand, Morgan might not resign, but continue to write letters to influential people."

Stanton smiles like I know who they are. Like I know as well as he does what has to be done.

"And influential people can, quite frankly, be a pain in the ass. Constantly hearing from them in behalf of Lieutenant Morgan et al could make <u>me</u> very unhappy. A second possibility would be to transfer you to another regiment, but the same problem might arise there, too. A contraband camp is out because you were assigned to one earlier, and it didn't work out."

"I was, Mr. Secretary, but I was placed <u>under</u> a captain who said he felt awkward giving a major orders."

"Yes, I remember now."

For a few moments, he doesn't say anything. All I can hear is the ticking of the clock in the corner behind me...and the faint cracking of ice.

"So from your point of view, reassignment is not simply a matter of transferring you from one place to another, is it?"

I nod hesitantly, but something tells me not to get my hopes up, not till I hear it all.

"From mine, there are several more...shall we say complications? First, it would certainly be considered as much my defeat as yours since I was the one who had you assigned to the 7th. It would allow Morgan to become chief surgeon, a position that neither the Surgeon General nor I think he is qualified for. Last, you are one of the few colored officers the army has. Congressman Stevens and your own Frederick Douglass, among others, see you as an important symbol of what the Negro race can become. They would be most unhappy if I were to remove you and appoint a less qualified white man in your place. Congressman Stevens, as Chairman of the House Ways and Means Committee, could be a very powerful enemy for the army."

You crafty old fox, I think, your trying to figure out some way to keep all the politicians happy. They're the ones you are really concerned about, not me--not even Morgan and Grange.

"You can see, Major Alexander, that Solomon's problem with the child claimed by two mothers was a simple one compared to mine."

He stops talking and studies my face for a long time--too long. Something tells me I won't like this Solomon's solution to my problem. I study his face for a hint. If it's not another regiment, not a contraband camp--what's left? Then, it hits me--he's going to ask me to resign, go back to Canada, and maybe transfer Morgan to a white regiment. Then all Mr. Secretary Stanton's problems solved. Well, he's overlooking one thing--I'm not resigning. No matter what. I'll fight. I'll write to Frederick Douglass and Senator Sumner and Congressman Stevens. They'll help me.

I stand up. "Mr. Secretary, I will not resign my commission."

Stanton couldn't look more surprised if I started taking off my clothes. "Resign...my good man...who asked you to do that?"

"I thought that's what you were leading up to."

"Good God no, man, your resignation is the farthest thing from my mind. I want you in the army. I want you in the 7th, but right now it will be better for both of us if you go back to Baltimore and examine recruits for the new colored regiments for a period of time."

"But sir, isn't that giving Lieutenant Morgan what he wants?"

"No, because it won't be a transfer, only a temporary change in duty station. You will remain the 7th's chief surgeon."

He starts smiling, "And as long as you are, Morgan and Grange will remain lieutenants. Mark my words, they'll request transfers soon, and I'll give my swift approval. Then, you'll rejoin the 7th."

Outside, the cold air feels good on my face. I walk down Pennsylvania Avenue to the train station by the Capitol, so I can think about what Stanton just told me. I don't really trust him. I see me as the big loser because I don't think Morgan and

Grange are going to ask for transfers as quickly as the secretary thinks. I think I am going to be up in Baltimore a long time. Still, there isn't much I can do about it right now. I turn my collar up and jam my hands in my pockets. Funny how cold it feels--all of a sudden.

Special Orders
No. 517

WAR DEPARTMENT,
ADJUTANT GENERALS' OFFICE,
Washington, February 17th, 1864

(Extract)

17. Seventh and Ninth regiments, U.S. Colored Troops report to encampment, Hilton Head, South Carolina on or about March 5th, 1864. Steamers <u>United States</u> and <u>Daniel Webster</u> to furnish transportation to said location via Portsmouth, Virginia.

By order of the Secretary of War;

E.D. TOWNSEND,
Assistant Adjutant General.

CHAPTER NINE
MARCH 1864

ELIJAH DORSEY
Hilton Head, South Carolina

Warm here. Warm as June back at Belmont plantation. Flies come at me soon as the Daniel Webster tied ta the dock. Nasty bitin' flies. Trees here like I never seen before. Tall, no branches, big leaves at the top. Somebody say they called palmettos. Never seen anything like 'em.

Bin on the Daniel Webster since we left Camp Stanton...let me see...five days ago. Seem longer--maybe cause the weather here like summer and it's still winter back in Maryland. Or maybe cause we only bin off this boat one time. Tha's the night we stayed in Portsmouth, Virginia.

Kinda funny us free colored soldiers here on this island right off the coast of South Carolina. Justa few miles over on the mainland, our brothers and sisters still slaves. Like they bin for 300 years. Like we ain't here. Like no white soldiers here either. Like they ain't no war.

"Prepare to disembark," Lieutenant Califf say. I swing ma pack up on ma back. Everything I need in this world in that pack: bed roll, mess kit, clean socks. It ain't much, but it's a whole lot more'n ever I have at Belmont.

Marchin' over ta the camp, we pass a bunch of white soldiers. One say, "Will you look at that? More goddamned niggers, ain't there no more white men left in the North?"

Funny, I thought it didn't matter what the color of a man's skin, long as he be willin' ta fight and die.

"Fall out for roll call," Lieutenant Califf say.

Everybody line up, and dress right without him tellin' us. Then stand at attention.

After all the names called, he say Captain Devlin volunteered us for a work detail with the 33rd regiment on the west side of the island.

"Hey, brothers, y'all ever seen such good lookin' niggers?" a black man leanin' on a pickaxe call out.

"No s-i-r," the rest of the work gang sing.

"Where y'all think they from?"

"Can't be from South Carolina."

"Why not, brothers?"

"Cause they too good lookin'."

Then all of 'em laugh hard as they can.

Lieutenant Califf give 'em a hard look, but they don't pay him no mind. They just keep on laughin' and laughin'.

They got no uniforms on. Just old work pants like all the field hands wear back at Belmont. And they got the kind of hard muscles field hands got.

"Is this the 33rd?" Califf ask.

They stop laughin' and look at the one who ask the first question. He turn all the way round like he's lookin' for somebody ta answer the lieutenant. We smile cause we know what he's doin'.

"Is this the 33rd regiment, U.S. Colored Troops, or isn't it?"

"Oh...you axin' me?" His voice so innocent soundin' that the lieutenant look embarrassed for bein' testy.

"Yes, I was. Sorry if I didn't make that clear.

"You made it clear enough, lieutenant. It's just Ransom and the boys like to play dumb, don't you?"

They stop laughin'.

The red-headed lieutenant with the faded blue shirt go on, "They don't mean any harm. It's just their childish idea of a joke."

Ransom and the "boys" look like they could kill him.

"Now answer the lieutenant's question properly, Ransom."

Starin' down at the dirt, like the answer writ on it, the one called Ransom say, "Yes sir, this the 33rd."

"That's much better. Now, all of you, back to work or it'll be punishment tonight."

Lieutenant Califf ain't said nothin', and he shake hands kinda half-hearted when the red-head introduce hisself as, "Lieutenant Herlihy, originally of the 3rd South Carolina Volunteers which is now called the 33rd U.S.Colored Infantry."

Califf tell him we're the work detail from the 7th he prolly lookin' for.

"Splendid," Herlihy say, "they're fine-looking bucks. We'll get a lot of work out of 'em."

Califf motion ta him, and they walk away from us. Califf say somethin' we can't hear, but Herlihy he laugh out loud. "You must not have much experience with niggers, lieutenant. Because you'd know you can't insult 'em. They don't have human feelings."

We bin workin' a hour or more draggin' heavy palmetto logs ta where Ransom and his crew makin' a wall by stackin' the logs and pushin' sand up in front of 'em. Four boys come with big water buckets, and Ransom tell us ta stop workin' and cool off.

"I sure don't like doin' this old heavy labor," I say time I have some water. "I'll be glad when we get over where the fightin' goin' on."

Ransom spit out some water, look me over real funny-like. "Just when do you think that'll be?"

"Any day. Colonel Shaw say we goin' ta the fightin' real soon."

Ransom come up close, put his face almost against mine's. "We hear the same thing in the summer of '63, but we ain't seen no fightin' yet. Work and more work all we seen here. Let me tell you somethin', Northern boy, the whites don't want nothin' outta us 'cept damned hard work. And the only fightin' we ever goin' ta do is 'tween ourselfs time we're drunk."

I don't wanta believe him, but lookin' deep in myself I see what he sayin' make sense. "Then, why they train us? Teach us drill and how ta shoot Enfields?"

"I don't know what they done up in Maryland, but let me tell you how it's bin here in South Carolina. If we do somethin' the white officers don't like, they put us on punishment. Y'all know what that is? It's standin' in the sun carryin' a heavy log on yall's shoulders. Or drillin' with a field pack full of stones. And we can't do nothin' about it. Cause the Rebels ain't too far from here. And the white officers can send us over ta them any time they want. So we gotta do what they say."

He take some more water in his mouth, spit it out. "So y'all best get usta workin' like this. Or y'all just might get sent over ta the mainland."

FLETCHER HOWARD

Baltimore, Md.
March 10th, 1864

Dear son,

I don't like botherin' you with home problems, but I got to. Your son Silas die last Tuesday from the typhoid. We done the best we could for him, but he was to weak from the fever and the stomach complaint. Now, Rebeccah and Little John Eager sick. I don't have any more money for medicine cause I ain't bin workin' steady since las' summer. So, you got any money, please send it, then Momma and me can buy medicine and nurse Rebeccah and the twins and maybe they be all right.

Your father,
Eager John Howard

"Captain Devlin, can I see you a minute?"

"Certainly, Fletcher, come in to my tent."

Not sayin' anythin', I give him the letter. He read it, then look up. "I'm very sorry to hear this. I know how worried you must be."

"Yes sir, captain, I am. I bin worryin' since this letter come yesteday, but I gotta do more'n just worry. That won't help ma Rebeccah get well, ma chil'ren either. Captain Devlin, sir, I got ta go home. I don't think I can do wha's right by the army long as they sick."

Devlin put his fingertips together, rest 'em on his lips, kinda stare down at them. I know he thinkin', so I don't say anythin'. But I feel everythin' inside me gettin' tighter and tighter.

"If we were still in Maryland, it wouldn't be too difficult to let you go home for a few days. But here, well, General Sickles may not be as agreeable as General Schenck because of the distance back to Baltimore. Plus, there's a time problem. I'm not supposed to tell you this yet, but the regiment's only going to be here a few more days. I've been told orders are being cut to send us to Florida."

He look up at me. "You understand what I just said? Knowing we'll be gone in about a week, General Sickles' staff will just send your request for a furlough back with a note to resubmit it when you get to Florida."

"And how much chance I got goin' ta Balmore from there?"

He put his thumb and first finger together. "Unless you're wounded...about this much."

"Captain Devlin, sir, don't say that--there's got ta be some way I can get leave. Rebeccah ain't had any money from me since I bin in the army. She and ma chil'ren been livin' off what ma mother and father give 'em. And you see what ma father said--he don't have any left, and I got none ta send. Ma wife might die she so sick with the typhoid. So, I got ta go home and take care of her and maybe find some money somewheres."

"Private Howard, I am not unsympathetic to your plight, but I just don't see any way..."

Then he get this look on his face, like he just think of somethin'. Somethin' he can't wait ta tell me.

"I can't do anything through regular military channels, but...and I must emphasize this is strictly off the record...you could go see Chaplain Gregg. He may be able to arrange something through the Christian Commission."

I start ta thank him, but he hold up his hand. "I didn't tell you that. You thought of it after I told you a compassionate furlough was out of the question." He give me a little smile. "I hope everything works out for you."

There's somethin' about tellin' a white man your troubles that don't set right with me. Maybe it's ma pride, or maybe I just don't trust 'em. But on the way over ta Chaplain Gregg's tent, I got the feelin' I'll never see Rebeccah or ma chil'ren again. And I call maself a damned fool for joinin' the army. For believin', for one minute, black people'll get somethin' out of this war. "Rebeccah, I'm sorry," I call out ta the empty night. "I shoulda lissen ta you."

I tell Chaplain Gregg about Rebeccah and the chil'ren and about 'em not havin' any money. I show him ma father's letter. I keep studyin' him real hard, but what he's thinkin' hid behind a face full of gray beard.

"Compassionate leave is possible under these circumstances, but very difficult to arrange. I would have to telegraph the Christian Commission, and a member or a local minister, would have to call on your family to verify that the emergency you described actually exists."

"Why, would I make up a story like that? If I didn't want ta be here, I coulda deserted in Maryland. Woulda been a lot easier and closer ta home." I look him in the eye, but he don't look back. That make me madder. "And you don't even believe ma Rebeccah sick with the typhoid and ain't got no money. No, you got ta have somebody verify. Well, you just send anybody you want ta ma house...even President Lincoln himself...and you goin' ta find out Fletcher Howard don't lie--not about somethin' important like this."

"Please sit down, Fletcher." He point over to a chair.

I don't want ta, but he said please. And the way he said it, personal-like, not in the white officer ta black soldier way everybody else use, make me feel like he mean it.

"I'm sorry it sounded as if I thought you were lying. That's not the case at all. It's only the army doesn't want to make it easy for anyone to leave his unit unless he's wounded and can be cared for better at home than in a military hospital."

I feel the tightness inside me let go justa little bit. Maybe I'll see Rebeccah again.

"Now, if you could give me the name of a minister in Baltimore, I can include his name when I telegraph the request to the Commission."

Before I open ma mouth, he add, "A white one would be best. The Commission might insist that a member accompany a colored one."

"Bishop Payne of the African Methodist Episcopal Church is a friend of ma father. Think the Commission trust his word?"

"Bishop Payne is an excellent choice."

Capt. James Gregg
Chaplain, 7th U.S.C.I. March 22nd. 1864

VISITED MRS. FLETCHER HOWARD (STOP) FOUND HEALTH AS DESCRIBED BY HUSBAND (STOP) FOUND ONE CHILD DEAD AND OTHER GRAVELY ILL WITH TYPHOID (STOP) HUSBAND'S PRESENCE ESSENTIAL (STOP) RECOMMEND IMMEDIATE COMPASSIONATE LEAVE (STOP)

/signed/ Daniel A. Payne Bishop, AME Church
Thomas M. Vincent, U.S. Christian Commision

CHAPTER 10
APRIL 1864

ELIJAH DORSEY
Jacksonville, Florida

"Forward march." Captain Devlin give the command. We step off real smart. Just like we bin practicin' all week. This's General Birney's big day. This dress parade's for him and the whole 54th and 55th Massachusetts regiments are watchin'.

The 54th the regiment that charged Fort Wagner las' July. Some of 'em even reached the top of the parapet and planted their regimental colors. But they hadta pull back cause they got no support. The 54th left a lot of good men on the hot South Carolina sand that day.

"By the left flank, march," and A company turn left real sharp like we one man. We practiced this over and over in the hot Florida sun till we can do it perfect.

"By the right flank, march," and we turn back the way we were.

"Left oblique, march." The captain showin' us off now. We make the sharp angle turn and head right for the 54th.

"By the right oblique, march."

The 54th showed black men could fight same as white men. They opened up the army ta the res' of us. Ask me...this parade should be for them, not Birney.

"Eyes right," and every one look at Birney who's givin' us a hand salute. Time we practicin', Captain Devlin say he want to hear our eyeballs click when we look right and snap when we look straight again. I didn't hear nothin' like that cause the band playin' so loud, but Birney look pleased, so I guess we done it right.

Colonel Shaw hold up his right hand. Officers and enlisted men of the three regiments all look at him. "I have an important announcement to read."

Everybody shut up and listen.

"From Brigadier General Rufus Saxton, Department of the South, U.S. Army. Effective April 14th instant, General William Birney will assume command of the Jacksonville District, this department."

Colonel Shaw turn and salute General Birney. He smile and salute back. Then Colonel Hallowell of the 54th and Colonel Hartwell of the 55th salute Birney. Birney, he just keep smilin' and smilin'. The enlisted men, like me, look happy too. We thinkin' time we go in a battle, we want Colonel Shaw leadin' us. We trust him more'n we do General Birney.

"What you boys goin' ta do pay day?"

That question asked over and over in our regiment, in the 54th and 55th. Everybody hear a equal pay bill in the Congress. Everybody hear it held up in a committee. Everybody damned pissed off.

"What <u>you</u> goin' ta do?" I ask the private from the 54th who ask me.

"We're havin' a meetin' t'night and decidin'. You can come if you want and bring your friends."

Solomon Greene and me deputized ta go ta the meetin'. Everybody mad about the pay bill bein' held up, but nobody willin' ta sneak away after lights out. They say, "You and Solomon got nothin' ta lose if you get caught."

So, time it real dark, we slip outta the camp and make our way best we can ta the clearin' in the woods where they already arguin'.

"I say we stack our arms and refuse ta do anything till this damn Congress give us equal pay. We proved at Fort Wagner black men can fight just as good as whites, maybe even better."

The sergeant speakin' was wounded at Fort Wagner. I hear he almost arrested before for talkin' like that.

"Talk's mighty cheap," a thin fellow wearin' glasses say. His name's Abram Simms, and they say he know Frederick Douglass hisself and bin ta Harvard College same as any white man. "Especially, since you seem to have forgotten what happened to William Walker."

Heads nod, voices say, "Brother, you forgot William Walker."

"Who's William Walker?" I ask the man standin' next ta me.

"He was a sergeant in the 3rd South Carolina. Back in November, he told his men to stack their arms. This February, he was shot for leadin' a mutiny."

"No, I ain't forgot him, nor our brothers in the 14th Rhode Island Heavy Artillery either, court-martialled and spendin' a year at hard labor. I say Walker, them and anybody else willin' ta take action as much heroes as any of our brothers who fell at Fort Wagner. And you know why?"

He don't wait for a answer.

"Cause they know this pay thing wrong. They know writin' letters and signin' petitions gettin' us nothin'. They know it way past time we told the whites runnin' the army and the Congress: you don't pay us right, we ain't diggin' no more ditches, we ain't haulin' no more supplies, we ain't fightin' your war any more. Brothers, they treat us like this when we're helpin' 'em whip the secesh, how do you think they're goin' ta treat us when they don't need us any more?"

"Same as before the war," a lot of voices round the smoky little campfire say. I say it too, cause I believe he's right.

"Hold on a minute, brothers," Corporal Simms say. "Sergeant Tibbs is most eloquent, and he certainly makes a most convincing case. But he overlooks two very important points. First, this is as much our war as it is the whites. They lose and a lot of you will be back in the fields pickin' massa's cotton or tobacco, feeling the overseer's lash when you're too tired to work. Your wives and chil'ren sold cause massa lost money at the races or gambling."

Other voices agree.

"And there won't be any North to run away to. Because slavery will be there too, just like in our grandfathers' time."

Now, he drop his voice real low. Make everybody lean close ta hear what he sayin'.

"On the other hand, if the North wins, we got a chance for something black folks have never known in this country. Something I can hardly say without feeling a chill run through me. I'm not talking just about an end to slavery. President Lincoln took care of that when he signed the Emancipation Proclamation. No, I'm talking about something that will affect black folks for generations to come...equality...full political equality--voting rights, property rights, education rights."

He got us now. We're hangin' on his words like he Jesus Christ hisself.

Sergeant Tibbs on his feet and fightin' back in a second. "I think brother Simms bin out in this Florida sun too long. Who goin' ta give us the vote and let us own property, the states...or maybe the Congress that don't want ta pay us same as whites?"

He laugh and a whole bunch laugh too.

"You're going to laugh out the other side of your mouth when I tell you Frederick Douglass himself said that Massachusetts is thinking about introducing a Constitutional amendment to give us voting rights. And once they're in the Constitution, nobody...North or South will be able to take 'em away."

It get real quiet. You can tell everybody thinkin' on what both said. Maself, I like what Corporal Simms say, and I got a feelin' a lot of others do too.

But Tibbs ain't licked yet. "Maybe Simms right. Maybe the abolitionists can do that, but so what? Ain't nothin' but a promise on paper. And after the war, white folks goin' ta say, 'We don't want niggers votin'. They might want to run things. We don't want niggers ownin' property. They might want to live next to us.' You know same as me what they goin' ta do then, brothers."

He pretend like he rippin' up a big piece of paper. And a whole lot say, "They're goin' ta tear 'em up."

"And where you all be then, brothers?"

"Same as before."

"No, brothers, you be worse off cause you'll know you bin made fools of again by white folks. You'll know you had the chance down here ta have things your way, and you were afraid ta take it. So, your children'll curse you, and so will your grand-grand-chil'ren and your great-grandchildren...and even onto the seventh generation they goin' ta curse you."

"No," everybody shout, "we're with you. We're tired bein' cheap soldiers. We ain't doin' a goddamn thing till we paid same as whites."

I look over at Simms. He got the saddest look on his face. Like he know we makin' a big mistake. Like we be real sorry for what we goin' ta do. And I shut up ma mouth.

Everybody follow Tibbs back over the camp, talkin' and laughin' about how they goin' ta show the whites. I kinda hang back and wait for Simms.

"You think they're wrong," I say.

He look at me over the top of his glasses, "I know they are. The army isn't going to stand for their foolishness any more than it stood for Walker's."

"You think they court-martial and shoot all of 'em?"

He shrug his shoulders. "Maybe not...but I do know...." He grab holda ma arm and squeeze it hard. "If the army thinks we are more trouble than we're worth, they will disband the black regiments. And the one chance we have to change our race's future will be lost forever."

He let go and walk away with his head down. I stay and kick sand on the fire, tryin' ta figure out which one's right.

Been layin' here waitin' for the bugle ta blow and hopin' it won't. Ever since the meetin' broke up, I bin thinkin' and thinkin' and thinkin'. Seems ta me Tibbs tellin' the truth about how we can't just keep waitin' and waitin' for the white folks ta do right by us. On the other hand, I know down in ma soul Simms right about the army. And if this regiment disband--what I'm goin' ta do? Where I can go? Old Taylor and even Mr.

Dorsey won't want me there after I run away. Can't go ta Balmore and get a free job cause I don't know nothin' but field work.

So, I lay here goin' back and forth--stand up with ma brothers or either play it safe. Which one, Lord, which one?

Then I hear reveille, louder'n I ever hear it blow before. Seems like it could wake up the dead. And ma insides tighten like they never done before. And I'm scared I'm goin' ta shit maself.

Then the buglin' stop...but I don't hear nothin'. No complainin'. No jokin'. No grab-assin' around. Just the buzz of fat, lazy flies.

"F-a-l-l out, everybody. Time to get the day goin'," Sergeant Hall say.

Don't sound like anybody payin' him no mind. A few minutes later, he say, "Everybody deaf or somethin'? I said fall out and I mean now."

Still no noise outside.

"What's going on here, Sergeant Hall? Why isn't A company lined up for morning report?"

"They won't come out of their tents, Lieutenant Califf."

"They won't, huh? Listen up, A company. If you aren't out here in five minutes, I'll have you all up on charges of insubordination."

It's real quiet for them five minutes.

"All right, if that's the way you want it. You're all on report.

I hear him mutterin' ta hisself while he's walkin' away. I want ta go outside and stand at attention, show the army I'm still a good soldier, but ma legs won't carry me nowheres.

"I don't know what the hell you men think you're doin', but tellin' you, you best get your asses out here before Captain Devlin come, or this's goin' ta be one sorry bunch of niggers," the sergeant say.

I'm afraid he may be right.

General Wm. Birney
Commander, Jacksonville Dist.
Jacksonville, Fla. April 17th, 1864

SEVENTH U.S.C. AND 54TH AND 55TH MASS. COL. VOLS. REFUSE TO LEAVE TENTS (STOP) REQUEST INSTRUCTIONS (STOP)

/signed/ James Shaw, Col., 7th U.S.C.T.
Edward N. Hallowell, Col., 54th Mass. C.V.
Alfred S. Hartwell, Col., 55th Mass. C.V.

Colonels: Shaw, Hallowell, Hartwell
Camp Mandarin, Fla. April 17th, 1864

TELEGRAPHED GEN. SAXTON (STOP) MEANTIME DO NOT PROVOKE INCIDENT (STOP)

/signed/
Wm. F. Birney, General
Commander, Jacksonville Dist.

Bin a long day in this tent. Six men layin' on they beds and the sun gettin' hotter and hotter. Six men who ain't had no food, no water since yesteday. Who ain't bin out ta the latrine either. Bin doin' our business and buryin' it inside. Now stink so bad in here flies don't have no trouble findin' us. They swarm round us like bees after spring flowers.

I count the flies tryin' keep from worryin' about what we're doin'. One, two, three, four...about what the army do if we don't come out...five, six...about bein' court-martialed...
seven, eight, nine...and bein' kicked outta the army...ten, eleven, twelve...or goin' ta prison...thirteen, fourteen, fifteen...and maybe end up standin' in front of a firin' squad...SIXTEEN, SEVENTEEN, EIGHTEEN, NINETEEN, NINETEEN, NINETEEN.

"Sweet Jesus, I don't want ta die like that."

"Wha'd you say, Lijah?"

"Nothin'."

"Don't lie. You say somethin' sound like sweet Jesus ta me."

"Mind your own damn business, Solomon. What I say ain't got nothin' ta do with you."

"Fuck you, plantation nigger."

I'm off ma cot and on top him before he know it. "I'll show you who's a nigger."

Before I hit him, Charles Waters grab hold ma arm. "Don't do it," he say. "We start fightin' between ourselfs, and we may as well give up right now."

I go lay down on ma cot and stare up at the flies. But I don't count 'em no more. Just lay there listenin' ta the rumble in ma belly. Somehow, I fall asleep and dream I'm back at Belmont and me and Mary out back of the tabacca sheds. I feel the smoothness of her thighs and ma dick so hard it hurt. In a minute we're naked, and I'm just ready ta go inside her.

"All right men of A company, listen very carefully."

"What the hell Captain Devlin doin' here?" Then a hand shake me, and I wake up.

"This is your final warning. If you are not assembled on the drill field in one hour, your absence will be considered a mutiny as defined in the Articles of War. You will then be subject to arrest and imprisonment as provided for in the Articles. Also, I must warn you Colonel Shaw has full authority from General Birney to request whatever assistance the officers of this regiment may need to exercise their authority. <u>One hour</u>, on the drill field, ready for duty. Be there."

I lay there listenin' ta the flies for a few minutes. Then I raise maself and swing ma feet down on the dirt floor.

"Where you think you're goin'?" Waters ask.

"You hear what the man say, Charles. We got a hour ta get ourselfs out on the drill field."

"So, you desertin' your brothers?"

I crouch down next ta his cot, so I'm lookin' him straight in the eye. "I may be a runaway slave, but I ain't stupid. I think if we don't come out, the Colonel's goin' ta call in white soldiers. And they's no tellin' what they might do--maybe shoot some, beat the rest. Maybe turn us all over ta the secesh."

"Tha's why you sellin' out, you scared...scared the white man goin' ta hurt you? You sure are one sorry nigger," Greene say.

I want ta hit him. I want ta hit him harder'n I ever hit anybody before.

"No, I ain't scared. Just let me tell you what Corporal Simms told me the other night after you run off with your hero, Sergeant Tibbs."

They quiet, so I go on. "He say refusin' our pay already makes us mutineers."

"Say what?"

"Tha's right, we could be doin' hard time right now if Colonel Shaw want ta press charges."

"So, why he don't?"

"Cause he don't think it's right how the army cheatin' us on our pay. And prolly a lot of other officers agree too. But we stay in here, and we on our own. We can't expect no help from them."

I stand up and say loud enough for the men in the next tent ta hear too." So, do what you want, but I'm goin' out on the drill field. Soon as I'm ready."

I pull a clean shirt outta the packin' case where I keep ma stuff. Put it on and open up the tent flap ready ta go outside.

"Wait up, Lijah, I think maybe I go with you," Waters say.

"I guess I will too," Greene add.

Most of A company--and from what I see--B and C companies already standin' round in bunches, not talkin', just kinda watchin' who come out on the drill field. Not exactly glad ta see 'em, but not sorry either.

"Company, atten-HUH," Lieutenant Califf call out. We snap to.

Colonel Shaw step in front. He don't look unhappy either. "It's good so many of you decided to be sensible. While your dissatisfaction with your pay is understandable, the army cannot condone insubordination or mutiny as a form of protest.

Therefore, everyone who did not muster yesterday morning is hereby ordered to perform one month's extra duty. Anyone still in his tent when this muster is finished will be arrested and held by the battalion Provost Marshal until a court martial can be convened."

While he talkin', I see others hurryin' ta take they place in the ranks. Looks like the 7th ain't mutinyin' after all.

"Finally, I have been informed that the 54th and 55th Massachusetts Colored Volunteers have been ordered back to South Carolina. Members of those regiments thought to be ringleaders are already under arrest."

"Officers, dismiss your companies," he say.

"They sure got us, don't they, Solomon?"

"By the balls, brother. By the balls."

FLETCHER HOWARD
Baltimore, Maryland

Feels like I bin travelin' since ma birth. First, on the steamer from Jacksonville ta Fortress Monroe. There, I almost got arrested for desertion. Somebody stole ma orders on the steamer. Had ta wait for the Provost Marshal ta telegraph General Birney. Had ta wait on a answer sayin' it's OK for me ta go home. Had ta wait on a steamer ta Balmore. Grabbed one ta Alexandria when I couldn't wait no more. Then, another long wait in Washington cause officers and wounded got first priority on the train cars.

Funny thing...I didn't worry about Rebeccah and the chil'ren till I left Washington. Now packed in this stuffy wooden car with all these wounded, I think about nothin' else. Want the train ta go faster, so I can find out if they're dead or alive.

But it don't. Keep stoppin' before every bridge, so the guards can check and see if the secesh put a bomb under it. Stop a hour in Laurel Factory, so everybody can use the latrine. Cuss under ma breath at every stop, every delay, but it don't do no good.

Finally, pass the guard post at the Balmore city line and rumble down Pratt Street. Feelin' a little sick time we get ta Camden Station. Got a funny feelin', I don't really want ta go no farther.

Standin' in the rain lookin' at ma house. Bin out here it for a long time. Wet as I am, I just can't get maself ta go inside. Long as I'm out here, I can hope everybody's all right.

"That you, Daddy?"

I turn and see ma daughter, Rachel.

She grab me. "Oh, Daddy, I'm so happy you're here," and she start cryin'.

"Your Momma...she...she...?"

Rachel look up at me. "Momma's still weak, but she OK."

She bury her face against ma belt. "But Silas and Little John Eager dead. Oh Daddy, I'm your only chile now."

I hug her and start cryin' too.

The room smell like camphor. Ma Momma think camphor can cure anythin', even typhoid, so there's a lot of it here. I tiptoe in, see Rebeccah sleepin'. Her big brown eyes closed. The quilt risin' and fallin' with her soft breathin'. I just stand and look at her. Wonder why I ever leave her. Why I think it's a good idea ta join the army. Say ta myself, "I'm never goin' back."

Her eyes open. For a second, she look at me like she don't know who I am. Then she say, "Fletcher," and smile.

I kneel down beside the bed. "Thank you, Jesus, for savin' ma sweet Rebeccah. Thank you, thank you."

"Fletcher," she whisper, "the boys are dead," and tears start down her cheeks.

"I know, honey, I know."

"Oh Fletcher, I'm so sorry. But there weren't anythin' I could do. I didn't have no money. And they...they had such bad fevers. I nursed 'em and nursed 'em. Set by their beds even when I had the fever too. When I couldn't set no more your Momma did. And your Poppa, Old John Eager, he brung water from the spring tryin' ta cool off their poor little bodies. But it weren't no use."

She turn her face away from me. Her shoulders shakin' with the sobbin'. "Just weren't nothin' we could do."

I put ma hand on her back. "Rebeccah, I ain't blamin' you. I know you done everythin' you could. This's all ma fault. I never shoulda joined the army and left you and the chil'ren like I did. And I swear, I ain't leavin' you again."

She turn back towards me. Hold up her arms. "Don't talk about that now. Just pray our sweet, dead boys with Jesus. And they don't miss us like we miss them."

I lay on the bed beside her, put ma arms round her, and cry like I never done before.

CHAPTER 11
MAY 1864

Special Orders
1711

WAR DEPARTMENT,
ADJUTANT GENERALS' OFFICE,
Washington, May 1st, 1864

(Extract)

5. Effective May 10th, 1864, William E. Birney, Brig. Gen., relieved command Jacksonville Dist. Reassigned Middle Department, Baltimore, Md. Brig. Gen. George H. Gordon assume command Jacksonville District.

By order of the Secretary of War;

E.D. TOWNSEND,
Assistant Adjutant General.

ELIJAH DORSEY
Camp Mandarin, Florida

Every day bin the same since the 54th and 55th gone back ta South Carolina. We called ta reveille at 5 o'clock in the mornin'. Then we cook breakfast from 5:30 to 6:30. Squad drill go from 6:30 to 10:30 and work detail from 10:30 to 1 o'clock in the afternoon. Roll call and dinner over by 2:30 and another work detail last till 4 o'clock. We drill again till 6 o'clock and have retreat parade and roll call. Supper's from 6:30 ta 7:00, then tattoo and roll call at 9 o'clock and taps at 9:30. Appears General Gordon don't trust us cause he have roll call so much.

He don't need ta worry about us desertin'. We be crazy ta try it this far south. There ain't no place where the secesh can't find us.

That don't mean we're happy. Everybody grumblin' about the extra work detail. Build somethin' one week, then tear it down the next. Dig trenches, then fill 'em in. Don't make sense.

And we ain't had school since we left Camp Stanton. Bin so long, I'm forgettin' ma letters.

"I hear they bin fightin' in Virginia. Some place called the Wilderness," Solomon say one mornin'.

I stop diggin' and lean on ma shovel. Too damn hot for diggin' anyway.

"Yes sir, this General Grant, he hittin' Old Bobby Lee with everythin' the North got. And what the hell we doin'?"

"Sweatin' and diggin', diggin' and sweatin'," I say and laugh. Solomon go on like this everyday now.

"You can laugh, but I'm tellin' you, we never goin' ta do any real fightin'. The army don't want us for nothin' but work."

"Which you ain't done much of t'day."

He mutter some more, but I don't pay him no mind. We got ta finish a ditch we bin diggin' so the swamp behind the camp can drain. Lot of the men got the fever, and General Gordon say prolly have somethin' ta do with the bugs in the swamp. They pesky all right, but I don't see how they can give a man the fever.

Twelve o'clock come and Lieutenant Califf march us back over the company area. Captain Haskell waitin' for us.

"Tomorrow morning after breakfast, Lieutenant Califf will take 20 men over to Cove Springs and arrest some smugglers. Lieutenant, pick your men."

Califf salute and turn round ta look us over.

Maybe not be real fightin', but it's better'n workin' in this hot sun. I look at Solomon, and can tell he's thinkin' the same thing.

"Lieutenant," I say, "I want ta go."

"Me, too," Solomon say.

Don't take others long ta figure out what we up to. They get round him in a circle and start sayin', "I want ta go too."

"The captain said twenty, and that's all I can take. So, let me see...Elijah, Solomon Greene, Charles Waters, Benjamin Lovejoy...."

Nobody tell us almost 20 miles ta Cove Springs. Or that they ain't no real road, just wagon tracks goin' through scrubby pine woods or passin' round a swamp. Sometimes, see a cabin like I live in over at Belmont, but it ain't never bin painted and got no window glass. And I can't hardly believe white folks live in 'em. And they kids stand and watch us with big, sad eyes. And sometimes a pale, skinny woman, barefoot and wearin' a old patched dress and holdin' a sick-lookin' baby, stand with the kids and stare at us too. Don't none of 'em say anythin' or even move a muscle. I swear, even they dogs don't bark.

Till I seen this, I never thought any white folks was poor. Always thought bein' white somehow made 'em rich. Now I see that ain't always so.

"Where's the men?" somebody ask. "Ain't seen nobody but women and chil'ren."

"They prolly over Virginia fightin' for the secesh," Waters say.

And I think, why would a poor white man go off and fight just so a rich white man can keep slaves? It don't make sense.

Time we left this mornin', it was kinda cool so nobody mind our blue wool uniforms. A hour later sun gettin' real warm, and the wool startin' ta itch. Justa little under the arms where the sweat runnin' down, and back behind the knees. Still, we think it's better here in the woods 'stead of workin' out in the sun.

By now we bin on the march almost three hours. And the bugs long ago found us. Every step I swat one and cuss softly ta maself. Inside ma pants I feel like I wet maself. Shirt stickin' ta ma back. Sweat runnin' down in ma eyes, makin' 'em sting. I keep hopin' the lieutenant say we can set and rest a while. But he don't. We just keep marchin'. And it keep on gettin' hotter and hotter.

"According to my map, Cove Springs is only about a mile down this road," lieutenant say. He got the map spread out on the ground in front of him. We all standin' round tryin' ta see.

"When we get to this crossroads," he point ta where two red lines come t'gether, "we're going to split up. Half will come with me up the right fork, and half will go with Sergeant Gates up the left. Sergeant, when you get to this creek, turn right and follow it for about two hundred yards. That should put you in back of a double cabin belonging to Josiah Henderson. He and his partners, Will Clinch and James Arnow, are the smugglers we've come to arrest."

Lieutenant go on and tell us how we suppose ta spread out in back of the cabin and wait for his signal. Then we suppose ta charge so Arnow, Henderson and Clinch be trapped inside.

"They are very important to the Confederates operating in this area, so there may be some soldiers guarding the house." He look at us, "Be very careful, everybody. They may put up a fight."

I'm hidin' in the tall sawgrass in back of Henderson's cabin. Seem like I bin here a long time. Waitin' like this give a man too much time to think. And thinkin's bad when somebody prolly goin' ta shoot at you any minute and maybe your life over quick as you can slap a mosquito. So I count the bugs flyin' round ma head, crawlin' up ma arms and legs, and the steps it take to get me to Henderson's back door. Over and over, I count them steps. So if I don't make it, I know how close I come.

Ain't bin much goin' on in the house. A few minutes ago, a dried up, chicken-faced woman throw some slops out the back door, and two pigs gobble 'em up. Sometimes hear yellin' like somebody playin' cards and gettin' excited. But other'n old chicken face, I ain't seen no people.

Hear two short, loud whistles, then two more. Tha's the signal. I'm up and runnin' for the house. Tighten ma grip on ma Enfield cause it the only thing that can keep me alive time I go through the back door. If I'm breathin', I don't know it. If ma feet hittin' the ground, I don't know it. I just hear a voice that sound like mine's sayin', "Twenty-eight, twenty-seven, twenty-six...fifteen, fourteen, thirteen...five, four, three...."

Hit the door with ma shoulder, not really knowin' I'm the first one, just relieved I made it. The door give way and swing kinda half way open, then stop and hang there crazy-like. Inside, I see two men with they mouths open, settin' at a pine table, playin' cards spread out in front of 'em. A plump woman with red cheeks and a broken nose settin' across from 'em. Chicken face, standin' at a fireplace over on the other wall, start screechin', "Nigger Yankees, Nigger Yankees," again and again.

Lieutenant Califf come through the other door, and point his pistol at the two men. "Are you Josiah Henderson and Will Clinch?" They nod. "Then, in the name of the United States Army, I arrest you two for smuggling arms and supplies to enemies of the Federal government."

"Like hell y'all will," Chicken Face say and throw a pot of somethin' she been stirrin' in the fireplace.

It splash on the lieutenant's arm, and he yell, "Jesus Christ." Red Cheeks, she grab a broom and hit his other arm so hard he drop his pistol. "Run for it," she shriek. Henderson or Clinch up end the table and cards go flyin' everywheres. One of 'em come at me with a chair, cause I'm the only man 'tween him and the door.

"Lijah," Waters shout, and I turn ma head and see Red Cheeks hit him with a iron ladle. Before I can turn back, a chair slam up against ma head. Room start spinnin' and gettin' real dark. I feel like whatever head I got left too heavy ta hold up. Feel like they ain't nothin' but rubber in ma legs.

Then, ma hand grab hold of somethin'. The fallin' stop. Try and open ma eyes. Don't see nothin' but a blur.

"Stop him," I hear the lieutenant say from far off.

Open ma eyes and a blur go by me. Shake ma head and the room come back some. See what look like the lieutenant pointin' at the door. "Clinch...getting away."

Tha's just what I need. March all goddamn mornin' in this heat, with bugs bitin' and I'm sweatin' like a mule--and let the two we come for get away? Not while I got any life in me, they ain't.

I force ma two heavy feet ta start movin'. One after the other like a train engine. Real slow at first. Seem like it take forever ta get ta the door even though it's only a couple steps. Outside, the sun hit ma eyes and they hurt like they on fire. I shake ma head again. Now everythin' real clear.

I see Clinch half way ta the woods. Don't waste no time hollerin' after him. Just start runnin'.

Now, I feel like a deer must feel when he run. I feel like I got all the air in me I'm ever goin' ta need. Like ma feet ain't even touchin' the ground. Like I can run like this all day.

Soon I'm close enough for Clinch ta hear me. He turn his head, give me a surprise look, try and run harder.

Five more steps and you're mines, Mr. Clinch, I think. Count ta maself: one...two...three...four...five. Dive at his legs, and he hit the ground.

"Turn me loose, nigger," he say draggin' us both cross the dirt.

"Show you who's a nigger you goddamn white trash," I say and hold on.

From somewheres he pull a knife. He try and kick hisself free so he can cut me. Time that don't work, he kinda half turn and slash at me with it. But I keep ma head real low and start haulin' maself up his britches real careful like till I'm on his ass, and he can't move no more. "Drop the knife, Clinch, you ain't goin' nowheres."

He don't pay me no mind. He keep strugglin' and mutterin', "Get your goddamn black hands off me," over and over.

Now, I grab ahold of his neck and push his face down in the dirt. "I ain't tellin' you again, Clinch, DROP THE KNIFE."

He drop it.

I grab his wrist and pin it against his back. "I'm gettin' off, and we're standin' up together. You try anythin'; and, so help me, I'll break this arm off and shove it up your skinny white ass."

Inside, everythin' quiet now. Red Cheeks and Chicken Face settin' on a chair with they hands tied behind 'em. Both look like they'd kill us if they get half a chance. Henderson's tied up and don't look like he got any fightin' left in him.

Lieutenant Califf's face swellin' up where the ladle hit him, but he try and smile time he see me bring in Clinch. "Good work, Elijah." He turn ta Clinch. "Now, maybe you'll tell me where your friend Arnow is. The other three seem to have lost their tongues."

"Gone ta fetch some friends," Chicken Face say.

"That don't sound good, lieutenant," I say. "Bound ta be lots of secesh round here, and we a long way from camp."

"A good point, Elijah." He look over at the four prisoners. "Waters, see if you can find some shoes for the women. They're under arrest too. Maybe some time in a Jacksonville military prison will cool off their hot secesh tempers."

"Y'all ain't never gonna see Jacksonville, nigger lover," Red Cheeks promise.

"Oh, I think we will. Your friends won't be likely to attack if they know you're with us."

Everybody real quiet on the way back. We almost double-timin' and that don't leave us breath for talkin'. Besides, we want ta hear any sound the secesh soldiers make behind us.

At one point, we hear rustlin' off ta the right. Clinch and Henderson look at each other. Chicken Face say, "Ain't nothin' ta be afeared of--only Cap'n Travers and his boys come ta make y'all sorry y'all ever come ta these parts." Then, she start cacklin' like she layin' a egg. The other three, they laugh too.

"Pick up the pace, men," the lieutenant say.

A mile down the road, we hear that rustlin' again.

"Only Cap'n Travers and his boys. Only Cap'n Travers and his boys."

Everybody give her a hard look, but she don't stop. She just keep sayin' it over and over.

Nother mile and we runnin'. Ain't worryin' about the heat, about the bugs, about nothin' except gettin' back ta the camp. Not worryin' about anythin' except not dyin' way out here in this stinkin' swamp.

Then...more rustlin'. On the left. On the right. Lieutenant Califf hold up his hand. We stop.

"What'd I tell y'all? Cap'n Travers and his boys come...."

"Shut up, secesh bitch," I say grabbin' for ma bayonet.

"I'll handle this," Califf say. He put his pistol right up ta her head and say, "I don't care if the whole damned Confederate army's out there. One more word and you're dead... and so are your friends."

Her eyes get real big as she feel the barrel pressin' on her temple. "I-I-I won't say no more. I swear."

Two more miles, and we're movin' in a pine woods. Nobody sayin' nothin', not even Chicken Face Clinch. No sun beatin' down on us in here, but the air heavy and hot like steam. And no breeze so the wool shirt and pants stick ta your skin and you smell like a wet hound. I feel a blister startin' on ma left heel, maybe on ma right too. Like ta stop and set a spell. Pull off ma shoes and soak ma feet in a cool river. Lean against a tree and close ma eyes.

Crack. Somethin' hit a tree right in front of me. Crack. Amos Albritten grab his side, hit the ground. Crack. Crack. Crack. Charles Waters grab his arm, yell, "Jesus Christ," and blood come oozin' through his fingers.

Cap'n Travers and his "boys" shootin' at us, but I can't move. Watchin' the minie balls flyin' round, smellin' the black gunpowder burnin' and all I can think is This ain't real; this some kinda dream.

"Rebs, hit the dirt," Lieutenant Califf yell, and the dream over. I'm on ma face in the dirt. Huggin' it like it's Momma's nipple and I'm a chile again, and I'm never lettin' go.

Over me, the crackin' gettin' louder and louder. And Charles yellin', "Please help me, I'm bleedin' real bad." And Amos moanin' and somebody cryin'. And the lieutenant shoutin', "Ball ammunition," "fire at will," and anythin' else he can think of.

Then Mrs. Clinch start cacklin' like she crazy and yellin', "Kill 'em, Cap'n, kill 'em. Kill all these nigger bastards, and thar nigger-lovin' officer too."

Somethin' go off inside me. I ain't scared no more, not of minie balls, secesh soldiers--dyin'. I'm up and runnin' before I even think. Grab the Clinch bitch and jerk her on her feet. Say real loud, "I got the Clinch woman and you best quit shootin' or else you might hit her."

I walk her out where they can see. But the shootin' don't stop. Then, Solomon grab Mrs. Henderson and stan' her next ta Mrs. Clinch. I motion for somebody ta stand up the two men. Then, I say, "You keep on shootin', and these four friends be dead real soon."

"Don't lissen ta 'em Cap'n. Kill 'em. Kill 'em."

I pin her arm up behind her back, hiss, "Shut up, you crazy bitch."

Somebody must see we ain't foolin' cause the shootin' stop. Can hear 'em talkin' back and forth for a couple minutes; then one say, "Let 'em go, nigger, and we won't hurt y'all."

"That mean we can go?"

"We cain't do that, but we promise y'all good treatment as prisoners."

I feel like laughin', but I don't. "Prisoners, huh? I know what you secesh do ta captured colored soldiers." I look over at the lieutenant, "and ta they officers. So, no thank y-o-u."

"Lissen, nigger, that's our best offer."

"Oh yeah, then you best lissen ta mine's. We takin' the Clinches and the Hendersons, and you lettin' us, or else they dead right now."

I motion ta Solomon, and he press his gun in her cheek.

"Don't worry none about me, Bill Travers. Jes' go ahaid and shoot."

Solomon ease back the hammer. "Open your mouth one more time, bitch, and...."

"Please, Bill, let 'em go. They gonna kill Sairy," Clinch say, soundin' like he goin' ta cry.

A long silence, "OK, nigger, Let's make a deal."

"I'm lissenin'."

"Y'all keep the Clinches and the Hendersons, and we'll let y'all go. Just outside your camp, let 'em go. Whatta ya say, nigger?"

Lieutenant Califf standin' behind me. He know well as I do...we prolly got no chance if they attack. But I don't know how he feel about lettin' the prisoners go. He's the officer. What he say, we do.

I signal for Waters ta take hold of Mrs. Clinch. Me and the lieutenant step back where nobody can hear us.

"I don't see that we've much choice, do you, Elijah?"

"Not without knowin' how many they are."

"But if we let the prisoners go, we'll have a lot to answer for."

"Maybe we won't have ta do that."

"What do you mean?"

I lean real close so I can whisper in his ear, "We only a mile or two from that big swamp. Real easy for a man ta slip away in there."

"And go and get help from camp."

We walk back to the prisoners. Lieutenant say, "Captain Travers, this is Lieutenant Mark Califf. We...uh...accept your offer. But, if you try anything, we will kill the four immediately. Do you understand?"

"Yes."

At the swamp, Simon Fleetwood slip in the weeds. Time we get over ta the other side, I ain't heard no shots, so I'm thinkin' he's on his way to Camp Mandarin. But I got no way of bein' sure.

Now the worryin' worse'n the heat and the bugs. Mile after mile, we go on. Knowin' the secesh followin' us, watchin' us. And over and over, same question goin' round in ma mind--in everybody's mind--did Simon make it?

The question answered a little over a mile from camp. We got ta pass through a big clearin'. We settin' ducks out there. I'm real dry in the mouth and ma blood poundin' so hard it make ma head hurt. I step out in the hot sun and see men wearin' butternut waitin' on us.

"And now, time for y'all ta let ma friends go," a tall one wearin' wha's left of a gray uniform coat say. Others come outta the woods behind us, on both sides of us. Thirty, maybe thirty-five, altogether. "But we aren't close enough to our camp," the lieutenant say.

"This's as close as any y'all ever gettin'," Travers say and grin a dirty kinda grin. "Now let ma friends go."

He point a pistol at the lieutenant, cock the hammer. But he don't get a chance ta squeeze the trigger. One of the cleanest shots I ever seen hit his shoulder and he drop the pistol. "Jesus Christ, I'm hit,"

Before any of the butternuts can raise a weapon, our men pour outta woods inta the clearin'. "You're surrounded. I'd advise you to drop your weapons and put your hands up," Captain say.

I never bin so glad ta see a white man in ma whole life. I feel like laughin' and cryin' at the same time, I'm so relieved.

The secesh see all the black men in blue uniforms comin' at 'em, and they do like they told. And they look at us kinda sheepish, like they sayin', "We didn't mean y'all no harm."

"Not a bad day's work, lieutenant, the smugglers and some of the guerrillas operating in the Cove Springs area. Well done." He reach ta shake the lieutenant's hand.

Califf look real uncomfortable, like he gotta say somethin' maybe he don't want ta, but he know it's the right thing ta say. "You're congratulating the wrong man, Captain."

Devlin look puzzled.

"Elijah's the one. He's the one who thought of taking the Clinches and the Hendersons hostage and of sending Private Fleetwood to get help." Then, he look real hard at somethin' on the ground. "If he hadn't been so quick-thinking, the rest of us would be back there in the woods somewhere--dead."

Devlin, he stand like he thinkin' on what the lieutenant say. After a couple minutes, he walk over and put out his hand ta me. "Then I'll shake your hand, Elijah, and tell you that the colonel is going to hear about what you did today."

Two weeks later, Lieutenant Califf read Special Order 1724 sayin', "Private Elijah Dorsey, 7th U.S. Colored Troops, is hereby promoted to Corporal, effective July 1st, 1864."

CHAPTER 12
JUNE 1864

Birney Barracks
Baltimore, Md.
June 1st, 1864

Brigadier Genl. W.A. Hammond
Surgeon Genl. U.S.A.
Washington, D.C.

Sir,

I have only recently seen your circular requesting that any surgeon on detached duty from his regiment report his whereabouts to you, once a month. Therefore be advised, sir, that I am on duty at this post as Examining Surgeon of Colored Recruits agreeable to Special Order No. 481 from War Department, dated Oct. 28th 1863.

I remain Sir,
Your Obedient Servant,
A.T. Alexander, Surgeon 7th U.S.C.T.

I check the letter for errors one last time. The title, Examining Surgeon of Colored Recruits, makes me smile sadly. The truth is I haven't seen a colored recruit in the last week or two. And I am not sure why. But since the defeat at Chancellorsville in April, there has been almost no one enlisting. The general feeling among black folk in this city is that the army can't beat Lee, so it's only a matter of time before President Lincoln has to agree to peace with the Confederacy.

"No, goddamnit, no," I say loud enough for two soldiers standing near the open window to hear. They look at me for only a moment, then turn their attention back to a small squad of soldiers drilling--the last ones recruited for the new 39th regiment.

"There has to be somebody in the goddamned Union army smart enough to defeat that old sonofabitch. There has to be."

I look down at the letter I so painstakingly wrote, "And here I sit, writing this same stupid letter month after month." I crumple it up. "The hell with this letter, the hell with the Surgeon General--the hell with this whole goddamned army."

Both look at me again and smile knowingly.

I grab my hat. "Going for a walk," I snap at the corporal sitting at the duty desk, who is too bored to care. "Need some fresh air."

A few minutes hard walking, and a little worry begins working on me. What if a white officer heard me? Any of them would be happy to tell the Medical Director--and Old Josiah Simpson would have me outta the army tomorrow. He has as much as told me he has no use for a black doctor on his staff.

Lost in worry and unhappiness, I don't pay attention to where I'm going. Soon, however, the smell tells me I'm near the harbor. I look around, but I'm not sure exactly where I am. Soon, I see someone pushing a rag cart down the street toward me.

"Excuse me, brother, can you tell me...?" There's something familiar about him, but he rushes past so I don't get a good look. Staring at his back as he hurries away, it comes to me. "The 7th regiment...Camp Stanton...last winter."

"Wait a minute," I call, but he just pushes his cart faster. Now, I regret the months sitting at a desk. After only a few yards of exertion, I'm already breathing heavy and no closer to the pushcart.

Two white men are leaning against the wall of a saloon on the corner. One yells, "Come on, nigger, you can ketch him." The other says, "I've got a silver dollar that says he can't." Both start cheering us on. Others pour out of the saloon and join in.

I will not be made fun of by white riff-raff. I stop running and begin walking at a very dignified pace. This really sets them off. They all curse at me until I reach the next corner and turn it. I almost bump into the man with the pushcart.

"Well, thank you, for making me a laughing stock."

"Sorry, Major Alexander, I didn't expect ta see nobody like you down here."

"Since you know who I am, am I correct in assuming you were in the 7th Regiment at Camp Stanton earlier this year?"

He studies the ground for a moment. "Yes sir."

"Then what are you doing here...with that pushcart?"

"I come home in March--ma wife and chil'ren have the typhoid. Ma two boys died, and I blame maself for bein' away. So, I didn't go back. I got me this pushcart, and I bin takin' care of ma wife and daughter."

"That means you're a deserter."

He looks me straight in the eye. "I don't see it that way."

"Maybe you don't, but the army does. If I inform the provost marshal, you will be arrested and possibly shot."

He lets go of the pushcart. It dumps its cargo of filthy rags on the street. His fingers tighten; the muscles of his arms knot up. A fist, the size of a small ham, threatens my face.

"You just go ahead. See if I give a fuck about you or thc whole goddamn army."

The muscles in his neck, the veins in his face seem ready to explode. But the fist trembles, and I sense his anger comes from the same source as mine used to--a feeling of powerlessness...a feeling that your life is always controlled by others. White others.

Looking at him, I wonder what happened to my anger. Has the easy routine of sitting at a desk day after day somehow put it out? Is there any way to rekindle it?

"You may not give a fuck, but you still owe the army three years of your life," I say with more intensity than I thought possible only moments ago.

"What about what the army owe me? What about the equal pay I promised and never got. What about signin' up ta fight and doin' only the same dirty laborin' I can do out here? The army don't want black fightin' men. It want niggers willin' ta work and keep their mouths shut. Well that ain't me."

I know who he is now. His attitude is unmistakable. I say, "Fletcher Howard," and some of the anger drains out of his face.

"I'm surprised you remember me."

"You caught my attention that first pay day in January."

"I just did what everybody else did."

"But the way you did it made you stand out."

Now, he manages a slight smile. "Sorry I got so mad at you, major, but I made up ma mind I ain't goin' back."

"I understand how you feel, but you can't just walk away from the army. If someone turns you in...." I don't finish because I suddenly realize threats won't make any difference.

I point to the pile of rags, the upended cart. "Is this really better than the army--being a rag man? Pushing a cart all day in the hot sun...for what? A few pennies?"

He looks a little uncertain, so I press in with, "And what about your daughter and any chil'ren you may yet have--do you want them doing this kind of thing?"

His anger flares again. "Major, don't try and tell me that old bullshit about how after the war all black folks goin' ta be free and equal with the whites. I seen how equal we were in the army."

He spits on the ground. It breaks into little dusty balls as it splatters.

"Bullshit is it? Frederick Douglass believes that bullshit. And so does Bishop Payne, and so do I. Listen, Fletcher, I know what it's like to live in a country that doesn't try to keep us down. I went to medical school in Canada, and white people there treated me just like I was one of them."

I put my hand on his shoulder. "This country can be that way. Your daughter could be educated and not be a maid or shuck oysters like her mother."

I let him think about that for a minute. "If we help the North win this war, they owe us. If they win it without us--they don't. And heaven help us if they lose. Because then, we all better head for Canada." I look him straight in the eye. "And I'm afraid it's that simple."

For a long time, we stand not saying anything. His eyes seem focused on a spot a long way from the shabby street we've been arguing in. From not so far away, I hear the sound of a ship's bell. Closer some boys arguing and the squeal of wagon wheels in need of grease.

At last, he turns his attention back to me. "You wastin' your time bein' a army surgeon. You oughta be a preacher. You sure got the gift."

"That's what my father said once."

He laughs, and I do too.

"Ain't you niggers got anyfing else ta do than stan' ina middle of the street all goddamn day?"

Without turning around we step apart, and the wagon I heard before passes between us. The driver stares at me for a moment, then shakes his head.

We watch it for a few moments, then Fletcher says, "I ain't comin' back if they try and put me in jail."

"They won't do that if you turn yourself in. But they may humiliate you in front of a regiment, just so they can say you were punished."

FLETCHER HOWARD
Baltimore, Maryland

"I'm goin' back ta the army."

Rebeccah don't say nothin'. Just look at me a long time.

"I bin thinkin' this's goin' ta happen. Told maself it's what you hafta do. Told maself it's the right thing for you ta do. But you know what?"

She startin' ta cry.

"Right this minute, don't none of 'em mean a damn thing ta me."

Now the tears runnin' down her cheeks. I ain't never seen her look so sad...or so pretty. I put ma arms round her and hug her as tender I know how. She rest her head on ma chest.

"First time you go, I feel like somebody tore ma heart outta ma body. I miss you so much I walk round all day like I'm dead. And every night, I lay in the bed and cry till mornin' cause you ain't with me, and I don't know if I ever see you again. Then one mornin', I say ta myself, 'Girl, stop actin' so crazy. Ain't up ta you, ain't up ta Fletcher, ain't even up ta Old Lincoln hisself. Only Jesus can end this war and bring Fletcher home safe.' So I get down on ma knees and pray. I pray in the mornin' before the chil'ren get up. I pray while I'm cleanin' the white folks' houses. I pray when I come home in the evenin'. I pray so much...one day they ain't no more prayers left in me. And I curse you for hurtin' me so much, and the damn white folks who started this war. I even curse Jesus for not answerin' ma prayers. But I shouldn't a done that cause then He send the typhoid and take ma two little boys ta punish me."

She cryin' so hard now her whole body shakin'. I don't know what ta do...or say, so I stand there pattin' her back like she a chile that fall down and skin her knee.

We stand like that for I don't know how long. Then the shakin' and sobbin' slow down and stop. I say, "Don't you worry none, Rebeccah I ain't goin' back."

She look up at me. Her eyes so big and brown and pretty and I think I must be crazy for ever wantin' ta leave her.

"No, you go back. Ain't fair of me ta carry on like this ta make you stay with me."

"But you just said."

Now she give me a little smile. "I said I was hurt and lonely the whole time you were gone. And I was. And I'm goin' ta be again, but I know you, Fletcher, and you gotta do what you think's right. If you think goin' back ta the army the right thing...then do it."

"But I ain't sure. I ain't sure about nothin' except I love you, and I don't want ta hurt you like I done before."

"Let's don't argue any more," she whisper and press herself against me. "Just kiss me real hard and carry me over the bed like you done when we first married."

It don't take a minute ta get our clothes off. Then her soft skin pressin' against me. Ma hands slide down her back and over the curve of her rear end. I pull her so close it's like we just one person.

"Now," she say.

I pick her up and carefully lay her on the bed. She open her legs.

"Inside me...please."

I ease ma dick where she want it. She bring her legs over ma back and cross her ankles. Soon as I start movin', she move too. Slow at first, then faster and faster, till they ain't nothin' in the world but her body, and her voice sayin', "Yes, yes, oh God, yes."

Turn rainy last night. The parade ground at Birney Barracks got big puddles all over it. Ain't rainin' this minute, but sky all gray and ugly. Perfect day for what they goin' ta do ta me.

"When the drum roll begins...."

"We march out at funeral cadence. We bin over this a hunnert times, Major. I'm sure I can do it in ma sleep."

"Fletcher, I want you to know I'm sorry I talked you into coming back," he say quiet-like. "I didn't realize how much they were going to humiliate you."

He look at me like he think I want ta say somethin'. Somethin' like, "Don't worry, Major, I don't blame you." But I right now I <u>do</u> blame him. I blame him for wha's goin' ta happen ta me. I blame him for makin' me break Rebeccah's heart again. Right now, I wish I never seen Major Augustus T. Alexander that day--or any other.

The drum roll start. Don't seem like I really hear it. More like it rumblin' inside me somewheres, turnin' me so cold I feel like I'm shakin' all over.

"Let's go," the major whisper, and we step off together. Left foot...pause...right foot...pause. And tha's the only thing in ma head: left foot...pause...right foot...pause till we're in the center of the parade ground where General Birney and the adjutant standin'. Then we stop.

Must be rainin' again cause I see little drops of water drippin' off the end of Birney's campaign hat.

He begin readin', "In as much as Private Fletcher Howard did fail to return to his regiment, the 7th U.S. Colored Infantry...."

I fix ma eyes on them little drops of water. They the only real things here. All this other stuff some kinda bad dream.

"He is hereby dishonorably discharged from said regiment." Finished, Birney step back, and the adjutant take his place.

Now, I look at the sky and don't feel the insignia of the 7th ripped off ma shoulder. The U.S. Army one ripped off the other. Quick strokes of a knife cuttin' off ma Army buttons.

The adjutant step back. "Guards, escort this man off the post," he say. Two men, bayonets fixed on their muskets come forward. The drum start again, and the three of us march toward the perimeter of the post.

For the first time, I look around. I don't see nobody. Only Birney, the adjutant, Major Alexander, these two guards and whoever playin' the drum see me "drummed out."

"We had to perform that little ceremony to make your...uh... separation from the 7th official," General Birney say. "Since it is irregular to drum a man out and re-enlist him on the same day, we thought it would be best to have as few witnesses as possible."

That explain why there ain't a whole regiment lined up on the parade ground.

"And now, I have to take you off the 7th's muster roll and put you on the 39th's." He take a pen and start writing next ta ma name. "I also must note that you overstayed your authorized leave, but you returned of your own free will." He blot what he just wrote. "There, that should do it."

"Now, in the absence of your new commander who is with the regiment in South Carolina, Colonel Silas Bowman, Chief Mustering and Recruiting Officer for Maryland, will administer the oath."

I hold up ma right hand and swear like I done last September. Only this time, I think maybe I mean it more. But, by the time ma hand come down, I'm already thinkin' how much I miss Rebeccah.

Special Orders
No. 1864

WAR DEPARTMENT,
ADJUTANT GENERAL'S OFFICE,
Washington, June 16th, 1864

(Extract)

1. On June 15th, 1864, the Congress of the United States passed, and President Lincoln signed an act authorizing equal pay for Colored and White soldiers of the Armies of the United States. Provisions of this law are retroactive to January 1st, 1864 for all colored troops and to the time of enlistment for those free as of April 19th, 1861. Regimental commanders will have full details in a few days.

By order of the Secretary of War;

E.D. TOWNSEND,
Assistant Adjutant General.

ELIJAH DORSEY
Camp Mandarin, Florida

General Gordon read us the Special Orders sayin' we gettin' same pay as white soldiers. Ain't nobody say nothin' for a minute; then he give the order, "At rest," and the cheerin' start. And we throw our hats in the air, and slap each other on the back. Everybody feelin' real good. Everybody talkin' about what they goin' ta do with the money. Cause now the pay equal mean we can take it next pay day. No more refusin'. I think I send some ta Momma.

Then it hit me. "What the General say about bein' free on April 19th, 1861?" I ask Lieutenant Califf.

"He said your equal pay will be retroactive to the time of enlistment only if you were free when the war began. That means ...."

"I know what it mean. It mean since Mr. Hammond Dorsey own me till I join the army, I don't get the difference back ta time I enlisted." I hold up ma hand. "It mean September, October, November and December don't count for me, but they do for somebody what was free. That ain't fair cause the free man and the runaway both need the money."

Califf put his hands on ma shoulders, look me in the eye. I feel like knockin' 'em off, but I don't need that kind of trouble.

"Twelve dollars, Elijah, that's all you're talking about. How important is twelve dollars? You could spend it in five minutes at a sutler's wagon on tinned meat and pies."

"It ain't just the money, lieutenant. It's the wedge it goin' ta drive 'tween us black men. The free ones be here next ta the white soldiers." I hold ma hand up in the air. "And the runaways still be down here."

Now I step back and look him in the eye. "And they didn't risk nothin' ta join the army like I did. No patrollers come after them with dogs. Nobody whip them for just thinkin' on runnin' away. Nobody chain them up in a slave pen. No sir, lieutenant, they didn't risk nothin'. They just walk over Birney Barracks and join up. And for that--they gettin' four months' extra pay. Ain't fair, lieutenant, just ain't fair."

He's real quiet for a couple minutes. Behind, I can hear other men mutterin' about the same thing. Maybe Califf hear 'em; maybe he don't.

"I don't know how much good it will do, but I will certainly convey your feelings to Captain Devlin to send up through channels. Perhaps, if there are enough complaints, something may be done about it."

"Thank you, Lieutenant."

He walk away, and I go over where the mutterin' the loudest. I tell 'em what Califf say.

"That proves what I bin sayin'." Solomon look round at the faces. "They're doin' this ta turn us against each other. That way we less trouble for 'em."

Everybody say, "Uh-huh," and nod they heads.

"But what we can do about it?" somebody ask.

It come ta me like a kind of message from God. "Same thing we done last time. Stick t'gether. Don't take no pay."

They look at me real hard. "Won't work," Solomon say. "The free-born got what they want. Why should they help us?"

"Cause we're all brothers, and whatever they can do ta us who bin slaves t'day, they can do ta the free-born tomarra."

Everybody real quiet for a couple minutes. Then Simon Fleetwood say, "He's got a point there, brothers." He look round at his friends. "Maybe, we oughta stand with them. What do you say?"

"We'll stand with our brothers," they say.

Major Gen. Rufus Saxton,
Dept. of the South
Beaufort, S.C. June 18th, 1864

TROOPS GENERALLY UNHAPPY WITH RETROACTIVE PROVISIONS OF EQUAL PAY LAW (STOP) FEAR NEW MUTINY (STOP) PLEASE ADVISE (STOP)

/signed/ Col. James Shaw, Jr. 7th U.S.C.I

Col. James Shaw, JR.
7th. U.S.C.I.
Camp Mandarin, Florida June 22nd, 1864

COLONEL HALLOWELL OF 54TH MASS. DEVISED ATTACHED OATH (STOP) RECEIVED FAVORABLY BY TROOPS IN 54TH AND 55TH MASS. (STOP) ADVISE YOU TRY SAME (STOP)

/signed/ Maj. Gen. Rufus Saxton,
Dept. of the South

Rained last night. First time in over two weeks. Still a lot of puddles on the sand here on the parade ground. All the officers here, even Colonel Shaw. Must be somethin' important ta bring him out. I hope it ain't bad news. Tired of hearin' how Lee and his army beatin' us.

"Regiment, Atten-huh," Sergeant-Major Jones call out and everybody kinda half-hearted obey.

"Men of the 7th," Lieutenant Lockwood begin, "Colonel Shaw has something very important to tell you. Please pay close attention."

"Like we got a choice," Solomon whisper in ma ear.

Colonel Shaw just stand there for a couple minutes, waitin' till everybody lookin' at him. Till breathin' the only sound on the parade ground.

"Many of you have expressed dissatisfaction with the equal pay law Congress recently passed. I personally think the retroactive provision is fair."

A very faint rumble make him pause, look round like he's not sure he oughta go on. Captain Devlin, Captain Pratt and other captains nod.

"Of course, it doesn't really matter what I think. You think it is unfair, and it's what you think that's important."

What you think that's important--the words have a nice ring to 'em. A ring that make the hair on ma arms, the back of ma neck stand up. Nobody ever say anythin' like that in front of me before.

Nobody.

"And all of you think you should receive equal pay back to your date of enlistment."

"A-men," we say.

"I have here," he hold up a piece of paper, "an oath devised by Colonel Hallowell of the 54th Massachusetts that I think will work as well for you as it has for that regiment. I will now ask you to raise your right hands and repeat the words Lieutenant Lockwood reads to you."

The adjutant take the paper, clear his throat, then read off, "I--say your full name--do solemnly swear that I owed no man unrequited labor on or before the 19th day of April, 1861. So help me God."

CHAPTER 13
JULY 1864

FLETCHER HOWARD
Petersburg, Virginia

"Ready with the ladders."

We swing 'em up over our heads.

"At the signal...charge."

A pistol go off, and we start runnin' cross the hot, dry grass, chokin' on the dust. At the first parapet, we stop. I hold ma foot on the bottom of the ladder, and the other two men stand it up. Then, we climb up the parapet, pull the ladder after us, and go down the other side. Run like hell with it to the next wall and do the same thing again. Over and over, till I think the surgeon have ta cut ma hands loose of the ladder, till I'm sure I can scale them parapets in ma sleep.

"Take a break," the lieutenant finally say, and we drop down on the hard ground.

"Your time is getting much better," he say, "but it needs to be even faster. Minutes are going to count on the 30th when you...you...." He see the captain shake his head.

Lieutenant Todd get real red in the face. "When you do what you are being trained for." He don't seem ta know what else ta say, so he go over by the captain.

"And just what the hell are we bein' trained for?" I ask the group round me. "Only thing I done since I bin in the 39th regiment is tote this damn ladder."

"Don't nobody know for sure, brother," a tall thin fella say.

"Somebody over in the 40th told me some white boys diggin' a tunnel so us coloreds can march right inta Petersburg and win the war."

"You a goddamn fool, Jeremiah," thin one--I think his name Cato--say. "Why're we totin' round these ladders all day if we're goin' through a tunnel?"

Everybody laugh.

"I wouldn't be so hard on Jeremiah," a voice behind me say. A voice that sound like the black surgeon in the 7th. I turn round half expectin' Major Alexander. Instead I see Corporal Horn. Somebody told me he went ta college in Ohio.

"I just got back from messenger duty at Division, and I think there's some truth in what Jeremiah said. One night when I was waiting to carry some dispatches to Colonel Sigfried at Brigade, I overheard General Ferrero and a Colonel Pleasants talking about a tunnel that's somewhere under the secesh lines."

He pause like a good preacher do. "And right now, it's being filled with enough gunpowder to blow that section of their defense works clear back to Richmond."

"That still don't explain what the damned ladders for," I say.

Before Petersburg, Va.
July 28th, 1864

TO: Brig. Gen. Edward Ferrero

Sir: You are requested to move the Fourth Division at seven o'clock to-morrow morning to a position in the second line of works. In addition, you are asked to move your command to the vicinity of Ninth Corps headquarters.

By order of Major General Ambrose Burnside:
Geo. A. Hicks, Capt.
Assistant Adjutant-General

I never seen the trenches before--not close up. And lookin' at 'em stretchin' away on the right and left and smellin' the damp comin' from the water seepin' in...gimme a kinda chilly, spooky feelin'. And I don't want ta be here--Frederick Douglass or no Frederick Douglass, cause or no cause.

Gotta shake this feelin' off, I think. Gotta act like a man, like a soldier. I come back in the army ta fight, and it look like this's where I'm finally goin' ta do some. The fear let loose some, but I'm still sorry I didn't write Rebeccah last night. Don't know if there be time t'night. Don't know if there be a tomarra night--for me.

Whole time we're filin' in the trenches, tired white eyes watch us, starin' at our clean blue uniforms--at our black faces. Lookin' at us like they know we ain't on no work detail.

Colonel Ozora Stearns standin' in front of us. The Colonel goin' ta tell us why we here...why we bin trainin' with the ladders. He ain't impressive-lookin', not like Colonel Shaw. Stearns kinda short and bow-legged. Got a belly pushin' out in front and a straggly moustache. Still, everybody tell me he's a good man.

"I have a message from General Ferrero that he wants me to read to you tonight."

He pause, look right at us like it's the most important thing we're ever goin' ta hear. Only thing I can think of--why his momma name him Ozora?

"Colored men of the Fourth Division, early tomorrow morning you are going to make history. Many of you may have heard rumors that a tunnel has been dug under rebel lines. Let me assure you that rumor is true."

I look over Jeremiah. He got this big smile and a "I told you so" look on his face.

"Even as you are listening to my message, final preparations are being completed. Early tomorrow morning, the kegs of gunpowder in the tunnel will be ignited, and a tremendous hole will be blown in the rebel lines. When that happens, you colored men will use your ladders to scale the forward parapets and lead the attack through the hole. God willing, we will all meet tomorrow night in Petersburg."

Don't nobody say anythin'. Guess maybe they all feel like me. Real proud we're leadin' the attack. Real proud our ladders goin' ta carry our whole race ta freedom. So proud we ain't got time ta think about the ball of fear in our guts.

"Your company commanders will give you the details of your individual assignments." Then Stearns drop outta his military voice and say, "Let me add my prayer that all goes well for you tomorrow."

Six o'clock...we're still stretched out along the Old Norfolk Road in little bunches of three, maybe four men, some pretendin' ta eat their dinner. Some braggin' on what they're goin' ta do time they get through the secesh lines. How they're goin' ta kill all the rebel sonofabitches. Easy ta tell they never bin shot at before.

I try eatin', but the salt pork and hardtack just lay like a big lump of lead in ma belly. They give me so much gas I fart and burp for hours.

I keep thinkin' I oughta write Rebeccah, but I don't know what ta say. Besides, we're goin' ta move up to the front trenches any time now. I don't want ta be startin' and stoppin' the letter. I think I'll wait till we settle down somewheres.

Half-past seven...the order come for us ta move real quiet-like upta the forward position.

"Keep your heads down," Lieutenant Todd say. "The rebel pickets can shoot the eye out of a hawk a hundred yards away."

Most everybody laugh, but it's a nervous laugh. It ain't cause they think he's funny.

On the way to the trenches, we pass General Ledlie's men headin' for the rear. They look happy ta be goin' the other way.

Almost half-past eight...we're in a small depression behind the forward trenches. I'm watchin' the big red sun go down. Wonderin' the whole time, if I'm ever goin' ta see it again. Now I gotta write Rebeccah. I want her ta know I bin thinkin' about her, missin' her t'night.

"Dear Rebeccah," I make the letters real careful, "it's gettin dark now, and early tomarra mornin Im goin in a battel. Colonel Stearns say this may be the one that get us through the secesh lines inta Petersburg."

The light so poor, I can hardly see. But I don't want ta get too close ta the coal oil lantern. I believe the lieutenant when he say how good them sharpshooters.

"I hope he's right, Rebeccah, cause we bin trainin hard all week, and the Colonel say we goin ta ketch the rebels by surprise, and we'll be in Petersburg tomarra night and in Richmond the day after. Then the war be over, and I can come home. I know I only bin gone from you a couple weeks, but it feel like years, I miss you so much."

A shot kick up some dirt near the lantern. A officer call out, "Put out that damned light. You want to get us all killed?"

"Rebeccah, I got a lot more I want ta say, but I got no more light."

As best I can, I write, "I love you, Fletcher." Then I fold up the letter and put it in ma pocket. They find me dead tomarra, maybe somebody send it ta her.

"Where the hell the ladders?" Jeremiah ask. "The ones we suppose ta go over the parapets with? I ain't seen 'em since this mornin'."

"Lieutenant say we don't need 'em. Engineers goin' ta knock the parapets down," I answer.

"Sounds like we goin' ta have a easy time of it."

A little past nine o'clock...a messenger come for the lieutenant and they both leave. Five, ten, maybe fifteen minutes later, he's back.

"We're moving back to the ravine near the Old Norfolk Road."

It's real quiet for a minute. Then everybody ask, "Ain't we leadin' the attack?"

"As far as I know, we are. But General Ledlie's division is going in too. And right now, General Burnside wants those men in this trench and us in the ravine."

We know all about General Ledlie's division. Since we come here, we heard about the attack he led back in June. How he so scared he got drunk and stay in the bombproof. How his men so gun-shy they quit attackin' soon as the secesh fire get heavy.

"I sure hope they ain't goin' with us," I say. "They likely ta be more trouble'n the secesh."

"Amen, brother," somebody say.

"I understand how you feel, but General Burnside himself made the change. And I'm sure the general knows what he's doing."

A few minutes after ten o'clock...Captain Thomas give us a little speech. "Get as much rest as you can," he say. "When the explosion goes off at three o'clock tomorrow morning, you must be ready to move rapidly through the gap blown in the rebel lines. We don't want them to know what hit them until all four of our divisions are through. Then, they won't be able to stop us. Petersburg should be ours in a few hours. I hope to see you all there tomorrow night."

The cheerin' keep up after he's gone. Then Lieutenant Todd tell us we best settle down. Like we can. Like we can forget this just may be the most important thing we ever do.

Eleven o'clock...twelve o'clock...one o'clock...no fires, no talkin' and, for me, no sleepin'. Feel too good one minute, too scared the next. Any way with all the black troops jammed in this ravine, ain't room ta really stretch out. So I just set and think about Rebeccah, about our dead chil'ren. Wonder if I'm killed, I'll see 'em with Jesus like the preacher say.

Two o'clock...still thinkin' about Rebeccah. About the first time we walk along the Jones Falls by ourselfs. I got real brave and took hold of her hand. Thinkin' how warm and soft it feel in ma hand. And how she look away, kinda shy-like, but don't take her hand outta mine. How we stop, and I pull her close; look down in her big brown eyes and see all the goodness and love in the world in 'em. How I kiss her lips and know there never goin' ta be another woman for me. Thinkin' how t'night ma heart, ma soul, ma body ache for her.

Three o'clock..."Any minute now," Jeremiah whisper, his words come out slow, like his mouth so dry it hurt when he try and talk. I just nod ma head. I keep thinkin' about Rebeccah. about when she carryin' our first chile, and I got drunk and beat her. How the next mornin' I was sorry, but she'd gone. How I go look for her, and finally find her by the Falls where we first kiss. Cryin', I tell her I'm sorry for what I done, and she say in a hard, cold way I never hear before, "You ever do that again, Fletcher, I cut your throat." Right now, I almost wish she had--I'm so scared.

For a minute, two minutes, five minutes, maybe longer, I wait. Ears strainin' ta hear the first sound tellin' me the attack begin. Lips prayin' it won't never come.

Half-past three...still no explosion, no orders, no nothin'. Jeremiah say, "Maybe they call the attack off."

"Maybe," I say, tryin' not ta sound relieved. For the first time, I feel like I got ta piss, and I hope he's right cause I don't want ta let it go here.

Four o'clock...we still in the ravine. The damp settin' in, gettin' in our bones, givin' the night air a heavy, wet smell. Nobody told us anythin' yet, but plenty stories goin' through the ravine. Some say General Ledlie's troops so scared they refusin' ta fight. Others say somethin' gone wrong with the powder in the mine. We get so loud, Lieutenant Todd say, "Quiet--Jeff Davis can hear you clear back in his bedroom in Richmond." I still got ta piss.

Half-past four...it's startin' ta get a little lighter in the east. Soon be day light, and we still ain't heard anythin'. Beginnin' ta look like we bin waitin' all night for nothin'. Bin thinkin' and worryin' and scared all damn night for nothin'. Bin prayin' and sometimes wantin' ta cry for nothin'.

Now I'm too tired and stiff ta care, ta worry, ta think anymore. I just let ma pee go. Let it soak ma drawers, ma pants. From the smell round here, I ain't the only one either.

Fifteen minutes ta five...I hear a rumble, just like a summer storm comin'. Then the ground under me shake. First one way, then the other. "The explosion," I say, and try and stand up. Another rumble--louder, longer, slower'n the first knock me down.

"Sweet Jesus, look at that," Jeremiah say, pointin'.

I look over at the secesh lines, and I don't believe it. The ground's risin' straight up in the air. Where it's bin mostly flat; now there's a hill. But the hill look like it's growin' inta a mountain. All of a sudden, it stop. For a minute it just hang there in the air; then real slow-like, it start ta break apart in pieces and fall back down. Then, this big flame shoot up in the air, and the blackest smoke I ever see come pourin' outta the biggest hole I ever seen. Followed by dust, huge clumps of dirt, chunks of wood, bits of metal, whole tents, and pieces of bodies that go flyin' everywhere.

"They blowed open the door ta hell," Jeremiah say.

Now, a boom even louder'n the explosion come from behind us. The ground shake, and I know our artillery startin' ta pound the rebels. In no time, smoke fill up the ravine, chokin' us and burnin' our eyes so we can't see.

The firin' go on till I can't hear it no more, just feel the poundin' in ma head. And the smoke get thicker and thicker till I can't smell or taste anythin' else. And I wonder if Jeremiah ain't right.

"Hell or not I'm ready ta fight," I say ta myself and swing ma haversack up on ma back.

But the order don't come.

Half-past six...the order still ain't come. We ain't even heard no rumors. Our artillery still poundin' away, shakin' the ground, but we also hearin' some answerin' from the secesh. Ain't loud like ours, but it worryin' just the same.

Seven o'clock...the sun up now. I'm already startin' ta feel hot. I ain't heard no more about attackin'. Still, I know some Union troops must be out there cause I hear more and more musket fire.

Half-past seven...da order finally come: "In columns of fours, move 'em out." A cheer loud as the explosion, loud as all the artillery go up. Officers wave their arms ta line us up. Slow, like we in some kind of dream, we march outta the ravine. Men so close, they almost walkin' on each other's heels. No time ta think now. No time ta worry, be scared now. We're goin' in the battle. Somebody start it; then, purty soon, up and down the columns everybody's singin', "We look like men a marching on;/ We look like men o'war."

Time we get ta the trenches, the 43rd regiment's startin' over the top.

"Not that way," one of their captains yell, "through the covered passage way in columns of two."

They stop. The 30th behind 'em stop. We stop. The regiments behind us do too. Everybody gotta wait while the columns squeeze down from four ta two. Whole thing seem like a damn stupid waste of time ta me. That covered passage only go from this line ta the next line of trenches.

Worse, the waitin' give me too much time. I hear the shells comin' and goin'...and wonder if more comin' than goin'. I hear musket fire and wonder if the secesh killin' more of us or we're killin' more of them. In ma gut, I got a feelin'--it's bin in there since round four o'clock--that somethin's gone wrong.
We're supposed ta be on our way ta Petersburg by now, not bunched t'gether like this. Not standin' round waitin' ta get from one damn trench to the other.

Finally, we squeeze through the passageway inta the front trench. All I can see is wounded white soldiers comin' at us. One of 'em stop and lean back on the log wall ta steady himself. He got a bloody rag tied round his head, but I can see part of his face gone. His one eye fix on me, and he say, "You're goin' straight inta hell, colored boy," spit out what look like blood, stumble on.

Behind the parapet, we stop again. Easy ta figure out why. There's a eight-foot wall of logs and dirt in front of us. A wall that ain't supposed ta be there. A wall the engineers was supposed ta knock down last night. But they didn't. Now we gotta climb over it--one at a time--on a ladder made outta bayonets stuck in the logs. Now that worry in ma gut feel big and heavy as a lead watermelon, "Sweet Jesus," I cry out, "where's the ladders now we need 'em?"

Lieutenant Todd just shrug his shoulders.

Seem like a hour before it's ma turn ta scramble up the bayonets. I almost don't make it cause I'm so loaded down with a haversack, a Enfield, a cartridge box. At the top, what I see make me feel so cold, I shake all over. In front of me, I see what's left of the rebel trenches, bombproofs, and rifle pits. Our men droppin' in 'em tryin' ta get outta the rebel fire sweepin' the ground 'tween us and the crater the explosion blowed in their lines. What I see may not be hell, but it sure close enough for me. I want ta climb back down in the trench and hide maself.

"Company B, over here," Lieutenant Todd shoutin' and wavin' his sword, doin' his best ta line us up. Other lieutenants and captains shoutin' for other companies ta line up on their guidons, their regimental colors. The whole time, artillery shells diggin' up the ground throwin' clumps of dirt and pieces of arms and legs up in the air.

Then for just a second, it's real quiet. I see Lieutenant Todd hold his sword up and look to his left. I fix ma bayonet and stand ready. When the bugle start blowin', he point that sword straight ahead, call out, "Company B...c-h-a-r-g-e," and start runnin' for the rebel lines. He don't get more'n a few yards when a shell hit him. We watch his head blow apart, and his body run a few more yards before it stop and fall down.

"Sonofabitches," I yell, "I goin' ta kill every fucken one of you for that," and start runnin'. I don't think, that can happen ta me. The rest of Company B see me and take off right behind, yellin' and cheerin'. Past what's left of rebel bombproofs and rifle pits and sections of trenches--all filled up with arms and legs and bodies. I swear, I never seen so many bodies.

Now, the smoke gettin' so thick I can hardly see the shells droppin' in front, behind, on the left, on the right. But, it ain't so thick I can't see the men blown apart. And their screams don't drown out the whistle rebel minie balls make cuttin' whole companies down like they was just blades of grass.

At the edge of the crater, we stop. I look in and I don't think hell can be no worser. Just below us I see what's left of General Ledlie's troops. Rebels on the other side of the rim keep firin' down on 'em like they was monkeys in a barrel. Some of 'em try and return the secesh fire. But each time one of our boys fire, he slide down the orange clay and hafta crawl back up. And they rebels doin' their best ta see not many make it back up. At the very bottom of the crater, I see legs and arms wearin' secesh butternut stickin' up in the air. Next to 'em, in a deep pocket, I see Union troops up to their waists in orange-brown water and packed in so tight they can't do nothin' but die.

"God help you," I say and turn ma head cause I hear Colonel Stearns yellin', "Not in the crater. To the right flank, to the right flank."

I do what he say.

Past the crater I see a rebel trench. On the right of it, what's left of a abatis. A few Union bodies hang on the stakes like they're rag dolls. I hear 'em moanin', but ain't nothin' I can do for 'em. The sharp points stick clear through their bodies.

Followin' the colors 'long side the trench, we're so close the secesh can shoot us in the legs without aimin'. Man after man just kinda fall down, and I know he ain't gettin' back up. But

I can't think on them or the trench. Or on the shells, or on what's down in the crater, or on dyin'. I can't think about nothin' except the red and white flag with the big, gold 39 on it and followin' it.

The colors stop and I stop. The colonel command, "By the left flank--march," and I do it. When I hear, "Charge," I do it.

In the rebel trench, a white boy look at me, his eyes get real big, and he say, "Nigger." And that's the last word he ever say. I ram ma bayonet in his gut and his eyes get real big and he look at me like he goin' ta remember me forever, wherever he be in the next world.

I pull ma bayonet out, and he look down at his belly, like he don't believe he's seein' his life seepin' out. Then he squeeze his skin t'gether real hard with both hands. Like this can stop the bleedin'. And he stand like that for a couple seconds watchin' his hands gettin' redder and redder; then, he let go a moan and double over.

I'm almost startin' ta feel sorry, when Jeremiah shout, "Fletcher, behind you," and I twist away just enough ta take a glancin' blow from a rebel rifle butt aimed at ma head. Jeremiah fire and that secesh's face just kinda explode.

I shake ma head ta clear it and follow him deeper in the trench. The clay stick on ma boots, makin' 'em heavier and heavier. And so many dead rebels, I can't help steppin' on 'em.

In the center two of 'em try and rally their troops by wavin' a regimental flag. Grabbin' ma musket by the barrel, I charge 'em and bring the butt down on the blond boy's shoulder so hard I hear his collar bone break. The other one--he look like he can't be no more'n fifteen ta me--let the flag fall. "I give up," he say.

For just one second, I stare at him, shakin' with all the anger I ever feel when a white man curse me, cheat me, make me feel like dirt. For just one second, I think I'm goin' ta pay every one <u>of you back</u>. I raise up ma Enfield. But I'm sweatin' so much, I gotta rub ma eye so I can aim. When it's clear, I see he's younger'n I thought and so scared, he's cryin'. I lower the gun.

"Gimme your weapon and them colors, rebel; war's over for you."

He start ta hand 'em over, when a officer I never seen before say, "I'll relieve you of those and the prisoner, private." Then, in a lot kinder voice, he tell the rebel ta come with him.

For a second, I want ta shoot 'em both. But I don't, and I ain't got time fa dwell on it cause I hear Colonel Stearns shoutin', "Form a line, form a line."

We do the best we can, standin' 'tween dead bodies, already startin' ta swell up and stink in the heat.

Then he shout, "For the Union, men--for the Union," and go up and over the parapet. Me and Jeremiah right behind him. The rest followin' us.

For just one minute, I think we're goin' ta make it. For just one minute, I can see the last secesh trench through the smoke. Past it, the Jerusalem Plank Road and...Petersburg. For just one minute, I think even without the ladders we're goin' on ta freedom.

Then, the rebel gunners and sharpshooters find us. Minie balls and artillery shells start cuttin' us ta pieces. On both sides of me, men twist and jerk this way and that before they drop. Explosions tear some apart and throw pieces of 'em everywhere. Pieces so hot they burn ma skin when they hit me. And there's so much noise and smoke and dust, I can't see the colonel, the guidon, or nothin'. And I ain't sure where I'm goin'.

Jeremiah holler, "I'm hit, I'm hit," and the smoke clear just enough ta let me see him fall. Somethin' hot tear ma trouser leg, but I don't pay it no mind.

"Back to the trench," the colonel order, I move over by Jeremiah, "Can you make it?"

He nod. "Take more'n a Confederate minie ball ta kill me."

I help him back in the trench we just left. There Colonel Stearns and what's left of the officers hunched t'gether--some pointin' back ta our lines, some pointin' to the crest behind the crater. A messenger come up and hand the colonel a piece of paper. He read it out loud. "General Ferrero says, 'If you have not already done so, you will <u>immediately</u> proceed to take the crest in your front.'" I don't hear what he say next, but I can guess. Another colonel come over and they both talk. Then Colonel Stearns shrug his shoulders and take out his sword again. The other officers do the same.

"Form a line," he say. "On my command...charge!"

For the second time, I'm up and over the parapet right behind him. Sweatin' like I never done before and gulpin' in thick mouthfuls of hot dust and smoke instead of air.

Everybody who's left from the four black regiments comin' too. But nobody's cheerin' or singin'. Not this time. We know...we take the crest or we all die.

Five yards and a major grab his belly and cry, "No, no," before he fall over on the ground. Four more yards and two lieutenants and a captain explode inta pieces. A part of a arm hit ma side. Three more yards and sergeants, corporals and privates around me are cut down like they so many weeds. One say, "I love you, Hannah," and fall on his face.

Just a couple more yards and we be there, I think, this time we goin' ta make it.

Then, "E-e-e-y-o-w-e-e-e-e-e-e-e," cut through the smoke. And the hair on ma arms and the back of ma neck stand up. And ma insides go ice cold clear down ta ma bowels. And I know we ain't never goin' ta make it. Cause that was the rebel yell, and now I see what look like all the devils in hell comin' straight at us.

And there ain't nothin' we can do but charge right inta the middle of 'em cause if we stand still they're goin' ta kill us all.

In seconds, the smoke and confusion and noise so bad I almost can't tell who killin' who. But I can tell we ain't stoppin' 'em.

"Fall back," somebody yell, "fall back."

For a minute, just one minute, I stand there, lookin' how close the crest, how close Petersburg. And I curse who it was keep us waitin' so long in the ravine we can't do nothin' out here but die.

Then I turn and start runnin' like everybody else with the rebels right on our heels, still yellin'.

The color-bearer stumble and fall. I can't do nothin' for him, but I can pick up the regimental flag and keep it movin'.

Some black men ahead of me jump in a trench, and the secesh jump right in behind 'em and start shootin'. I see three or four rebels bayonet the same man, then leave him bleedin' and screamin' with pain. Any who throw down their weapons and beg for mercy on their knees, get beaten till they can't beg no more.

I want ta stop and help, but I can't. Not with the whole secesh army pushin' the rest of us toward the crater.

At the edge, I stop and look down; see what's happenin' ta all the white and black men packed in there. Secesh mortar shells droppin' right on 'em, blowin' 'em apart. When the bloody arms and legs, the heads, and the chunks of bodies stop flyin' round, the livin' men pile 'em up and tryin' ta hide themselves from the fire. The heat, the stink, the dyin' worsen anythin' I ever seen before. And again I curse the stupid sonofabitch who condemned them poor bastards down there ta hell.

I turn round. "You fucken secesh just come on. This far as I'm goin'." Then, I wave 39th's flag hard as I can. Men see me and stop runnin' down in the crater. Black men from ma regiment and the 30th and 43th. White men from the 45th Pennsylvania, the 115th New York, and 57th Massachusetts. They all come and stand with me. Ready ta fight and die up here on top.

A Captain Wright, first officer I seen for some time, join us. "Form a line," he say, "form a line."

We do it. "Wait for my command," he say. When the rebels so close we can almost touch 'em, he shout, "Fire." We open up and the first rank don't even know what hit 'em.

"Fire," he say again and we do the same thing to the second rank.

"Fire at will," he say, and everybody shoot and reload. Shoot and reload over and over, sweatin' and cussin' the whole time.

And we keep doin' it till so many dead secesh piled up in front of us the rest of 'em pull back outta our range.

"Hallelujah," somebody next ta me shout.

"Praise the Lord," I yell, and cheerin' go up and down our thin, blue line. We showed them secesh we can fight as good as them.

I turn ma head and see Jeremiah. "Where you bin?" I ask.

"Down in the crater, till I see you wavin' that flag and carryin' on like a fool. And I think, *He goin' ta get himself killed if I don't go up and pertect him*."

"You, pertect me...." I don't get ta finish. Colonel Stearns find us and order us ta take cover behind the crater rim. "Dig in as best you can. We've got to be ready when they come back."

Two more times we beat back their charges. So they stop chargin' and dig in close enough ta keep up a steady rifle fire at us. And from somewhere behind the crater, their mortars keep droppin' shells on us. But that ain't the worse. Now, the early mornin' clouds gone, and the sun beatin' down on us. Some already faintin' from the heat, and some are startin' ta talk outta their heads.

"You think we're ever gettin' outta here?" Jeremiah ask, tryin' ta sound easy and off-hand-like...but not makin' it.

"Why, don't you?"

"Tell you the truth, Fletcher, I ain't sure about anythin' right now."

I give him a real good look, and I see a dirty rag tied around his arm for a bandage. And I see that rag--and the whole sleeve--caked with blood. And I see in his eyes that wound hurt real bad. And I see him kinda shiver, and I think maybe he got a fever from that wound. And I think his canteen empty as mine. And, for a minute, I wonder if he's right. "Can't think like that," I say ta myself. "Can't think about nothin' but keepin' this flag flyin' and killin' secesh." But I feel kinda cold for a second or two.

Half a hour later, nothin' much changed. A couple more of us are dead or wounded. Not much smoke now, so the sun's beatin' down on us harder and harder. The poom, poom of mortars firin' on us and the troops in the crater about the only sound comin' from their side. Moans and cries for water, the only ones comin' from our side. We're still holdin' our line, but don't nobody know for how long. We're runnin' so low on cartridges and water we soon be out.

When the rifle fire die down, the colonel send a detail down in the crater ta look for cartridges. I see 'em turnin' over dead bodies huntin' for their cartridge boxes. He have four men collect canteens and head for our lines ta get water.

A hour later, ma mouth dry as dust. My lips cracked and I can't taste nothin' but salt on 'em. I don't know how much longer I can go without a drink.

Jeremiah's so quiet I think he's dead, and I shake him. He open one eye a little and ask, "The water come yet?"

"Soon," I say. "Prolly the reinforcements bringin' it time they come."

He smile, "You never was a good liar," and drift back inside himself, far away from the heat and the dyin' I hope.

A few minutes later, a sergeant from the 115th New York stand up and shout, real crazy-like, "We'll fight 'em till we die, won't we boys?" Then he fall down. I can't tell if he's shot or passed out from the heat. Least he don't have the feelin' I got that our army give up on us. That no water or reinforcements comin'. That soon the heat or the secesh goin' ta kill us all.

The time keep draggin' on till I think I always bin here, always bin this thirsty, and maybe I be the next one ta go outta his head. And sometimes I think dyin' can't be no worsen this... bein' trapped tween the secesh and the crater. And I wonder if water in the river Jordan sweet and cool like folks say.

I hear a voice. I rub the sweat outta ma eyes and see Colonel Stearns. "Private Howard, we're falling back to our own lines. I'd be obliged if you would bring the regimental colors and stay beside me so the others can follow."

"Yes sir," I say.

He move away, and organize the others. I bend over Jeremiah and lift him up. "What you doin'?" he ask.

"Colonel say we pullin' back, and I ain't leavin' you here."

He smile just a little and say, "Bless you," so quiet I almost don't hear 'im.

When the order come, I grab up the flag in ma left hand, and put ma right arm round Jeremiah ta support him. Then I fall in next to Colonel Stearns and keep up with as best I can.

The rebels see us and open fire with everythin' they got. Jeremiah moan. I tell him, "Don't you worry; we're goin' ta make it."

And I just keep runnin', sometimes stumblin' on the dead bodies and the ground throwed up in crazy ways by the explosions. But I don't let go of him or the flag. I keep sayin', "We're goin' ta make it. We goin' ta make it," over and over like it some kinda prayer.

Jeremiah moan some more and then he go limp and get real quiet. So, I'm draggin' him when I finally see our forward trench. "Just a few more yards," I say, "just a few more yards."

The men on the parapet see Colonel Stearns, me holdin' up the 39th's flag, the others followin', and open fire on the rebels chasin' us. Some climb down ta help us. I hand the flag to a white corporal, but won't give Jeremiah ta nobody. I struggle up the ladder with him.

On the other side, I see the bayonets still stickin' in the logs from when we went over this mornin'. Seems like a hunnert years ago now.

I let Jeremiah down on the ground real gentle-like. "Fetch me some water, somebody. My best friend wounded real bad."

"A private hand me a canteen, but shake his head. "Your friend don't need water now."

"Mind your own damn business," I growl and snatch it outta his hand. I open it and splash some water on a rag ta clean Jeremiah's face.

Now, I take a good look at him, at his nostrils what ain't movin', at his eyes starin' and not blinkin'. Even so, I won't believe it. There're things your mind can accept that your heart can't. I clean the sweat and dust and dry blood off my best friend's face. Tell him over and over, "We're safe back in our own trenches. And you'll soon be in a hospital over at City Point, where surgeons can fix your arm good as new." The whole time, he don't move.

Finished, I cradle his head in ma arms, hear maself say, "Please, Jeremiah, don't be dead. Please, please, please."

I stay like that till I feel a hand on ma shoulder and hear Lieutenant Gates from D company. "Your friend's dead. Best leave him for now and go back and get some food. You've been through a terrible ordeal today."

I lay Jeremiah's head back down on the ground. Whisper, "Good-bye, friend" while I close his eyes. Then, I stand up, look down at him for the last time, and walk away.

A few hunnert yards this side of the Old Norfolk Road, I see the ladders, stacked up right where we left 'em. And I think about Jeremiah ...the men in the crater...the ones in the trenches. And I see them useless ladders, and I can't keep all the anger, all the pain inside no more. "What goddamn good you ladders doin' here? Why weren't you at the parapet this mornin'? Why weren't you at the crater helpin' them poor bastards get out? Why're you just layin' here...useless...when men needed you?" I run over and start smashin' at 'em with ma rifle butt, yellin' "Why? why? why?"

Hands pull me away. Take ma Enfield from me. Lead me back ta the others. "Why did all those men hafta die?" I sob.

Back in camp, I come ta our tent. Inside Jeremiah's things waitin' on him. Tomarra or the next day, I'll get 'em ready and send 'em on ta his wife. But not right now. T'day I gotta rest and stop thinkin' about all the killin' I seen.

I stretch out ma bedroll and ease myself down on it. Lay there, starin' up at the dirty canvas over ma head. The words of our marchin' song come in ma mind:

<u>We look like men,/ we dress like men,/ we fight like men of war</u>.

Then I think on what happen t'day, and I don't ever want ta sing it again.

A couple days later, Colonel Sterns tell us the four colored regiments t'gether--27th, 30th, 39th and 43rd--had 781 men killed, wounded or missing. He tell us the army holdin' a court of inquiry ta find out what went wrong with the attack. He say him and Colonel Sigfried, and even General Ferrero goin' ta testify we fought bravely and well. Last, he read ma name off a list he say goin' ta Ninth Army headquarters for special commendations.

Don't make me feel any better. A commendation can't bring back Jeremiah or any of the other 780 dead men.

CHAPTER 14
AUGUST 1864

Special Orders
No. 474

WAR DEPARTMENT,
ADJUTANT GENERAL'S OFFICE,
Washington, August 3rd, 1864

43. By direction of the President, a Court of Inquiry will convene at 10 a.m. on the 5th instant, or as soon thereafter as practicable, to examine into and report upon the facts and circumstances attending the unsuccessful assault on the enemy's position on the 30th of July, 1864. The Court will report their opinion whether any officer or officers are answerable for the want of success of said assault, and, if so, the name or names of such officer or officers.

Detail for the Court: Maj. Gen. W.S. Hancock, U.S.V.; Brig. Gen. R.B. Ayres, U.S.V.; Brig. Gen. N.A. Miles, U.S.V.; Col. E. Schriver, inspector-general, U.S. Army, judge advocate.

By order of the Secretary of War:

E.D. TOWNSEND
Assistant Adjutant General

FLETCHER HOWARD
Near Petersburg, Virginia

The building's one of them country churches you see. Made outta brick with a little white steeple on the top. Course, since we came here, it ain't bin a church. All the pews and the pulpit gone from the inside. Dry mud so thick on the floor you can't tell where one plank end and the other begin. The stained glass window in the back wall's the only thing still give the place a churchy look. But even that's got a hole in it made by a cannon ball. Now, John the Baptist and Jesus both ain't got heads.

Only eight o'clock in the mornin', but wool pants already itchin' ma legs. Don't know how I'm goin' ta sit in 'em all day.

"Inside you men," a sergeant say. And all us black soldiers who have bin called ta testify file inta the buildin'. I sit down on a bench so new it still smell like fresh-cut wood. I look round the room. On the back wall, I see a table and five chairs. Under the headless Jesus and John the Baptist, a Union flag bin put up. In front of the table, two smaller ones facin' it, and a chair 'tween 'em kinda facin' both. The rest of the space from the door ta the tables filled up with benches and chairs.

Hope they call me soon, I think. Goin' ta be hotter'n hell in here this afternoon.

Next, some white soldiers file in and sit in the other two sections. White officers come in and sit in the chairs. A tall lieutenant come in and say, "At-TEN-tion."

Everybody snap to and a major general, two brigadier generals and a colonel come in and stand in back of the other chairs.

"By authority of the President and the Secretary of War, this special court of inquiry to investigate the mine explosion of Saturday, July 30th, 1864 is hereby called to order."

The major general look round the room and say so everybody can hear, "Please be seated."

Chairs scrape on the floor and all the officers set down. The lieutenant tell us enlisted men we can set.

The general clear his throat and say, "As president of this court, I want everyone to understand that this is not a trial court. We are not here to determine guilt or innocence. Our purpose is to investigate as fully as possible the events on and before Saturday, July 30th. To accomplish this, we will call witnesses and question them concerning their knowledge of, or participation in those events. Our findings will be sent to General Grant who will then recommend to the Secretary of War what actions are appropriate."

Then, he introduce the members of the court. He's Winfield S. Hancock, the two brigadiers are Romeyn B. Ayres and Nelson A. Miles. The colonel's Edward Schriver. He's a judge advocate, and he's goin' ta ask the questions.

The colonel thank the general and address the room in a loud, clear voice. "With the court's permission, I call Lieutenant Colonel Henry Pleasants of the 48th Pennsylvania Volunteer Infantry as the first witness."

Colonel Pleasants kinda dark-skinned for a white man. I guess he's maybe round thirty. And he's got a shiny black beard.

Colonel ask him, "I understand it was your idea to tunnel under the rebel lines?"

"Not really...a young man in my regiment, a hard coal miner from Schuylkill County, Pennsylvania, said to me one day, 'You know, colonel, we could blow that damned Rebel fort out of existence if we could just run a mine shaft under it.'"

"And you agreed with him?"

"Not right away. But later that afternoon, I spent some time on the parapet studying the fort and the whole line of secesh defense works. I came to the conclusion that the young man was basically right. That fort was just about the only thing between us and Petersburg. If we could get rid of it, we could smash through their lines and reach Petersburg in hours. The war could be over a lot sooner."

"At that point, did you inform General Burnside of the idea?"

"No, I studied the location of the fort for several hours; even made some sketches of the terrain and then went back to my tent and calculated how deep the tunnel would have to be and the best route to dig it. I even did some preliminary figures on the amount of powder it would take to destroy the fort."

"And how much was that?"

Pleasants fiddle with his mustaches. "Based on my experience digging a 4,000-foot railroad tunnel through the Allegheny Mountains, I decided about 300 kegs oughta do it."

"For those of us who aren't mining engineers, how much black powder is that?"

"Well, each keg holds 25 pounds, so 300 kegs would hold a total of around 7,500 pounds."

"A total which turned out to be far too high."

I can see the sweat breakin' out on Colonel Pleasants' face, guess he prolly thinkin' about the crater.

"I had no way to determine the actual composition of the hill the fort sat on. The Confederates were certainly not about to stop shooting and allow me to make test borings. I had to guess, particularly about the amount of rock in the hill."

His voice drop down real low. "As it turned out, there was almost no rock, so I greatly overestimated the amount of powder."

Colonel Schriver lean forward. "I'm sorry, Colonel Pleasants. We didn't hear everything you just said. Would you repeat it for the court, especially the last part?"

"I said, 'As it turned out, there was almost no rock, so I greatly over-estimated the amount of powder needed.'"

The colonel don't say anythin'. He just look at the officers of the court, then at us. So quiet in here, I can hear flies buzzin' outside the windows.

"After you estimated the amount of powder, what did you do?"

Pleasants talkin' down to the floor, so it's hard for me ta hear him now. "I...uh...took my sketches and calculations to General Porter. And, he was the one who arranged a meeting with General Burnside."

One of the generals settin' in the officers' section give Pleasants a hard look. I guess he must be General Porter.

"And what happened next?"

"Two or three days later, General Porter told me that General Burnside liked my...idea and that we both were to meet with him the next day to discuss details."

Schriver look over at General Porter even before Pleasants finish. Porter frown like he wish he told the colonel ta go ta hell that day. Pleasants fix his eyes on the floor.

Schriver turn back ta Pleasants and ask him in a almost friendly way ta describe his meetin' with General Burnside.

"It was a very hot night when General Porter and I reached General Burnside's tent. He was sitting in his shirt sleeves smoking a cigar. He listened very intently while I explained my plan. When I was finished, he pulled out a silk bandanna and wiped the perspiration off his forehead and said, 'Excellent, excellent.' Then, he thanked both of us for coming and promised he would take my sketches and calculations to General Meade in the morning."

"Did he say anything else?"

"He said I should get started."

"And did you?"

Colonel Pleasants take out his bandanna and wipe sweat off his forehead. "Yes...I rounded up all the anthracite miners I could find, organized them in details, and began digging the shaft around the clock."

General Hancock lean forward. "I'm sorry to interrupt you, Colonel Pleasants, but did I understand you to say that you started digging the tunnel?"

"Yes, I did."

"Before you had General Meade's authorization?"

Colonel Pleasants don't say anythin' for a long time. Everybody wait.

Then real slow-like Pleasants say, "I did not, in fact, have his authorization when I started the tunneling."

"What made you feel so sure you would get it?"

Colonel Pleasants put away his bandanna, square his shoulders, look right at General Hancock. "First, sir, because General Burnside was so enthusiastic about the plan and, second, because I felt certain that if General Meade's army engineers raised any objections on ventilating or shoring grounds, I could answer them."

"And did they?"

"Yes sir, they did. But, I was able to convince General Burnside the tunnel could be dug safely. A few days later, a message came from his headquarters that Generals Grant and Meade had given their approval."

"How far along were you by that time?"

"We needed timbers to start shoring up the roof."

We go outside for a brief break after Colonel Pleasants finish testifyin'. Some of the men smoke. Some get out the cards and start a game. I just loosen ma coat and sit down under a tree hopin' a breeze come by and cool me off.

Course it don't, and I sit there thinkin' on Jeremiah.

"The court calls Sergeant Harry Reese as the next witness."

A big man with a round, flat face and deep eyes, sit in the chair. It's so hot in here now, the whole front of his tunic dark blue from sweat.

"Colonel Pleasants has told us that you were the one who actually supervised the tunneling."

"That's right, sir," Reese say in a loud voice. "I organized the men in shifts and saw to it they got what they needed to do their job--just like any good mine boss."

"How did the digging go?"

"The diggin' went good, but gettin' the supplies we needed from the army--that was...well...a damn big problem right from the start."

"In what way, sergeant?"

"Well, we couldn't get anythin' from 'em. I mean, we started out diggin' with bayonets because we didn't have any picks or shovels. When we finally got 'em, they weren't right for tunnelin'. So, me and Colonel Pleasants...I mean...Colonel Pleasants and I...went to the blacksmiths and showed 'em how to change the picks so we could use 'em."

Colonel Schriver kinda frown. "Are you saying, sergeant, that it spite of General Meade's authorization, the IX Corps did not really cooperate with you and your miners?"

Reese come out with a "that ain't the half of it sir." Then, he give a example. "When we needed timbers for the shorin', we had to go tear down an old railroad bridge and use the wood from that. We had to make our own handbarrows outta cracker boxes and use the iron hoops from pork barrels to hold 'em t'gether. We even had to fill our own sandbags. Why if General Burnside himself hadn'ta telegraphed a surveyor friend of his for a theodolite, we mighta dug right past the fort and been clear on the other side of Petersburg by now."

Everybody, even the generals, laugh.

"Yet, in spite of this lack of cooperation, the tunnel did get dug?"

"Yes sir, in three weeks we was under the Confederates, and so close we could hear 'em tramping around right over our heads. Then, Colonel Pleasants had us dig a 75-foot side shaft, so the whole tunnel looked like a T with a very long shank and a short cross-piece."

Reese say some more about the tunnel. About how the secesh dig holes tryin' ta find it, but never could. Then, Colonel Pleasants come back and tell how he set the fuses. And how he gotta go in the tunnel and find out why the powder didn't explode the first time. I try and listen, but it's so hot ma tunic and pants all wet and I smell worsen a dog what bin out in the rain all night. And I ain't the only one either. Finally, General Hancock say, "This special court of inquiry is adjourned until tomorrow at eight o'clock in the morning. I guess he startin' ta feel the heat too.

"General Burnside, yesterday the court heard in testimony from Colonel Pleasants and Sergeant Reese that you were the only general officer who had any faith in the mine tunnel. And that at several key points, you alone kept the project moving."

General Burnside ain't much ta look at. He bald and even fatter'n General Birney. The side whiskers he so famous for seem like they just tryin' ta hide his heavy jowls.

He sound kinda far away when he say, "I had faith in Colonel Pleasants' idea because I thought it was the kind of bold stroke we needed to break the stalemate here at Petersburg. I said as much to both General Meade and General Grant."

"What was their reaction?"

"General Meade was cool toward it, especially after his engineers said the tunnel couldn't be properly ventilated or shored. And as for General Grant...well...he just wanted to break through the rebel lines and give the President a victory before the fall election. I don't think he cared much how we did it."

"And do you attribute the problems that Colonel Pleasants and Sergeant Reese mentioned--the lack of timbers and proper tools, the need to requisition men and to improvise--to the commanding generals lack of enthusiasm?"

The generals shoot surprised looks at Colonel Schriver. He act like he don't see 'em.

General Burnside don't sound so far away now. "I'll grant you those problems might have been solved more easily if there had been more enthusiasm for the operation. But they were the kinds of problems field officers are accustomed to dealing with. And by and large, I think the colonel and I did a good job solving them."

The generals like his answer.

Burnside wipe off his forehead with a silk bandanna. "Besides, those were not the ones that caused the operation to fail. I'm sorry to say, there were decisions made after the tunnel was finished which, though made for the best of reasons, contributed to the attack's failure."

Now, I forget about it bein' hot in here. Forget about ma itchin' wool uniform. I lean forward so I can hear every word. So I can find out why so many good men died...why ma friend, Jeremiah died.

"Please explain, general."

He kinda puff himself up like a cat do just before a fight.

"Glad to."

He stare right at a red-faced general sittin' in the officers' section, who look away real quick.

"After assuring myself that Colonel Pleasants' tunnel could really be dug, I started thinking about my tactics--what kind of attack should follow the explosion. I reviewed my records and discovered that three out of the four divisions in my corps had been in the trenches for over a month. The men were tired, and the kind of attack I envisioned could be carried out only by fresh, well-trained troops."

He stop, wipe off his forehead again. Like a good preacher, he know he got everybody in the room waitin' on him.

"I summoned General Ferrero to my tent because his 4th Division had not been in the trenches long, and it made sense to me it should lead the attack. When I spoke to him, he said his regiments, particularly the 39th, had no combat experience and very little training."

"Given the generally unfavorable view many whites officers have about colored soldiers' willingness to fight, didn't you have reservations about using them to lead the attack--especially after what General Ferrero said?"

There some mutterin' from the black men sittin' around me. We're all thinkin' the same thing, What the hell we gotta do ta show you we can fight good as any white man?

Burnside sit back in his chair. Puff himself up even more.

"Not after I questioned him at some length, and he assured me that the problem was not willingness, but readiness. By the time he left that night, I had written an order to provide his division with the additional training we both thought it needed."

"And how did that training go, general?"

"Very well, the colored men quickly learned how to use the scaling ladders; and, had they been allowed to lead the attack, I think the outcome would have been quite different."

A soft "Amen, brother," come from our benches.

General Miles give Burnside a funny look and ask, "Are you suggesting, general, that the attack failed because the colored troops were not allowed to lead it?"

Burnside turn redder. "Sir, there were several...shall we say...miscalculations that caused the attack not to achieve its primary objective. But, I think General Meade's last-minute decision to use the 4th only for support, even though it was made for the best of reasons, was one of the worst."

A tall, thin general with grayin' black hair and straggly mustaches give Burnside a look nobody can mistake. He must be General Meade.

It's so quiet General Miles' voice sound loud as a cannon when he ask Burnside ta explain.

"General Meade was afraid the army would be accused of using the colored troops as cannon fodder if they were sent in first. I argued with him for almost an hour, but he refused to change his mind. Then, I appealed to General Grant, but he agreed with General Meade."

Burnside look straight at the three generals. "Much against my better judgment, I then altered my plans so that General Ledlie's division could go in first. From that moment on, practically nothing went right."

He wipe more sweat off his face. Then go on and tell how he have his baggage packed and he go ta a battery only a few hunnert yards from the entrance ta the mine. How he spend the rest of the mornin' there gettin' messages from the front and telegraphin' 'em back ta General Meade.

And the whole time he's talkin', I'm thinkin', *General Meade didn't want us ta be cannon fodder*. *And what the hell did he think we was--out there on the rim of that crater*? *And what the hell was the men down in the crater*? *And what the hell was Jeremiah*? *If he wasn't cannon fodder--what the hell was he*?

In the afternoon, General Meade testify. He make me so mad I want ta leave. Sittin' there talkin' about why he don't let us go in first. Sayin' he weren't sure if us colored troops would really fight the rebels. How we might look good in drill and trainin', but he weren't ready ta put us against the best of Robert E. Lee's troops.

He sit there talkin' like there weren't no 54th Massachusetts attackin' Fort Wagner or 36th U.S.C.T. destroyin' so many rebel supplies on the Rappahannock last spring. No he just sit there and say he afraid we might turn tail and run, so he play it safe and send in Old Whisky Ledlie's troops what ain't got enough sense ta stay outta the crater and get themselfs trapped and we gotta go save 'em, and instead of bein' in Petersburg now, we sittin' in this hot room listenin' ta why it all went wrong, and a lotta good men died for nothin'.

"Scuse me," I say to the soldier sittin' next ta me. "I gotta go outside." He let me pass.

"General Ferrero, yesterday you heard General Meade testify that he did not want your division leading the attack because he was not sure how they would behave in a real combat situation. Please tell us how your men did, in fact, behave under fire."

"Let me assure the officers of this court that the colored men of the 4th Division acquitted themselves most honorably on the morning of the assault. After delays that would have unnerved the most battle-tested veterans, when given the order to charge, they did so gallantly and without hesitation. The leading brigade engaged the enemy at a short distance in the rear of the crater, where they captured some 200-odd prisoners and a stand of the enemy's colors, then proceeded to the crest of Cemetery Hill."

"But, isn't it true, general, they subsequently had to retreat from that position?"

"Yes, Colonel Schriver, that is quite true. However, they regrouped and charged again. The second time, they remained on the crest for almost half an hour before they were driven back by very heavy artillery and musket fire from the enemy. Even so, they withdrew back only to our first line on the rim of the crater where they remained the rest of the day."

Ferrero then look straight at the generals. "With your permission, sirs, I would like to add that my troops were, for the most part, recruits with very little training. However, their determination and bravery that day more than made up for their deficiency in that regard. Furthermore, had they been permitted to go in first, when the enemy fire was light, I am sure they would have been able to hold the crest of Cemetery Hill."

I ain't supposed ta, but I can't help standin' up and cheerin' after General Ferrero stop talkin'. And I ain't the only one. All the other black men do the same, and even some of the whites.

General Ferrero and General Burnside look kinda pleased, but General Meade don't. General Hancock bang on the table and say loudly, "Order, order in the court."

After a few minutes, we stop.

"I realize feelings are still very strong, particularly among you colored men," he say, "but I will not tolerate such outbursts." He look round the room real slow, like he waitin' for his words ta sink in. "And I want to remind you all that this is not a trial. We are here only to gather as much information as we can."

He wait for a few minutes again like he want his words ta sink in. "So far, we have heard only from the officers who planned and authorized the mine and the attack. After our noon recess, I think we should hear from some of the officers and men who actually participated in the attack."

He turn to the other generals. They all nod. "Good, court is adjourned until two o'clock."

Colonel Sigfried of the 48th Pennsylvania, first one ta testify in the afternoon. He tell how his brigade suppose ta follow General Ledlie's division, but they can't get through our lines.

"The parapets of our rifle pits had not been dug away as I was told they would be. Therefore, General Ledlie's 14th New York had to stick bayonets into the logs and climb over on them. On the other side, they had to clear a path through our abatis because it had not been removed either. In my opinion, both of these delays caused a mere trickle of men to be where a flood should have been and allowed the rebels sufficient time to recover from the surprise of the mine explosion."

"Who had the responsibility for removing the parapets and the abatis," Colonel Schriver ask.

"It was my understanding that IX Corps engineers had that responsibility."

"Do you know why they did not?"

"I was told they had never received the order from General Meade's headquarters to do so."

After Colonel Sigfried finish, Colonel Stearns tell how we train with the ladders. And how we suppose ta lead the attack. He tell about we sit in the ravine off the Old Norfolk road waitin' and waitin', and then we told we ain't goin' in first.

"How did you feel about that decision?"

"I am a soldier and not used to questioning my superiors' orders. However, I was surprised at the change, given General Ledlie's...ah...reputation."

Schriver turn real fast and look him right in the eye, "And what is his reputation, colonel?"

First time I ever see the colonel not sure what ta say. He look down at the floor for a long time. So long, General Hancock ask him ta answer the question.

"It...uh...has been rumored that during an attack on June 18th of this year, he was...ah...too intoxicated to lead his troops."

All the eyes in the room look over at General Ledlie, but he act like he ain't heard a word.

Schriver start ta ask a question, but General Ayres do it first. "Colonel Stearns, while you were with your troops on July 30th, did you at any time see General Ledlie?"

"No sir, I did not."

"Did you have any idea where he was?"

"No sir, I did not."

"What was the situation of his men when you first saw them?"

"It appeared to me that most of them in the crater were salvaging or sight-seeing. There was almost no discipline. A few officers had organized parties to rescue rebels trapped under debris from the explosion, a few others were trying to organize an attack, but most seemed happy to let us go on to Cemetery Hill while they joined their men rooting around in the crater."

"Did you attempt to impose any discipline on them?"

"No sir, I did not. By the time my regiment reached the rim of the crater, the rebels had sufficient time to regroup and lay down a very heavy fire. Since my orders were to take the ridge at all costs, I had to keep my men moving forward in the face of that very heavy fire. There was no time to deal with the situation in the crater."

"Colonel Stearns, could anything have been done to prevent the situation you saw in the crater?"

"Firm leadership would have."

"And do you think the Third Division lacked that?"

"Yes sir, I do. The attack's success depended on the element of surprise. By not pursuing its original objective, the Third Division allowed the rebels time to recover and regroup. Once they had done that, they were virtually impossible to defeat."

Everybody look at General Ledlie. Ain't no doubt who goin' ta testify next.

General James H. Ledlie look tired. His face kinda sunk in. His eyes got a look in 'em like they seein' somethin' far away. His voice low and raspy, and the words come out real slow.

He first tell how the Third Division been here since May. He tell how they built the trenches, parapets and bombproofs everybody bin usin'. "These fortifications are the best piece of work I've seen since before the war when I was an engineer in charge of new construction for the railroad in New York. Why, some of the boys that built these trenches helped me put up the longest single-span bridge across the Hudson River. No sir, you won't find any better engineers than what we've got in the Third Division."

Schriver read from a memorandum General Burnside send ta General Meade about Ledlie's men, "They are worthless. They didn't enlist to fight and it is unreasonable to expect it of them."

"That's what I been trying to tell you. They were engineers and heavy artillery men. They had no business being in the trenches in the first place. Besides, they were tired of being shot at and just wanted to go home on leave for a while."

"When you met with General Burnside, did you communicate this information to him," Schriver ask.

"I most certainly did. And he assured me that my division would not be directly involved in the attack on July 30th. So I went right back to my headquarters and told my brigade commanders that General Ferrero's colored boys were going in first. And they all seemed as relieved as I was."

"Please describe for us, general, the meeting with General Burnside that took place on the evening of July 29th."

"Amos...General Burnside...called Bob Potter, Orlando Willcox and myself to his tent and explained that George... General Meade...was dead set against using the colored boys. Burnside said Meade was afraid the mine wouldn't work, and the colored boys would be cut to ribbons by the secesh. Then, the Black Republicans in Congress and the Abolitionists would be after his and Grant's scalps for making cannon fodder out of 'em."

Them words sends the blood boilin' in me again. Poundin' in ma head so I can't hardly even think.

"Then General Burnside said one of us had to go in first. We protested our boys were tired. Some of 'em, Orlando's I think, have been in the fight since Antietam. Amos said it was out of his hands."

"How was the actual selection made, General Ledlie?"

Everybody quiet like they dead and, low as he say 'em, Ledlie's words ring out, "General Burnside had us draw straws, and I drew the short one."

<u>It all happen cause he draw a short straw</u>? I can't believe what I hear. I can't believe the army run that way. I want ta get up and ask can he say that again. In fact, I feel maself stand up, but then I can't get ma mouth ta open.

"Fool, what the hell you doin?" a voice whisper.

"I want ta ask the general a question," I say.

"Fool, you don't ask the general nothin'...not if you want ta stay outta the guardhouse."

"But I got a right ta ask. My friend dead on account a him."

"You know you ain't got no rights in this here army. So you best set."

I let him pull me back down.

For a long time, I don't hear anythin' cause of the poundin' in ma head. Finally, from the other side of the poundin' I hear Schriver ask, "And after you saw that the parapets and abatis had not been removed, what did you do, general?"

"I told my men to use their bayonets to get over the wall; then, I went to the bombproof to direct the attack."

"While you were in the bombproof, did you have any further contact with your brigadiers or other officers?"

"I did not."

"Then how did you direct the attack?"

"Whenever a runner brought me a report, I would see to it that someone took it back to General Burnside. And when one came from him, I saw to it that it went to the appropriate line officer."

General Hancock look at him kinda hard and ask, "Did you at any time witness any of the actual fighting?"

"No sir, I did not."

I see now why everythin' go so bad. This general weren't doin' nothin' but hidin' in a safe place.

"While you were in the bombproof, did you have anything to drink?"

"You mean alcohol?"

Hancock nod.

"I...ah...might have. Purely to...ah...steady my nerves."

Colonel Schriver hand General Hancock a piece of paper. He read it then say, "I have here a sworn statement by a surgeon in your division that you consumed at least one bottle of medicinal rum on the morning of July 30th."

Ledlie don't look tired no more. And he say in a loud, but kinda shaky voice, "Yes, I had some rum that morning. But I wasn't the only one, not by a long shot. Old Eddie Ferrero was with me in the bombproof. And, by God, he had a couple pulls on the bottle too."

Everybody look at General Ferrero. His face show Ledlie tellin' the truth.

"And you would've too--if you had to do what we have to do. Send boys out into a battle to die day after day. Why I couldn't look my boys in the eye when I sent 'em out that mornin'. Not after I told 'em they weren't goin'."

His head droop a minute like he thinkin', then it jerk back up. "And why did I have to send 'em out that mornin'? Because higher-ups didn't want to look bad if something went wrong. They didn't want the colored boys killed, so mine had to go instead.

He stare at General Meade, at General Burnside, at the officers of the court. Well, gentlemen, something did go wrong, and it wasn't all my fault. Far as I can see, we all look plenty bad now."

The poundin' and boilin' too much. I stand up. Look at this sorry excuse for a general. Want ta damn him ta hell. Open ma mouth, but again no words come out.

"Sit down, fool," voices say round me. Hands try ta pull me down, but I break loose. Run outta the room.

Outside, I stand and look up at the outside of the stained glass window. "Jesus," I say, "what kinda army use straws ta pick fightin' men? What kinda army let a drunken fool lead a attack? What kinda army?"

CHAPTER 15
SEPTEMBER 1864

Birney Barracks
Baltimore, Md.
September 1st/64

Brig. Genl. W.A. Hammond
Surgeon Genl. U.S.A.
Washington D.C.

Sir,

I have the honor to report that I am on duty at this post as Examining Surgeon of Colored Recruits, agreeable to Special Order No. 481 from War Dept. dated Oct. 28th 1863.

I remain Sir,
A.T. Alexander, Surgeon 7th USCT

ELIJAH DORSEY
Near Petersburg, Virginia

We got here about a month ago. Soon as we march off the steamer Varuna at the Bermuda Hundred and reach our camp, General Birney waitin' for us.

"Welcome to the real war," he say, "here you will see more fighting in a day than you did in Florida in a month."

"So we don't think he lyin', the secesh artillery start droppin' shells on us, and we lucky only three wounded before we move outta range."

Birney in command of the Xth Corps and got us, the 8th and 9th U.S.C.T. and the 29th Connecticut Colored Volunteers. Don't take long till we see he still don't know nothin' about leadin' troops.

On August 14th, we help take a piece of the Kingsland Road from the rebels. And round ten o'clock, we cross over the James River and march most of the night in a drizzly rain. Next mornin' we cross the river again and camp for a couple hours. We just got time ta dry off and rest some before Birney come and point out a little road goin' off in the trees.

"Colonel Haskell, I want you to march your men down that road until you find the rebels, then attack," he say and ride away.

We march on a piece; then we see the road leadin' back ta our own lines. The colonel send Birney a message tellin' him, but he say, "Proceed as ordered."

We do and soon we bein' fired at. We give it back best we can till we find out we shootin' at our own men in the 2nd brigade.

Whole thing don't last no more'n twenny minutes, but some good men in both units wounded.

Then about a week ago, we're up workin' on the bombproofs in the trenches. I climb up a parapet cause I want ta see the crater I bin hearin' everybody talk about. I only got time for a real quick look before a minie ball hit the ground a couple inches from ma foot. But I got enough time ta see why men got trapped in it.

Comin' back from that work detail, we go by where the 39th camped. And who do I see in B company--Fletcher Howard tha's who. I ain't seen since he left us back in March cause his wife and chil'ren got the typhoid. I walk right up and say, "Good ta see you back, Fletcher."

He look me over for a second like he wonderin' who the hell I am? Then he remember. "Sweet Jesus, if it ain't Elijah Dorsey."

I stick out ma hand. He do the same, and in a minute we poundin' each other on the back like we really long-lost brothers. I ask him about the crater fightin'.

"Worse day of ma life," he say. "Times I wasn't sure I'd get out alive."

He tell me about friend Jeremiah and how he die on the way back ta our lines. "And you know what make me madder'n anythin' about the whole damn business?"

I shake ma head.

"The army let General Ledlie resign his commission and go back ta New York. And send General Burnside on extended leave."

"Brother, you know how white folks stick t'gether," I say. "Wha'd you think they'd do?"

"Take that stupid fool Ledlie out and shoot him."

I look at him real long before I say, "They can't do that. Cause then they have ta shoot half the generals in the army and send the rest home."

He laugh.

"You're sure right about that, brother."

This mornin's a little cool. The first mornin' the air feel like maybe summer about over. I just put ma coffee pot on the fire when Lieutenant Spinney come by. "We workin' on the bombproofs and parapets again t'day," I ask him.

He shake his head, "No, Captain Weiss is taking four companies up on the line for skirmish duty."

He don't need ta tell me B company one of 'em. I study ma coffee pot for a long time after he gone. Don't see it boilin' and boilin' cause ma head too full thinkin' on skirmish duty. About bein' up on the line tryin' ta draw out the secesh fire so our officers can guess how many of 'em dug in and where.

"Fool, what're you doin'?" a voice ask. A hand reach down and pull ma coffee pot off the fire.

For a minute, I don't see the voice belong ta Charles A. Fleetwood.

I don't say "good mornin'" or "thank you" or nothin'. I just look him straight in the eye and ask, "Charles, you ever get a funny feelin' inside. Like somethin' bad goin' ta happen ta you?"

He laugh. "Tha's why you so solemn face this mornin'?"

I nod.

"Don't think nothin' more on it. A change in the weather, that's all. Cool mornin' make you think on home and folks you love. Ain't nothin' else."

"You prolly right," I say, "just the change in the weather." But when I drink ma coffee, it hurt deep down in ma gut and I know more botherin' me than a change in the weather.

One o'clock, four companies leave the main regiment and head over a field called Strawberry Plain. Course ain't no sign of strawberries, just a lot of grass startin' ta green up again after all the hot weather. I think it's a shame we're trampin' it down again. Pretty soon, we settle down 'long a swale and wait for orders. Maybe half a hour later, Captain Bailey who's General Birney's adjutant ride up. The funny feelin' come back. "Bailey bein' here can't mean nothin' good for us," I whisper ta Charles.

"Man, you just like a old woman with that worryin'."

Bailey dismount and give Captain Weiss a piece of paper. He read it, and everybody can hear him say, "The general wants us to...to take a fort with a skirmish line?" Bailey nod, and the two of 'em put their heads t'gether for what seem like a long time. Can tell they arguin', but can't hear what about.

When Bailey get on his horse, Weiss say ta him, "You tell General Birney I'll try and do what he ordered. But in my opinion, it can't be done--not with only four companies."

Bailey dig spurs in his horse and ride away without even answerin'.

Captain Weiss call us t'gether. He's a short fella, kinda round face, from a farm somewhere near Harrisburg, Pennsylvania. He look worried when he say, "Simply put, General Birney wants us to advance across this plain and take Fort Gilmer."

He expect us ta take a rebel fort with only a hunnert and twenny men? Do what the whole Xth Corps ain't bin able ta do since we bin here? Now I'm sure he's a fool or else plain crazy.

There's mutterin' from other men thinkin' the same as me.

Lieutenant hold up a hand. "We may have private misgivings about this operation, but we cannot disobey the direct order of a major-general in the U.S. Army."

He look round and the mutterin' stop. "Fix bayonets, and on my command we will move out in quickstep along the swale until we are in the open area in front of the forts. Captain Bailey has assured me the fort on our left is unoccupied."

We hook on the bayonets and, on his signal, we start runnin', kinda slow-like in the beginnin'. The only sounds the poundin' of feet on the ground and jinglin' of cartridge boxes.

"Companies halt," Weiss say.

About 500 yards in front of us, we see the two forts with a v-shape line of rifle pits 'tween 'em. A deep ditch in front of both forts. Dirt from the ditch piled up ta make the parapets. It don't look like a whole army be able ta get over them walls.

Seem like Captain Weiss think the same. "Form a line," he say, "and on my command advance on the rifle pits."

While we line up, seems like all the sound's gone outta the world. No firin' from the fort, no noise from birds or even flies buzzin'. It's so quiet; I look up at the sun ta make sure I ain't dreamin'.

"For-ward," he call, and we start runnin' again--but faster.

Fort Gilmer didn't look so far away a second ago, now seem like it's on the other side of the state. And ma shoes feel like I got lead cannon balls in 'em. And I can't hardly ketch ma breath. And still no sound but us poundin' the ground and breathin' so hard.

We almost ta the ends of the V when all hell break loose. The secesh open fire on us from both forts at the same time. Two men on ma right fall on the ground. I look back and see one got no face. Just a bloody hole where it usta be. I want ta throw up, but don't dare stop and do it.

A shell hit on ma left so close the dirt from it like ta bury me. For a minute I can't see nothin' and stumble over somebody layin' on the ground moanin'. Another shell hit in front of me and a arm and a leg go flyin' by. Somethin' hot sting ma face. I reach up and tear off a piece of human skin.

Then the rifle pits open fire--pop, pop, pop, pop. Seem like for every pop, a man fall down. So much smoke and dust now I can hardly see anythin'. Still I keep runnin' forward. Can't do anythin' else.

"Fall back," somebody holler through the smoke and dust.

I stop and start runnin' back the way I come. Only now so many bodies on the ground I keep steppin' on 'em. "Sorry, brother," I say over and over, but none of 'em answer. Minie balls whiz past ma head and kick up so much dust the air too heavy ta breathe.

"Companies C, D, G and K form a line. Form a line," that voice holler again.

I stop, turn round and wait for somebody ta get next ta me.

"Charge," the voice say when there's enough ta make a line. And I see the 7th's guidon goin' off ta the right.

For a second, I think *I ain't goin'*. *I ain't goin' ta try and get across a ditch and up a parapet with every rebel in Virginia shootin' at me*. Then, I see Charles's carryin' the guidon. "Wait for me," I yell and take out after him.

Halfway ta the ditch ma chest hurt, ma legs 're shakin', and ma arms so tired from carryin' ma Enfield I think maybe bein' dead ain't so bad. Least I can lay down and rest.

At the edge of the ditch, ma eyes burn so much from the heat and smoke and dust for a minute I can't see nothin'. I rub 'em real hard so they water, and then I'm sorry. The ditch six or seven feet deep and maybe ten, twelve feet wide. Worse, the parapet go almost straight up on the other side. Ain't no way a man can climb outta that ditch and up the parapet by hisself.

No tellin' how long we bin huggin' dirt at the bottom of the parapet. Somebody say we're waitin' on reinforcements. But we ain't in a hurry for 'em ta git here cause right now we're safe as we're goin' ta be. This close to the parapet the secesh artillery can't fire on us without hittin' they own men. And the rebels inside the fort can't shoot at us without showin' themselfs on the parapet. And our artillery stop firin' at the fort so they don't hit us by mistake. For the first time, I'm thinkin' I just might live through this. Then, Lieutenant Spinney come over. "The captain says we can't wait any longer for reinforcements. He wants everybody to get ready to charge."

I look at him. "How we gettin' up there?" I jerk ma thumb at the parapet.

Spinney kinda laugh. "The captain's already worked that out. Two men will give the third one a boost."

He weren't jokin' neither. In a few minutes I'm standin' 'tween Abel McKinnon and LeRoy Harris waitin' for the command.

"Up and over," Captain Weiss say, and they boost me up. I cradle ma Enfield and dig in hard with ma knees, elbows and feets till I'm on top the parapet. For just a second, I wish I'm back down in the ditch. The secesh open fire, and I pray ta Jesus this ain't goin' ta be ma grave. Then, I follow the captain down inside the fort.

Somebody yell out, "Niggers, they sent goddamned niggers," and I see secesh everywhere. They're firin' at us point-blank and cussin'. One jab at me with a bayonet.

"You white sonofabitch." I swing ma Enfield up and let him have it right in the face. Before I can reload, a minie ball hit ma arm so hard I drop the Enfield like it's on fire. "Jesus," all I can say cause another one hit ma shoulder and nearly knock me on ma ass.

"Back to the ditch," I hear from somewhere in the smoke and confusion. "Everybody back to the ditch."

Shoulder and arm bleedin' like hell, I scramble up the slope best as I can.

Back in the ditch, we're worse off than before. Everybody got some kind of wound. And the rebels keep firin' down on us with everythin' they got. Moanin' and callin' comin' from everywhere.

Captain Weiss say somethin' ta Lieutenant Ferguson. He stand up and say he's goin' ta lead a charge back up the parapet.

"Everybody who isn't seriously wounded form a line," he say.

I stand up best as I can.

"Same as before," he say and I get ready ta help boost the man 'tween me and Charles.

"Ready," he say and dirt from minie balls kick up in ma face so I can't hardly see.

"Now," he say, and I push up a foot hard as I can. Then, I got ta set cause the pain so bad I feel like I'm goin' ta faint.

Most of 'em don't get to the top of the parapet before they rollin' down again dead or wounded. Even Lieutenant Ferguson come slidin' down with a big gash cross the top of his head. Right behind him come a bunch of lit shells what roll on the wounded and go off.

It's real quiet for a minute. A voice yell down, "Y'all niggers best surrender."

Perry Wallace stand up. "I'll show you rebs how we niggers surrender." And that's the last thing he ever say.

Captain Weiss get with the other officers. I can see they arguin', and I can guess about what. A few minutes go by, and they all nod they heads. Then, I see Captain Weiss raise up his sword with a white handkerchief tied on it. And I feel cold inside, colder'n I ever feel back in the cabin at Belmont when the wind was blowin' snow in. Colder'n when I had the fever and almost die. And I know this cold I'm feelin' ain't the kind no fire can chase away cause it's the cold of fear.

Captain wave his sword, call out, "We surrender," and every eye fix on that white handkerchief, and we all know we're good as dead.

"Officers come up here with your hands over your heads," a voice say.

We help Weiss and the others up the side of the parapet.

Seem like a awful long time before we see Weiss on top. He cup his hands and call out, "Lay down your weapons and march around to the rear of the fort in columns of two...with your hands over your heads."

Movin' away from the ditch, I look back just one time and see all them black men layin' there. And I think on how stupid this whole day's bin. On how many dead. And I ask maself--<u>for what</u>?

Inside Fort Gilmer, the rebels carry on like we broken down old hound dogs. They kick us, swear at us, spit on us. They take everythin' but what we're wearin'. One of 'em tell me take off ma boots. But others laugh and curse him for stealin' "a nigger's boots," so he get mad and smash his musket butt in the shoulder I'm shot in. Hurt like hell, and I go down on ma knees. Feel the whole world spinnin' round and gettin' real blurry. But I grind ma teeth and hold hard as I can cause I ain't lettin' no goddamn secesh see me faint or nothin' like that.

Soon as it's dark, they line us up. A captain say, "March 'em back to Richmond," and we head on outta the fort. Big moon shinin' so it's almost like day time. We go about a mile and come on a column of secesh headin' for they lines.

"What the hell y'all got there?" one of 'em call out.

"Bunch of niggers thought they was soldiers," a guard answer.

"Where y'all takin' 'em?"

"Libby Prison in Richmond."

"Prison's too fucken good for 'em," one say.

"Let's kill 'em right here," others say, "just like our boys did at Fort Pillow."

The column halt, and scarecrows wearin' rags rush over.

Captain Weiss step out in front. "These men are soldiers in the United States Army. If you try to kill them, you'll have to kill me first."

One aim a musket at captain's head. "Suits me, Yankee nigger-lover."

Captain stare right at him. He stare at the captain.

"Come on, Lem, shoot 'im, so we can get outta here."

"What's goin' on here?"

The one with the musket lower it. Others get real quiet, stare at a officer on horseback.

"Nothin', General Lee, sir," me and the boys just havin' a little fun with this here Yankee."

"Well, I suggest, you stop and get to your positions without further delay."

They salute and General Lee ride away.

Couple hours later, I don't think I can go no more. Ma shoulder and arm...sweet Jesus...how they hurt. And we ain't had no food since yesteday mornin' and no water either. Seem like I feel weaker every time I put ma foot down. When I can't go no more, I just lay down in the road.

"Get up, nigger," guard yell at me.

I try, but I can't.

"I said, get up, nigger." This time he kick me.

Again, I try, but can't get on ma feet.

"What's goin' on?" another guard ask.

"This here nigger fell down and won't get up."

"Shoot 'im. One less ta worry about."

I close ma eyes and wait for the minie ball. Think, don't matter. Better ta die here instead of rottin' in Libby Prison or bein' worked ta death on some plantation.

Feel a hand roll me over. Pull open ma tunic. "Hell, he's bleedin' real bad," the guard say. "Ain't no need wastin' good powder on 'im. He'll be gone by mornin' any ways."

"Let's make sure of that," other guard say. They both beat me with they muskets till I pass out.

Time I open ma eyes, I ain't sure where I am. So, I lay real still and listen. Don't hear nothin' or nobody. Try and raise maself, but I hurt so bad I pass out again.

Next time I come to, I remember Fort Gilmer and bein' in the ditch and the captain surrenderin' and us marchin' on the road ta prison in Richmond and fallin' down and bein' beaten.

Got ta git outta here, I think, before the secesh come and shoot me. Try again ta git up but feel like they broke every bone in ma body when they beat me. Still I keep tryin' till I'm on ma feet. Walkin's even harder. I'm sweaty and dizzy before I take more'n a couple steps.

I set down. Ain't no use, I think, I'm too weak busted up inside ta make it back over the Union lines.

Then, I think on what them rebels done ta me, and I make maself get up. "Better you die tryin'," I tell maself, "than settin' here waitin' ta be killed like a sick dog."

I walk some, I rest some. I fall down plenty a times cause I'm so weak. And I'm so thirsty I could drink ma own piss. So hungry, ain't no tellin' what I would eat. But I can't stop ta look for anythin'. Got ta keep on movin' till daylight. Then look for a place ta hide.

All day I bin layin' in tall weeds next ta a old shed. All day the sun bin beatin' down on me. All day the gnats and flies bin pesterin' me, landin' on ma face, gettin' in ma eyes, ma nose, ma ears. I'm scared ta swat 'em cause I hear horses and wagons and men goin' by all the time.

Hour after hour I lay, ma head feelin' like it's on fire. Ma body hurtin' so much I got ta bite ma hand so I don't moan. Ma mouth dry like the dirt I'm layin' on. And I keep thinkin' I'm back at Belmont with Momma. And how good the water outta the well taste. And how good her stew and greens taste.

Late in the afternoon, I'm finally in the shade. Now I know I'm on the east side of the shed. West on the other side. Got ta remember that...got ta...got ta...I say over and over till I fall asleep.

I wake up, and it's real dark. Time I'm sure nobody's round, I get up on ma feet and slowly start walkin' west. Every step hard cause I'm sweatin' with fever and so weak ma feet feel like they made outta lead.

I want ta lay down and die a hunnert times, maybe more, but every time I stop walkin' I think, Fool, you ain't dyin' here behind secesh lines. That's the same as dyin' a slave. And you ain't dyin' a slave. So, I keep movin'.

I follow the road best as I can. Sometimes, I lose ma bearin' and wander off. Sometimes, I got ta hide cause secesh wagons or troops passin', and the whole time I'm prayin' ta Jesus they don't find me. Other times, I'm so hungry and thirsty and burnin' up with fever, I pray they do.

Finally, I think I best turn south or I'm goin' ta walk right in a rebel camp. When I come ta a fork, I stand a long time and think on which one ta take. I don't know for sure if I'm still goin' west cause no stars out t'night. So maybe the left fork's south; maybe it ain't. Only thing for sure, I can't stay here. "Jesus, please be with me," I say and take the left road.

Soon, the road just a path goin' through a pine woods. I come ta a creek and lay down and drink all the water I can. Splash it on ma head ta cool it down some. I think about stayin' here cause I'm so weak and tired. But if I do, I know the rebels might find me. Weak, tired and hungry...I make maself get up and move on.

On the other side of the woods, I got ta cross a open field. Grass ain't high enough ta hide me, so I hunch down low as I can and walk like that. Past the field, I find a road and follow it, but got no idea where it's takin' me.

And I'm thinkin' about Momma all the time now. I come round a bend and swear I see the "street" at Belmont and the cabin...and Momma standin' out front. She's wavin' ta me ta hurry. I start runnin', callin' out, "Momma, I'm comin', I'm comin'."

She see me and smile.

"I'm comin', Momma; I'm comin'." I run hard as I can. I see her open her arms like she waitin' ta give me a big hug. I raise up mine. I'm almost touchin' her when I feel ma ankle turn in a rut, and I start fallin'. Ketch a funny look on

Momma's face, like she scared for me and she want ta help me, but they ain't nothin' she can do. Then she's gone, and I just keep fallin'...down, down, down inta somethin' what ain't got a bottom.

From somewhere, I hear a voice say, "Be careful; he's badly wounded."

I feel hands lift me up. Lay me down on somethin' soft. I open one eye, see a white face with a heavy black beard. "I almost got away from you rebels," I say.

"Good heavens, man, we're not secesh. This is the main camp of the 45th Pennsylvania. You're behind Union lines."

I raise maself and see he's tellin' the truth. All round me nothin' but blue uniforms. "Praise, Jesus," I say and pass out again.

Next thing I know I hear screamin' and force ma eyes half-open. Everythin's hazy, but I can make out I'm in some kinda big room. I raise up on ma good elbow and see the room lit with coal oil lamps. They're ten or twelve tables like the one I'm on and they're filled with wounded soldiers...some white, some black like me. And the whole floor got men layin' on it. And some more over by the walls. I can't really see 'em, but I hear 'em moanin' and cryin' out for water. And the ones on the tables, they're moanin' and cryin' out too.

<u>This must be hell</u>, I think.

Then, I hear, "Damnit, Jason, hold that lamp closer. I can hardly see what I'm doing." I look over ta ma right, and see a big man wearin' a bloody leather apron. Sweat and blood all over his face, in his beard. His sleeves rolled up, but they got blood on 'em too. One big hand's holdin' somethin' down; the other's workin' a saw.

"For Christ's sake, Jason, hold that lamp steady. I'm almost finished," he say.

Then, the one name Jason pick up somethin' and fling it over in a corner like he's throwin' some old piece of meat ta a dog. It pass near me, and I see it's a leg. I look in the corner and see a whole big pile of arms and legs. And I think I'm goin' ta throw up.

But I ain't got time. The big one wipe off the saw on his apron and come over ta me. The one holdin' the lamp right behind him.

"Lie down," the first one say ta me, and I do what he say.

The second one cut ma tunic off me. Feel the first one's fingers move along on ma shoulder.

"Hmm...collar bone's definitely broken," he say, "and there's a bad wound in the shoulder as well."

Then, the fingers move on ma arm. "There's another wound in the upper arm, just above the elbow."

I hear a nose pullin' in air. "And, unless I miss my guess, the one in the arm is badly infected. It smells like it's beginning to suppurate. Bring me the chloroform. I'm goin' to amputate this arm."

I set up. "You ain't cuttin' off ma arm," I yell. "You ain't, you ain't."

"Good God man, you're arm's infected. If I don't take it off, you...you could die. Anyway, I don't have time to argue with you about it. There's plenty more in this room that need my attention. Jason, where in the hell is the chloroform?"

I look straight at him. He's a older white man, look sorta like Captain Weiss, but taller and heavier. "I'm a colored man. I got a hard enough time in this world if I got ma two arms and two feet." I hold up ma arm. "You cut this off; I got no chance--no chance at all. I be better off dead."

He look straight at me, shrug his shoulders. "Have it your way." He walk away, Jason right behind with the lamp.

I lay down again on the table. Tryin' not ta hear the moanin' and cryin' round me. Tryin' not ta think about how hot ma head feel and how the pain in ma arm and shoulder gettin' worse and worse. Tryin' not ta think the surgeon right and I'm the biggest fool in the army.

I don't know how long I lay there like that, but finally two mens come and start loadin' me on a stretcher. "What you doin'?" I ask.

"The sawbones needs this table, so you goin' for a little ride ina ambulance."

"Yeah," other say, "to the hospital over in City Point."

"What they do ta me over there?"

"Fix you up like new," first one say. Then, he look at the other one, and they both laugh.

I bump along in the ambulance till I pass out again. Sometime later, I feel maself bein' lifted up and carried. I open a eye and see a hazy sky and a big orange sun. Raise maself up on a elbow and see I'm bein' carried to a whole city of tents. "Wha's that?" I ask.

A voice behind me say, "City Point Depot Field Hospital."

"Them tents?"

"Them tents and a whole lot of pavillions you can't see," he say. "There you stay till you walk out or we take you out in a pine box."

I lay back down, hearin' the clump of they feet on boards while they carry me, turnin' this way and that, till we get wherever we're goin'. I hear one of 'em say they brung a wounded man from the 7th, and somebody tell 'em what tent ta put me in. Then, I drift off again.

I see ma brother playin' in the dirt in front a the cabin. "What you doin' here? You sold away years ago."

He stop playin', just look at me sad-like for a long time, and don't say nothin'.

"Momma, Momma," I call out, "I'm home."

She come ta the door and see me. "Oh ma God, Lijah, what happen? You got blood all over you."

"I bin wounded, Momma. And they want ta cut off ma arm, but I won't let 'em. I won't."

She walk over ta me. "You done the right thing comin' home. I'm goin' ta take care of you."

I put ma arms round her. Lay ma burnin' head next ta her cool cheek, and the fire go right out. And I feel so good and so safe I fall asleep holdin' onta her just like I'm a chile again.

Then, I'm back in the ditch and the rebel shells come rollin' down on me. I see bodies blowin' up, and blood and pieces of skin cover me till I can hardly breathe. I try and get outta the way, but I can't move. I try and holler, but no words come out.

Now, I'm in the line marchin' ta prison in Richmond. And I fall down, and the secesh beat me and beat me, and I hear ma bones breakin' and ma skull crackin' and feel blood pourin' outta me. They stop, and I beg 'em ta shoot me. I can't stand the pain.

I hear somebody say, "Get ready." And I know ma time's come. I try and get ready ta meet Jesus.

"Now," the voice say, and I feel fire go in ma shoulder and ma arm. And it hurt so bad, I holler out, "Jesus Christ," so loud I hear it and open eyes.

I see faces lookin' down on me. One have a red beard. On the other side, I see a black face--a black woman's face. "Where I am?" I ask.

The woman smile. "In the Union army hospital at City Point. And the doctor here, he just cauterize your wounds."

"Tha's what hurt so much?"

She smile again. "Yes, but y'all heal a lot better now."

She put somethin' cool and wet on ma head. "Just close your eyes and go back ta sleep. Y'all need rest."

I do like she say.

I don't know how long I sleep. When I wake up, ma head ain't so hot, but ma throat real dry. "Water, "I kinda whisper, "can I have some water?"

"Just a minute," a voice say. And I wait, hopin' it's the same black woman I seen before.

"Here's your water," the voice say, and it's soft and full of sunshine like Momma's when she's real happy.

I raise up ma head a little and a hand go behind it and another one bring a cup ta ma lips. I start sippin' slow cause ma throat so dry it hurt. But the water make it feel so cool I don't want ta stop.

"That's enough," she say when the cup empty. "Y'all get some sleep now cause sleep the best thing for a wounded man."

She let ma head back on the pillow and slide her hand out.

Before I close ma eyes, I look on her face. She got the biggest eyes I ever seen. They're so big and deep brown I think I can see way down inside her. And I think I see she a kind and good woman. She see me lookin' up at her, and she smile. And somethin's in her smile I ain't never seen before. Somethin' that make me feel warm inside where I ain't felt warm for a long, long time. Then, she put the cool, wet rag on ma head again. I open ma mouth ta say somethin', but she put a finger on ma lips and say, "Shh, go ta sleep. We can talk later."

I wake up sweatin' and hurtin' worse'n I ever hurt before. And I know this ain't no dream. I raise up as best I can and look for her ta help me. Only I can't really see much cause it's night time and they just one smoky lamp burnin' in the tent. Finally, ma eyes get use ta the dark, and I see somebody sittin' over by one of the cots.

"Miss," I say, "I hurt awful bad. Can you help me?"

The voice that answer ain't hers. "I'm sorry, but I can't. I have to keep pressure on this man's artery, or he'll bleed to death. When my relief comes, I'll get you something for the pain. I promise."

I ain't happy with that answer, but I can't do nothin'. I lay back on the cot and shut ma eyes. Try not ta think how much I hurt.

Maybe I sleep; maybe I don't. From somewhere I hear voices talkin' real low so I can't make out what they sayin'. One time, I think I see Momma lookin' down on me. 'Nother time, I think I see that hawk from back at Belmont, only this time he's so close I think I can reach up and grab him. Soon as

I try, though, he fly off. "Take me with you," I holler loud as I can. "I want ta be free like you."

I try and raise maself up out the bed. Soon as I do, I feel somethin' holdin' me so tight I can't move. "Lemme go," I say, "lemme go," and I try and tear off wha's holdin' me down.

"Orderly, somebody get an orderly. This man is tearing off his dressings."

I open ma eyes and see the black angel and she's frownin' at me. I look at ma arm and see I pulled the bandage off and they blood on ma hand. Now, I know I'm awake, and I done somethin' stupid.

"Sorry," I say, "I hurt so bad I can't stand it. And every time I go ta sleep, I have a crazy dream."

"Never mind," she tell the orderly, "he'll behave himself now."

She ease me back down on the pillow, put her cool hand on ma cheek. "You lay still for just a minute, and I'll fetch the doctor. He'll give you somethin' for that pain."

I grab hold of her arm. "Don't go. Stay with me a few minutes. I feel better when you're here."

She smile, put her hand on mine. "I won't be long. I promise."

She's good as her word. In a few minutes, she come back and give me a big spoonful of medicine. "This's laudanum. It'll cut the pain and let you sleep."

Then, she put the cold cloth on ma forehead, and I feel maself driftin' off.

"Anythin' else I can do for you?"

"Yes ma'am, wha's your name?"

"Florence...Florence Crittenden."

I feel real warm inside, and I know it ain't only from the laudanum.

CHAPTER 16
NOVEMBER 1864

Birney Barracks
Baltimore, Md.
November 1st/64

Brig. Genl. W.A. Hammond
Surgeon Genl. U.S.A.
Washington, D.C.

Sir,

I have the honor to report that I am on duty at this post as Examining Surgeon of Colored Recruits, agreeable to Special Order No. 481 form War Dept. dated Oct. 28th 1863.

I remain Sir,
A.T. Alexander, Surgeon 7th USCT

How many more times, I wonder, am I going to write this same stupid letter to the Surgeon General. How many more times is a clerk in his office going to note its contents and file it away?

I look out the window at the parade ground so over-grown with weeds it's useless. There hasn't been a parade on it since...let me see...late August right before the last recruits left.

And I sit here, day after day, with nothing to do. It occurs to me that I'm as useless as the parade ground, and I suddenly feel angry. "Damn Stanton for letting me rot here while the war goes on." I stand up and walk to the window. "I should be in

Virginia with my regiment performing useful service for my race and my country," I shout at the empty parade ground. "And damn me too for not standing up to him and telling him how stupid his idea was and then throwing my letter of resignation in his face."

I march back to my desk and pull out another sheet of paper, telling myself that <u>this</u> <u>time</u> I'm really going to write the letter.

Half an hour later, the only thing on the page is "Dear Secretary Stanton." I curse myself for being a fool and a coward, but it does no good. I just can't write it.

I wad it up and throw it in a corner. I sit staring at the parade ground until I hear feet echoing down the empty hallway.

"Letter for you, Major. From Washington. From the White House. Looks real important."

I take the envelope with the President's seal on the flap out of the private's hand, and in my excitement to open it, forget to dismiss him. He watches me slit the seal and unfold the single sheet of stationary inside.

"Dear Major Alexander," it begins. "Would you be able to attend a meeting of the Contraband Relief Association on November 10th at Israel Bethel AME Church?" I don't bother reading the rest, but drop down to the signature. The name "Mrs. Elizabeth Keckley" almost leaps off the page at me.

"Yes," I say out loud, completely disregarding the grinning private. "Yes, yes, yes."

"Good news, sir?"

"The best, Simon, the very best." I wave the letter in front of him. "Mrs. Keckley herself has invited me to a meeting."

For the rest of the afternoon, all I can think about is that, at long last, I'm going to meet the remarkable Elizabeth Keckley. The woman who was born a slave in Virginia...was later taken to St. Louis by her mistress. There she became such an accomplished dressmaker that she made enough money to purchase freedom for herself and her son. Then, just before the war she moved to Washington. Now, she's Mrs. Lincoln's modiste and, many say, her closest friend and confidant. Moreover, she's also the acknowledged leader of black society in Washington and the founder and head of the Contraband Relief Association.

Sometime during the afternoon--I don't know exactly when--a plan begins forming in the back of my mind. A plan so simple, but so bold, I'm not sure I dare to carry it out.

Moments later, I decide against it. "It's not right to cultivate Mrs. Keckley's friendship," I tell myself, "only to try and get her to intercede with Mrs. Lincoln on my behalf."

After staring at the empty parade ground for almost an hour, I change my mind. *It's worth trying*. *Anything's better than rotting away here*.

November 10th is a cold, rainy day. By the time I walk from my rooms on Mulberry Street to Camden Station, all my careful brushing and pressing and polishing are undone. My uniform is spattered with orange mud, and it smells vaguely like the dirty water collecting in the puddles on Pratt Street. I catch a glimpse of myself in a mirror and sigh...I wanted to look my best. *Well*, I think, *maybe it'll stop by the time I get to Washington, and I can repair some of the damage there*.

Of course the train is crowded, and I have to stand up the whole way. Dripping umbrellas and cloaks have left the aisles wet and slippery. Worse, the swaying car is full of cigar smoke and the sounds of sneezing and coughing. And to pile annoyance on top of the discomfort, the train stops at every little bridge so that troops can search under it. There have been recent reports of rebel spies being seen between Elk Ridge, just outside Baltimore, and Laurel Factory, a village about twenty miles from Washington.

Finally, the train reaches the B. & O. Station, which is just south of New Jersey Avenue in Washington City. I get off with the rest and, knowing I'll never be picked up by a horse cab, I walk up C Street to First, turn left and walk to the horse car shed at the foot of Pennsylvania Avenue, just outside the iron fence that encloses the Capitol grounds.

The rain is so hard now that, by the time I reach the shed, my coat is heavy with all the water it has absorbed. Worse, the shed is crowded with people waiting for a Georgetown-bound car, and they make a point of letting me know I'm not welcome. And I wonder once more what's in store for us.

A car finally comes, but it's so full that no one can get on. The next one isn't much better, yet a few ladies...Patent Office clerks, I think...manage to push their way on.

I take out my pocket watch, hoping it will lie to me. It doesn't. If the next car comes soon, I still can be at the church on time.

I see it coming toward us along First Street, and it doesn't look too crowded. Even before it reaches the shed, I've made up my mind, <u>I'm boarding this one</u>. As soon as it stops, I make a dash for it, grab the pole and swing myself up on the rear platform.

"And where the hell do you think you're goin'?" the conductor asks, blocking my way.

"To the Israel Bethel Church up on Fourteenth Street."

"Then you best move up front with the driver. No coloreds inside the cars--it's the law."

Everybody inside the car is looking at me. The ones standing behind me in the rain are already starting to mutter. It would be so easy to comply--what's one more little humiliation? I start to turn, but before I can shift my weight, something inside me rebels.

"I will not," I say loud enough for everybody to hear. "I'm a human being as well as a major in the Union army." I open my coat so they can see my insignia. "And I will not ride outside in this pouring rain."

"Then you won't ride at all," the conductor says giving me a hard shove that sends me sprawling in a puddle of dirty brown water.

They all laugh. "Serves you right," one of the women says, "for forgetting your place."

"My place--I'll show you my damn place." I pick myself up and go around to the front of the team pulling the car. Grabbing the bridle of the lead horse, I say, "This car isn't going anywhere without me."

"Let go of that, you sonofabitch," the driver shouts, "or I'll run ya over."

I act like I don't hear him.

The white crowd stops muttering and watches as he raises his whip. "Giddap," he says, cracking it well above my head.

The horses try to move, but I throw my weight against them.

"Giddap, damn it," and the whip cracks again, only inches above my head.

The horses strain against me, neighing with fear as the whip cracks even closer. The men in the crowd yell at me "to get my black ass out of the way," and someone throws a half-eaten apple at me. But, I won't budge.

"All right, you asked for it." This time, the whip sends my hat rolling across the broken cobblestones into a foul-smelling puddle.

"Let go, or the next one'll split your black hide."

I duck my head down below the horse's, so he'll hit the horse before me. For an instant, I think I have a chance. For an instant, I think I'm going to show them this is one "nigger" who isn't going to take any more pushing around.

Then, hands grab me from behind. A cane, or stick, or club slams down on my forearms, and I let go of the bridle. A cheer goes up from the whites as rough hands drag me to the gutter on the north side of the Avenue and push me face down in it. "Let that be a lesson, you uppity black bastard," these pillars of the white community say and, reassuming attitudes of dignity, walk back toward the horse car.

A few moments later, car 32 of the Navy Yard-Georgetown Line resumes its slow progress up Pennsylvania Avenue. "So much for standing up for myself and my race," I say softly as I get back on my feet and try my best to brush off the mud and bits of garbage clinging to the wet wool of my coat and trousers.

Then, with a slow, tired step, I begin my own journey up the Avenue toward the Israel Bethel AME Church.

As I open the wooden door of the church hall, the wind catches it and bangs it against the side of the building. A small group sitting near a large cast-iron stove looks up and sees a soaking wet me framed in the opening. A very handsome light-complected woman stands up and asks, "Are you Major Alexander?"

I nod.

"We didn't think you were coming. We've just about concluded the meeting. But, won't you join us?" The other board members of the Contraband Relief Association shift their chairs to make room for me.

"I don't think I should, ma'am. My uniform is soaked clear through. I'll ruin anything I sit on."

"Nonsense," she says and insists with quiet authority that I remove my coat and go sit by the stove before I "catch my death."

I'm too wet, too tired and too disappointed in myself to protest. I remove my coat, hand it to her, and wearily drop on the chair she indicates.

Of course, she notices the mud and bits of garbage clinging to my coat. "Did you fall down, major?"

"No, I had a disagreement with a horse car conductor, and it ended badly for me."

"Please tell us about it."

I try to make it clear I don't want to, but she urges me in such a kind, concerned way that I find myself relating the whole miserable experience, ending with, "After I picked myself up out of the gutter, I had no choice but to walk here."

When I finish, there is silence for a few minutes. I stare at the stove. I know they think I'm a coward, and I don't want to see the disapproval on their faces.

"It is absolutely intolerable," Mrs. Keckley says at last, "that one of our fighting men--a major no less--can't ride a horse car, in weather like this, and the lowest life white man in this city can. Absolutely intolerable."

She turns back to the group at the table. "Bishop, Senator Sumner must be notified of this outrage at once."

A man I recognize as Daniel A. Payne, bishop of the AME church, agrees with her and asks me to give him a full report before I leave Washington. "The senator," he says, "has been preparing a bill to outlaw discrimination on the horse cars. There is, of course, much opposition; but I'm sure when he learns how badly a man of your rank was treated, he will redouble his efforts to secure its passage."

I assure the bishop he will have the report before the evening is over. "And if it can play a part, however small, in ending this odious form of discrimination against our people, I will think the indignities I suffered today were worth the cost."

A young woman enters the hall with a steaming cup in her hand. She smiles very sweetly and presents it to me with the suggestion I drink it while it's still hot.

It's a steaming cup of coffee. Taking a long, long sip, I close my eyes and enjoy feeling the warmth spreading through my insides.

"I'm so sorry to disturb you, Major," Mrs. Keckley says, "but Bishop Payne has another meeting to attend, and we would like you to join us for the last item of business."

"Gladly, Mrs. Keckley, gladly." I take another hearty sip and join the group seated at the table.

Mrs. Keckley introduces me to them, beginning with Bishop Payne and the Reverend Rufus Simpson, "who is our interim pastor while the Reverend Henry Turner is on duty as an army chaplain with the 1st regiment USCT," and ending with Miss Sallie King, the young woman who brought me the "coffee."

"For some time," Reverend Simpson begins, "many of us have wanted to remove the word contraband from the name of this organization. We think it's . . ."

"We think it makes our brothers and sisters sound like property instead of human beings, and isn't the property vs. human being issue what this war is all about?" Sallie asks, looking first at the bishop, then at Reverend Simpson, then at Mrs. Keckley.

"Please don't misunderstand me, Sallie," Mrs. Keckley replies. "Basically, I think you're right. But from the time General Butler first called escaped slaves 'contraband of war' at Fortress Monroe to protect them from their former masters, the term has come to stand for safety and the promise of freedom. As such, it is very important to many of our people, especially in the South."

"To change it at this point might well cause confusion among them," the bishop adds.

"Mrs. Keckley, what you and Bishop Payne say is true, but I also believe the term has outlived its usefulness. At this point in the war, we must show that this organization is no longer concerned with the promise of freedom for our people, but for the reality of freedom. Furthermore, removing contraband from our name will say to all who have escaped the bonds of slavery that you are no longer a chattel, but a human being."

She looks straight at me. "Don't you agree, Major Alexander?"

My face feels hot as I realize I was paying more attention to the deep brown of her eyes and to the sweep of the long black lashes above them than to what she was saying. Now, I have the terrible feeling that everyone is waiting for me to say something important. But all I can do is stammer, "I...er...most definitely agree...with...with everything you say."

"Then, you think Freedmen's Relief Association would be a better name?"

Those deep brown eyes are on me, urging me to be on her side. I can't resist them. "Yes...yes I do...and I think you should broaden the group's scope to include the families of our soldiers as well." I explain that even though the pay has been equalized, it is still low and comes at irregular intervals; consequently, many soldiers' families are destitute and need assistance as much as the freedmen's do.

"That's a wonderful suggestion, major." Turning to Mrs. Keckley, Sallie says, "Madame Chairman, I would like to propose a motion to this board that we change the name from the Contraband Relief Association of Washington to the Freedmen and Soldiers' Relief Association of Washington."

There is, of course, a lot of discussion. But finally, the board votes to change the name. Afterward, the bishop makes his apologies and rushes off--he is so very late for his other meeting.

"Mrs. Keckley, may I have a word with you?" I ask.

"Certainly, major, but I have a small favor to ask of you first." She motions to Sallie to join us. "I need someone to escort Miss King home. She came with Bishop Payne, but he had to leave and...."

"Say no more, Mrs. Keckley, I will be honored." I offer my arm to Sallie, who is tying her bonnet.

"What did you want to speak to me about, major?"

I look at Sallie, think about the chance to be alone with her, even for a few minutes. "It can wait. I'll write to you about it."

Sallie links her arm with mine. I feel her light touch on my forearm, and I'm not so sure I want to leave Baltimore. After all, it's only a few hours away by train.

MAJOR AUGUSTUS T. ALEXANDER

Near Petersburg, Virginia
November 21st, 1864

The Hon. John T. Sherman,
U.S. Senator from Ohio
Washington, D.C.

Sir,

I write to you as a fellow Ohioan to ask your help in correcting a most grievous wrong. I am an assistant surgeon in the 7th U.S.C.T. and have been since my appointment in November last.

When I received my appointment, I had no knowledge that the regiment's chief surgeon was to be a colored man, Major Augustus T. Alexander. If I had known, I certainly would have refused the appointment. I do not harbor any ill feelings toward Major Alexander personally; however, I think it is grave, unjust, and humiliating to place a white man, such as myself, under the command of a colored officer.

After repeated appeals to Surgeon General Hammond and Secretary of War Stanton, Major Alexander was placed on temporary duty in Baltimore examining recruits, where he has been since February of this year. However, officially he remains the chief surgeon of the 7th U.S.C.T., even though he has not been with the regiment for over eight months and has not attended to any of the wounded in the various engagements and battles the regiment has fought in. That burden has fallen on myself and the other white assistant surgeons who have labored long hours caring for the wounded and dying. Yet, we cannot be rewarded or promoted for our efforts as long as Major Alexander remains chief surgeon.

Therefore, I urgently and respectfully request that you exert whatever influence you may have in the Government to have Major Alexander permanently transferred to some camp for Contrabands or some General Hospital for Colored Troops, where he may care for his people and not have white men as his subordinates.

As stated earlier, I am not opposed to Major Alexander personally, but I am opposed on principle to mixing the races in this manner. Perhaps, when I have reached a much higher level of maturity, I may not object to having a colored man as a superior officer. However, at this time, I am far from that state of perfection.

Most Respectfully,
Your Obt. Servant,
Lt. Joel Morgan

Once again, the clerk ushers me into Secretary Stanton's outer office. Once again, I stand at one of the tall windows and pretend to be interested in the Indian Rock which sits between the War and Navy Department buildings. Once again, while I wait, my mind runs over the possible reasons for me being here.

"The secretary will see you now," the polished voice says, and a white-gloved hand opens the heavy mahogany door.

"Your friends at the 7th have been at it again," Stanton says as a sort of greeting to me. "Lieutenant Morgan has gone so far as to put pressure on me through Senator Sherman."

He hands me Morgan's letter and drums his finger nails on his desk while I read it. When I finish, I am sure this time Morgan will have his way. I know that John Sherman is General William Tecumseh Sherman's brother, and a man to be reckoned with in Washington City.

"And that's not all. Read this one from your boss, General Simpson."

He hands me what is clearly a reply to a letter Stanton wrote about my position at Birney Barracks. Simpson stated quite clearly that I was "the only officer on duty" and that my duties were "very light." Furthermore, the letter said, "his services could be dispensed with, and an Acting Assistant Surgeon assigned to perform such duties as might, from time to time, be required." I feel myself already on the way to a contraband camp in Washington. <u>Oh well</u>, I think, <u>at least I'll be able to see Miss Sallie more often</u>.

"Do you realize how easy it would be for me to grant Lieutenant Morgan's request?" He waves the Simpson letter. "This certainly suggests you are not indispensable right now." He smiles slightly, "And how pleasant it would be not to <u>ever</u> hear about you from Morgan again. Do you have any idea what a relief <u>that</u> would be, major?"

I know I'm not supposed to answer. That this is leading up to an announcement of the decision he has already made. I brace myself as best as I can.

He slams both letters down on his desk blotter so hard that I flinch a little from surprise.

"But damnit, man, I don't like being told what to do, especially by whining little pipsqueaks like Lieutenant Morgan, who think all they have to do is write to some politician and I'll jump through hoops for them."

Then, he looks at me for a long time like he's seeing me for the first time. "You know what Morgan's real problem is don't you?"

I certainly do know, and before I can check my tongue, I blurt out, "I'm an intelligent, educated black man."

He bangs a fist on the blotter. "Exactly. You challenge his most basic beliefs about himself and the world he lives in. Colored people who are the equal of whites--it goes against everything he's learned since childhood. It's like...."

"Putting the bottom rail of a fence on top?"

"Yes, as far as he's concerned, that's exactly what it is."

"Then, let me ask you point-blank, Mr. Secretary, do you intend to reassign me just so Lieutenant Morgan and the others won't have their assumptions of racial superiority challenged?"

My question catches him by surprise. It surprises me a little too, but I think <u>Damnit, I'm tired of this game</u>. <u>If Stanton doesn't want me in the army, he can say so right now</u>. <u>If he does, then let him openly declare himself on my side</u>.

For what feels like a very long time, he doesn't say anything. In spite of the November chill outside, I'm sweating.

"Lieutenant Morgan's racial assumptions have already been challenged, and my guess is they will be again and again in the years to come. Because when this war's over, he may be living in a country far different from the one he knew before it started."

He looks me up and down again. "A country where you count as much as he does. And I don't need to tell you--he <u>already</u> doesn't like that idea."

Stanton puts his finger tips together just touching his lips; his eyes focus on the desk blotter. He seems to have forgotten I'm in the room. I wonder if I should leave.

Finally, he turns his attention on me again. "I just can't justify reassigning you to myself...no matter how hard I try. Therefore, you are to stay as the 7th's chief surgeon."

I start breathing again.

"However, I think you ought to go where you could be useful.

City Point Army Hospital might be such a place."

"Thank you very much, Mr. Secretary, I...."

"And as for Lieutenant Morgan, I think I'll leave him right where he is for a little longer. Who knows? One day he may thank me for helping him get ready for the post-war world."

Some minutes later, I leave Stanton's office. Outside, the wind has picked up considerably and is blowing leaves around and around in circles. I feel as confused and as helpless as those leaves. I have no more control over what happens to me than they do. And I seem to have no more understanding of Stanton than they do of the wind. On the one hand, I want to believe what he said about the future, yet I can't completely rid myself of the suspicion he said it just to buy himself a little more time. He may think that, sooner or later, either Morgan or myself is bound to give up.

CHAPTER 17
DECEMBER 1864

Near the James River, Va.
Dec. 5, 1864

Mrs. Fletcher Howard
10th St.
Balmore

Dear Rebeccah,

Every night I dream the same dream. The war is over and Im home with you again and we walk till we go out past Mt. Carmel Cemetery. Then we lay down in the grass and I touch your face and your skin soft like a baby and you smile and I think no prettier woman, colored or white, in this whole world. And I hold you and kiss you and love you and Im so happy just being with you I think this must be what Heaven like.

And when I wake up, I miss you so much I think I will desert again and take you with me up to Canada where we never hafta hear about this war again. Only then I think of my friend Jeremiah and them other men who died in the Crater and I know I got to stay and make the secesh pay for what they done that day. And keep making them pay till they give up. And dont nobody know how long thats going to be. I dont know and General Grant dont know and President Lincoln dont either. Maybe not even God himself know.

So what Im saying Rebeccah, I dont know when I can see you again. Maybe not for a long, long time. And when I do come home, I aint never leaving you again. Meantime, there aint a hour go by I don't miss you.

Your loving husband,
Fletcher

P.S. Kiss Rachel and Momma and Daddy for me.

I fold up the letter like I always do and take it ta the 2nd Brigade Post Office. Drop it in the outgoin' box and hope Rebeccah get it before Christmas.

Course don't nobody tell us where we goin' time they load us on the creaky old Paramus at City Point. When that's full up, rest of us go on the Montauk with the 4th Colored Troops. Their sergeant-major, name of Christian Fleetwood, say the 6th and 30th Colored loadin' too. Later on, I hear sailors talkin' about white regiments like the 47th and 48th New York, the 76th Pennsylvania, 6th and 7th Connecticut, and the 3rd and 7th New Hampshire already bein' on their transports.

And loaded's the right word. The Montauk's so full, men down in the hold layin' on top of the coal. They're jammed in 'tween the decks. They take up every inch of space on the top deck. This steamer's so crowded nobody can scratch his ass without stickin' his hand in somebody else's pocket.

Early the next mornin', we leave City Point and make our way down the James River and out inta the Ches'peake Bay. A couple days later, we stop somewheres off what I'm pretty sure's the North Carolina coast. Men who bin sayin' we're goin' down ta Savannah and join up with General Sherman change their mind and say we're goin' ta Fort Fisher.

"What're we waitin' for?" everybody keep askin'. For two days the Montauk and the other troop ships ain't moved. We just bin settin' here bobbin' up and down on the tide. Worse thing-- nobody's allowed ashore. And for two days every one of us bin wantin' ta get off this crowded old tub. Stretch our legs, fix some good, hot coffee, breathe air what ain't bin fouled by other men's farts. So for two days we bin askin' the same question. And for two days we ain't got a answer.

This mornin', right after reveille, the Montauk start rockin'. A hour or so later, I can't hardly stand up on the deck. About a hour after that, all the troop ships head south for Beaufort. Time we get there, storm's blowin' so hard transports can't dock, and we hafta ride it out on board.

I hope I never get that sick again. I throw up everythin' in ma belly. Then, feel like I throw up everythin' what's ever bin in ma belly. Still, the heavin' don't stop. Sometime durin' the night, Fleetwood come over and ask me ta join him in prayer. I can't hardly lift ma head, but I mumble 'long best as I can. Others join in, and he say, "You see what I bin tellin' you? When you're really scared, there's nothin' like prayer."

Storm finally end, but we still don't get off the Montauk. Food, water and coal loaded on, and some who are too weak from bein' sea sick are taken off. Rest of us stay on board, and the ships leave Beaufort and head back up the coast ta Fort Fisher.

We hear the boomin' before we're close enough ta see anythin'. And it keep gettin' louder and louder till it seem like there ain't nothin' else but the noise of the bombardment. Like the whole ocean shakin' from it. Finally, the Montauk close enough so I can see our ships firin' at what look like a row of sand hills, connected t'gether with rows of logs and earth walls, stretchin' way up the beach.

"You think we're goin' ta attack from this side?"

"I don't think so," Sergeant-Major Fleetwood say. "My guess is those hills are hiding major batteries just waiting to catch us in a cross-fire the minute we set foot on that beach." He look off ta the north. "I think we'll probably land up there and try to take the fort from the land side."

Sometimes, the firin' stop for a minute or two, and maybe, a young soldier look over the fort and say, "What're we waitin' for? Let's go and get this over with. Can't nobody be alive after all that shellin'."

And I tell him, "They're alive all right, and a lot of us are goin' ta die findin' out."

It's real quiet now. The troop ships moved a couple miles north of the fort. Officers movin' up and down the *Montauk's* deck givin' orders in soft voices. Then, we see the Navy launches comin' towards us, and we check our Enfields, makin' sure they ready ta fire. Some pin letters on their backs, but I don't cause I got no letter. I try and write ta Rebeccah early this mornin', but I got nothin' ta say I ain't said before. Fightin' in this war gettin' ta be like a job. I know what I got ta do, so I just want ta do it and get it over with.

Soon as we're on the beach, a new lieutenant, his name's Wrightson, come next ta me. "You were at the Crater last summer, weren't you?"

"Yes sir."

"Was it really as bad as everyone says?"

"Yes sir, every bit as bad."

He don't say nothin' for a minute. Then, he get that look white folks get when they goin' ta tell you somethin' they don't think they oughtta. "I've never been in a charge against works like this before."

Or against anythin' else, I think.

"So I...would appreciate it if you would stay with me when we... we...."

He don't finish. He don't hafta. I can tell he scared. I just nod ma head and say, "Yes sir."

We're marchin' down some ruts in the sand the secesh got the nerve ta call the Wilmington Road. Round a bend, we come on a column of prisoners bein' escorted by troops from the 117th New York.

"What've you got there?" Lieutenant Wrightson call out.

"Some secesh boys callin' themselves the 4th, 7th and 8th North Carolina Junior Reserves."

"Junior is the word; most of them don't look old enough to shave yet."

Everybody laugh till they look in them young faces and see how ashamed they feel for givin' up. I almost feel sorry for 'em, but then I see 'em pointin' and hear 'em whisperin', "Can y'all believe that--the Yankees have niggers in their army."

"Rebel sonofabitches," I say, "ain't never goin' ta be a end ta this war till they all dead." And I spit on the ground.

For the last hour or two, we bin choppin' down trees and draggin' 'em up ta a point 200 yards from Fort Fisher so the 142nd New York can build up some rifle pits the rebels left. Whole time our officers and theirs runnin' round barkin' orders like we ain't never done this before. I think maybe the same thing's botherin' them that's botherin' us. Up close the land side of the fort's mighty imposin' lookin'. The Wilmington Road cross over a wooden bridge and go right in the fort through a little gate. It's the only openin' in a earth wall that stretch east far as I can see. In front of the wall's a log palisade goin' cross most of it. The spooky thing's, we ain't seen no rebels up there. Some already sayin' this goin' ta be real easy.

It's gettin' dark. A captain from the New York regiment come over and tell Lieutenant Wrightson ta move us back ta the landin' site. "The rest of the breastworks can wait till morning."

Don't none of us mind goin' back ta the Montauk. It's better sleepin' there than rolled up in a shelter half on this cold sand.

We're about half a mile up the Wilmington Road when it get real quiet. "Guess the Navy quit for t'day," I say turnin' ma head ta look back at the fort.

"Good, then we can get some sleep t'night," fella next ta me say.

We go on maybe a hunnert yards, and we hear firin'. Some of it's artillery, some small arms.

"Sound like the white boys attackin' the fort," he say.

Seem kinda funny ta me, doin' that this late. But, what the hell, this army do some funny things.

"Bother you if they take it without us?" he ask.

"Don't bother me at all. They take it t'night, and we can go on ta Wilmington tomarra. But, just 'tween you and me, I don't think they can do it t'night."

I don't say nothin' more ta him rest of the way back ta the landin' site. I don't want ta get friendly with nobody...not since Jeremiah killed.

Started rainin' this mornin'. Cold, drizzly kind of rain. Weather bad enough, but we find out New Yorkers didn't attack the fort. They're here on the beach waitin' ta be taken off same as us, but the sea's too choppy. Lieutenant Wrightson say General Butler call off the attack. That we're all goin' back ta Fortress Monroe soon as the navy can get the 117th off the beach. Much as I like General Butler, seem stupid ta get that close to Fort Fisher and don't even attack it.

ELIJAH DORSEY
Depot Field Hospital City Point, Virginia

Bin real cold last couple days, so I'm glad ta be in a pavillion now. With the stove full of wood, it's warm enough ta lay on top of ma blankets durin' the day.

Ma shoulder and arm healin' thanks ta Miss Florence takin' such good care of me. I don't see her so much now, and I kinda miss her. Time she come, I try and keep her with me long as I can.

T'day I see her soon as she come in the ward. I don't mind her stoppin' at each bed ta say somethin' or do somethin' like fluff up pillows or take a letter ta mail. I feel warm inside knowin' soon she goin' be with me. And t'day, I'm hopin' she have time ta help me with ma writin' so I can tell Momma about bein' wounded and this hospital and...about Miss Florence.

"Good mornin', Miss Florence, you look real purty t'day."

Tha's what I bin sayin' ta her last couple times I seen her, and usually she smile. T'day she don't.

"I wish you wouldn't say things like that."

The way she say it make me think somethin's wrong. But I don't want ta hear it right away, so I ask her, "You help me with a letter ta Momma?"

She start ta say somethin', stop, make a funny-kinda face, then say, "Yes," and move a chair next ta the bed.

I get ma paper and pencil and start writin' up at the top of the page, "Deer Moma."

"Don't you remember, Elijah, dear is spelled with an a, not two e's?"

I rub it out with the eraser and write "Dear Moma."

She don't say nothin', so I go on. "How you bin feelin? Im fine."

I look at Miss Florence, but she ain't watchin' me write. She's starin' out the window.

"Somethin's troublin' you, Miss Florence, ain't it?"

"Yes," she say real soft-like, "somethin's troubling me. What I've got ta tell you's goin' ta hurt. And I'm sorry. I really am."

"You got a husband, ain't you?"

First, she look surprise, then just sad. "I won't lie, Elijah. I do have a husband, and I got a letter sayin' he's bin wounded real bad. He wants me ta come home and nurse him." She close her eyes a minute, open 'em, then look straight inta mine. "Day after tomarra I'm goin' ta Hilton Head and take care of him. I won't ever see you again."

I wish I was a little boy again, so I can cry. I ain't never hurt in ma whole life the way I'm hurtin' now. Not when them secesh shot and kicked me and left me ta die. Not when Old Taylor whip me.

And I want ta grab her hand and plead with her, "Don't go. I love you and want you ta stay and be ma woman and love me." But I can't. I just set there starin' at her like ma eyes can tell her what ma mouth can't.

After a couple minutes, she get up off the chair. "I hafta go. But I'll send somebody ta help you finish your letter."

I just nod ma head. I can't do nothin' else.

She's about half way up the ward, time ma voice start workin'. "Miss Florence," I call out, and I get up off the bed and start down the aisle after her.

She stop and turn around.

When I get close, I can see she's cryin'.

"Miss Florence, they somethin' I got ta tell you."

She put a finger on ma lips. "No, you mustn't. Not now, not ever."

She take a handkerchief outta her sleeve and wipe her eyes.

"I shoulda guessed how you felt and told you weeks ago about ma husband. But, I didn't and now I hurt you very much. I'm sorry, Elijah, sorrier than you can know."

In spite of what she say, I hafta tell her, "Miss Florence, I love you."

She reach over and touch me on the arm. "Oh, Elijah, you make it so hard ta leave you."

Then, I know she love me too. And I know she's tellin' me she care for me, but she got a duty ta her husband. I understand that. And I tell her I do.

She reach up and kiss me on the cheek, like a sister or a momma, and say, "Thank you."

She walk outta the ward. Watchin' her go, I feel so sad inside I don't want ta live no more.

MAJOR AUGUSTUS T. ALEXANDER

It's a very cold day. I see now the disadvantage of wooden buildings on a point between two rivers. The wind whistles through the cracks in the wall and under the door. No matter where I am in the room, I can feel it. I stand in front of the wood stove soaking up heat long after I should have started my rounds. I stand remembering last night--how much it was like my arrival at Camp Stanton. First, there were the surprised looks on the faces of the officers who came down to meet me.

And no one spoke to me on the long ride past the wharves busy even that late in the day as hordes of stevedores struggled to unload steamers, sailing barks, and barges and move their cargoes to the empty cars waiting on the military railroad tracks. Finally, we reached the wooden buildings of the hospital situated near General Grant's headquarters on the point between the Appomattox and James Rivers. I don't know how long I waited in the orderly room while someone went to see, "if my quarters were ready." Or how many times I asked myself last night, "Why didn't you just stay in Baltimore?"

"You've got to face it sooner or later," I say to myself, pull open the door and step outside. The first blast of cold air from the James River hits me, and I want to go back inside and stay there. But I can't turn back now.

In spite of the way the wind stings my face, I almost enjoy the walk from my lonely quarters to the ward buildings. Out here, the cold and wind are harsh, but I can protect myself from them. But in there...I can't protect myself from the cold treatment I get from my fellow officers.

Too soon, I reach the first building and stand for a moment looking at its low, unpainted sides. Finally, I grab the knob and push the door open. Get on with it, I think, there are wounded men inside who need you.

The rush of warm air fogs up my spectacles, and I have to wait a few moments for them to clear. When they do, I see the row of cots on either side of the center aisle. I see the dark faces on those cots staring at me in wonder. I see the smiles begin and hear the soft "u-huh's" of satisfaction spreading up and down the rows. This is where I belong, I think, right here where I can be of real service to my brothers.

After examining everybody in the first row, I cross the aisle and stand by the first bed on the other side. "Excuse me, young man, you must turn over. I need to look at your shoulder."

"Ain't nothin' wrong with it."

"Maybe not, but I'm the new surgeon in this ward, and I have to look at it."

No movement, no response.

"Soldier, I have to look at your wounds. Now, turn over. That's an order."

"Yes sir."

As soon as I see his face, I recognize him. "Elijah... Elijah Dorsey," I say.

He looks at me for a second or two, then smiles. "Major Alexander, sure good ta see you here, sir."

"It's good to see you too, Elijah."

For several moments we smile at each other like two old friends instead of officer and enlisted man. Then, we both remember where we are, and the smiles fade.

To fill in the awkward silence, I ask the nurse to remove the dressings so that I can examine his wounds.

"This doesn't look good," I say and gently push on the shoulder wound. It oozes, and I can easily smell the suppuration. The one in his arm looks better. "Your shoulder is seriously infected."

"Don't matter."

"Of course it matters. You could die."

"That don't matter either."

I look at his face and see that he means exactly what he said.

I sit down next to him on the bed. "You have everything to live for, Elijah. Why...when this war's over, you'll be a completely free man. You'll be able to do whatever you want--live wherever you want to."

"Way I'm feelin' got nothin' ta do with that."

"Then, what does it have to do with?"

He turns his head so I can't see his eyes.

"Don't turn away. If you tell me what's troubling you, maybe I can help."

He doesn't respond.

"Elijah, I'm giving you a direct order. Turn over and tell me what's bothering you."

Slowly, reluctantly, he moves just enough for me to see the pain in his eyes. I may not know everything about the human heart, but I know to guess a woman is involved somehow.

"Did your woman take up with another man since you've been gone?"

"You really want ta know?"

"Yes, I do."

He doesn't say anything for some time. And I start to feel pressure--I've got a lot of other patients to see. Maybe, I should move on; let him cure his melancholy in his own way.

"They were a nurse in this ward," he says just as I'm about to stand up. "Pretty and kind, and she take good care of me. I like talkin' ta her, and havin' her fuss over me. Before long, I know I'm in love with her. Then, last week, she say she got a husband and she got ta go down ta Hilton Head and nurse him cause he bin wounded. And she say, 'Good bye, Lijah'."

His voice breaks, and he struggles to control his feelings.

"And since she bin gone, I don't care nothin' about livin' or dyin'."

What can I say to him? Are there any words that will take away his pain? If there are, I don't know what they are.

"You know, major, everythin' different back at Belmont. If you love somebody and she love you, you just move in with her. If chil'ren come, Mister Dorsey give you extra food and presents at Christmas cause you give him more slaves ta grow up and do his work. Why ain't it simple like that out here?"

"Because Belmont and every other plantation is a closed little world where the master made all the decisions and you, the slave, had to obey them or be punished. Out here, you are free to make your own decisions based on your needs and wants, but so are other people. And sometimes, what a person decides has serious and painful consequences for another person. That's the best answer I can give you."

For a few minutes he just looks at me, and I'm sure he hasn't understood a word I said.

"So, you sayin' bein' free goin' ta be a lot harder'n I think back in slavery?"

"I think it's going to be a lot harder for all us black folks than any of us ever thought it would be."

I wish I hadn't said that. I came to help him and, instead, I laid another burden on him...a worse one. Maybe, the best thing I can do now is leave him alone.

"I'm going to have the nurse wash out the wound with carbolic acid and put on a new dressing. I'll check on it tomorrow."

"Sure, major, sure, you just go on about your business."

His sarcasm freezes me.

Moments later, I stand up, still not certain what I should do. A glance down the aisle tells me I have to move on. A glance back at Elijah tells me he needs me more than ever. I put my hand on his good shoulder. "I'll come back tomorrow," but he has already turned his back on me again.

I'm back at the side of Elijah's cot.

For the third morning in a row, I ask, "How are you feeling today?" For the third morning in a row, he doesn't answer. He just opens his eyes half-way and then rolls over on his side.

"I'm gettin' real worried about him, major," the nurse says. "He doesn't do anything all day but lay there with his eyes half-closed. And he hasn't eaten since the day before yesteday."

It's clear I've got to do something, or he'll die. But what? Send him home on convalescent leave? To the plantation he ran away from? What will happen when he gets there? Will anyone take care of him? Or should I transfer him to a hospital in Washington City? Would that be enough of a change to bring him out of his melancholia?

I have to think. Turning away from the cot, I walk down the aisle and through the door. Outside, the cold air feels good on my face. I walk past General Grant's headquarters and sit down on a tree stump on the bluff overlooking the two rivers. For a hour or more, I argue with myself. Slowly an answer starts forming. There's a good chance he may die no matter where he is. Wouldn't it be better for him to spend his last days in a familiar place...with whatever kin he has...instead of in an army hospital?

...

"You're going on leave."

Elijah had already turned away from me. Now, he turns back. The normally half-closed eyes open a little more. "What you mean?"

"I've requested a convalescent leave for you. The papers are already on their way to General Meade's office. I don't anticipate any problem there--the General's staff don't usually question medical leaves."

"Where I'm goin'?"

"Why home, of course. And depending on how soon all the details can be worked out with Quartermaster Corps, you may be there in time for Christmas."

Now, his eyes are fully open. For the first time, I see real interest in them.

"First, you have to travel by army transport to Fortress Monroe, be examined by a surgeon there, and then proceed on to Baltimore. The tricky part, of course, will be getting you out to that plantation. What did you call it?"

"Belmont."

"I know people at Birney Barracks who may be able to help."

For a long time, he doesn't say anything.

"Of course, you have to start eating so that you build up your strength. I can't send you that far on a stretcher."

Again, he doesn't say anything for a long time. I'm starting to think that I made a mistake. He isn't interested. He just wants to lie there and die.

"It be good ta see Momma and the home folks again. Bin almost a year now."

On my way out of the ward, I tell the nurse, "See that Elijah gets a double helping of dinner. He's going to be very hungry."

She looks puzzled.

One thing I didn't count on was how long it would take to arrange all the details of Elijah's trip home. Finally, on a cold, overcast afternoon in the middle of December, I help the orderly wheel him down to the landing where the launch will take him down the James River to Fortress Monroe.

"Keep him wrapped up in this blanket. He mustn't get chilled." The corporal from the launch doesn't even look surprised when I give him the order. He grunts something that sounds vaguely like, "Yes sir," and starts pushing Elijah up the ramp to the launch.

"Have a safe journey," I call after him, "and I'll see you back here in a month."

If he heard me, he doesn't acknowledge that he did.

I watch him move onto the deck and then into the cabin in the middle of it. There's a brief burst of activity; and, the next thing I know, the launch is heading out into the river's current.

"Take care of him, Lord," I say softly, over and over, until the launch rounds a bend, and I can't see it any more.

It has been threatening to snow all day. Now, on the way back to my quarters, it begins--tiny, wind-driven flakes, feeling like ice as they strike my face.

Back in my room, I shake them off my overcoat and hang it up. It feels almost as cold in here as it did outside. Opening the cast iron stove door, I stick in some paper and kindling and soon have a fire going. For a long time, I stand there staring at the greedy flames eating up the wood, thinking about Elijah and wondering if it was too soon to send him off...in his condition, in this kind of weather.

<u>Maybe, I should never have come here</u>, I think. <u>Maybe, I'll end up doing more harm than good</u>.

A sudden chill snaps me out of my thought, and for a moment, I'm puzzled as to why it's so cold. "Fire's gone out," I mutter touching the top of the stove. When I glance over at the window, I'm surprised to see how dark it is outside. "Must've been standing here a long time." The stiffness in my knees tells me I'm right.

In a few minutes, the fire is burning again, and I make myself a pot of coffee. I pour some into my enameled cup, walk over to the pine table and sit down.

By the time I've finished half the cup, I feel a little better. *It won't do any good to fret night and day about him*. *His life's in the hands of the Lord, now.*

I say a little prayer for Elijah; then, I raise my head and wonder what I can do--right now--to get my mind off him for a little while.

"I'll write to Miss Sallie," I say aloud. "I owe her a letter anyway." And the more I think about it, the more appealing the idea becomes. I turn around and from the shelf behind me take down the old hardtack box I keep my personal papers in.

For some time, I've been reading and re-reading the one letter she wrote to me several weeks ago, smiling at the girlish chatter in some places and marveling at the mature reflections in others. Finally, I put it down and pick up my pen. With a determined hand, I write tomorrow's date, my address and "Dear Sallie."

Sounds too familiar, I decide, wad up the sheet of paper and throw it on the floor. Taking another out of the box, I begin again. This time I write, "My dear Miss King."

Too formal--sounds like I'm writing to somebody's maiden aunt. That piece of paper also ends up on the floor.

Half an hour later, there are several more crumpled up pieces on the floor, and I'm standing at the window, looking out at the snow and wondering if Elijah has reached Fortress Monroe or if the small launch has met with some accident in the storm. "Enough of that," I say and make myself walk back to the table and sit down.

I pick up my pen, write the date and my address, then stop. "Why is it so damned hard to write a simple letter?" I ask.

"Because you're afraid," I blurt out before I quite realize what I've said.

"Afraid of what?"

"You know damned well of what. Afraid that a young lady as pretty and sweet as Miss Sallie King already has a man. Not a husband like Elijah's Florence, but someone she cares for. Someone younger and more handsome than yourself."

I take my looking glass out of the box. In it, I see a face that's getting jowly, a head that's losing its hair. I don't need the glass to tell me I've put on weight around my middle.

"Let's face it, Augustus; you're not much of a catch for a woman as young and as pretty as Sallie King."

I have almost decided not to write the letter, but then I picture her soft eyes and golden brown complexion in my mind's eye. I can almost hear her sweet laughter. Can almost smell the faint scent of lilac in the air. Can almost feel the warmth that radiates from her.

I look again at the face in the mirror. "Augustus, old man," I say to it, "you're in love with her." The face smiles at me.

"And what do you propose to do about it?" it asks.

"I've heard that a faint heart never won a fair lady," I reply.

"Damnit, don't spout cliches at me." I put the looking glass back in the box. I put my stationery back in the box.

"This nonsense has gone on long enough," I mutter, putting the box back on the shelf. "I'm going to bed."

An hour, maybe two later...the room is cold, and I'm still awake. A hundred times, I've started to get up and write the letter. A hundred times, I've talked myself out of it.

For the hundred and first time, I call myself a coward for being afraid to write to her. This time...I don't argue back. This time, I say loud enough to wake up all of City Point, "A man who wasn't afraid to take on the whole Union Army certainly is not afraid of trying to win the woman he loves."

A few minutes later, wrapped in a blanket and with only the flickering light of a candle, I begin the letter again.

Dear Miss King

It has been several weeks since I received your charming letter. I regret the duties of my new post have kept me from replying sooner....

CHAPTER 18
JANUARY 1865

ELIJAH DORSEY
Fortress Monroe, Virginia

I bin in this hospital, near as I can tell, two weeks. I don't remember much after the launch left City Point. Seem like the snow start comin' down real hard, soon as we left the dock, and the water got so choppy the pilot had trouble steerin'. Then, the next thing I know, somebody's helpin' me onta another dock.

"This Fortress Monroe?" I ask him.

He say, "Yes," and that's the last thing I can recall.

Time I open my eyes again, I'm in a warm bed, the sun's shinin' and a white doctor's examinin' ma arm and shoulder.

"Wha's the day t'day?" I ask him.

"January 1st, 1865."

"Then, I miss Christmas."

"Christmas? Good heavens, man, from the way you looked when you arrived that night, I thought we would be burying you long before this morning. Obviously, I was wrong."

He bend down and study ma wounds real close for a couple minutes. Sniff 'em, then straighten up lookin' kinda pleased. "As a matter of fact, I see no reason why you shouldn't be on your way to Baltimore in a week or so."

<u>See Momma...in a week or two</u>. For the first time, I start feelin' excited. Excited about seein' Momma, even if I ain't so happy about goin' back ta Belmont.

Just like the doctor say, in two weeks I'm on the packet, <u>John B. Anderson</u>, headin' for Balmore. It ain't a interestin' trip cause I got ta stay in the cabin by the stove. Time the packet dock, I'm glad it ain't snowin' or nothin' like that cause I got ta walk ta the Birney Barracks.

I stop where Camlin's Slave Pen usta be. Standin' cross the street and lookin' at it, I still feel a little scared, even wearin' ma army uniform. *Maybe, I ain't really safe here*, I think. *Maybe, I oughten go over Belmont*. *No tellin' what Old Taylor do time he see me*.

I see two white men come round the corner, and I don't like the look of 'em. "I best be gettin' outta here," I say ta maself, and move off down the street fast as I can. I don't even look back ta see if they followin' or not.

A white lieutenant and a black private goin' with me ta Ellicott Mills. We got ta ketch the train in the President Street Station in Balmore, and I'm a little nervous waitin' on 'em ta buy the tickets. Bin attacks on Union soldiers here on and off since the war start.

Time I hear somebody behind me talkin' about uppity niggers, I don't pay him no mind. But he keep on, gettin' louder and louder. Finally, I turn ta see what he's goin' on about. I can tell right away he's drunk and lookin' for trouble.

"What the hell you starin' at, nigger?"

I ain't in any condition for a fight, so I turn ma back on him and hope the lieutenant get here real quick. But when I ain't lookin', the drunk grab ma kepi, throw it on the dirty platform floor, and stomp on it.

I turn round mad as hell. "Why you do that?"

"Do what?"

"Knock ma kepi on the floor."

He turn ta some rough-lookin' white men standin' behind him. "You see me do anythin' ta this here nigger?"

"Naw, he's a lyin' sack a shit," they say.

He stick his face up close ta mine. "I don't like niggers, and I 'specially don't like lyin' ones." Then, he hit me in ma wounded arm with a club he bin carryin'.

It hurt so bad tears come in ma eyes.

"Hey lookit this. The nigger's cryin'."

The rough-lookin' whites crowd on in. "Aw, did he hurt you?" one of 'em ask and blow smoke in ma face.

"No, you white sonofabitch, I'm a Union soldier, and I bin fightin' in the trenches outside Petersburg since last summer." I open ma coat and show 'im ma uniform. "No tap from the likes of him can hurt me."

"Soldier, my ass," the drunk say, "you prolly robbed some poor, drunk white man. Grab 'im, boys. First, I'm gonna take back that stolen uniform; then, I'm gonna make him sorry he ever opened his mouth."

They grab holda me, and he cut ma suspenders with a knife and try and pull down ma pants. I bring ma knee up, but he jump back.

"So, it's kickin' you want, is it?"

He like ta bury his foot in ma belly.

All the air go outta me; and, for a second, I can't suck any back in. When it come, ma muscles tighten and breakfast go all the drunk's face.

"You fucken black bastard, I'm gonna kill you," he scream and hit ma arm hard as he can.

It start burnin' like all the fires in hell. But I ain't goin' ta just stand still and take it. I spit in his face. "Tha's what I think of a man who'd beat up on a wounded soldier."

I jerk ma head outta the way of the club, but it hit ma shoulder. I see bright spots a light, and I can't hardly hold ma head up. Ma legs feel like they goin' ta let go any second.

"What's going on here?"

I lift ma head and see the lieutenant pointin' a pistol at the drunk. The other ones let me go, and I straighten up best as I can.

"Nothin', I was just teachin' this boy some manners."

"This boy, as you call him, was wounded twice in the service of our country, and he certainly doesn't need any lessons in manners, or in anything else, from street thugs and bounty-jumpers like you."

He give his pistol to the private. "Benson, keep an eye on these men while I go get a provost guard to arrest them."

. . .

It take us almost a hour ta go ta the Provost Marshal's office on Balmore Street, swear depositions, and have the ones who attacked me locked up. A small crowd's waitin' outside and start followin' us. Time we go down the street ta the Marsh Market, it's a lot bigger and a couple men start hollerin' we're the ones got poor Mike Rooney and his brother arrested, and "They was just mindin' their own business."

Some stones come flyin' at us. The lieutenant fire his pistol in the air once. "Disperse immediately," he say. "Or this trooper and I will begin firing at you."

They look at him and his pistol. Then, they look at the private with his Enfield pointin' at 'em. They stand a long time mutterin' and threatenin' us. Some even throw a few more stones.

When he's tired a waitin', the lieutenant fire another round up in the air. This time they slink away like wild dogs driven off by a hunter.

Back at the President Street Station, we just in time ta ketch the last train ta Ellicott Mills. "Hell of a welcome you got back there," the private say.

"Yeah, good ta be home."

Funny, I think lookin' at Ellicott Mills as the train pullin' in the car shed, all ma life I live only four or five miles from this town, but this the first I ever bin here.

At Archer's Livery Stable, we hire three horses and ride real slow out the Frederick Road. The whole time I keep thinkin' on Momma and how good it be ta see her again. I don't give maself no time ta think on what the white folks might do.

Seem like we get ta where the lane meet the Frederick Road too fast. "I got ta stop and go behind a tree," I tell the lieutenant.

"Hurry up," he say. "I hafta get back to the barracks before dark."

The private prolly know wha's really botherin' me cause he say he got ta piss too. Behind the tree, he say, "Don't worry, brother, can't nobody put you back in slavery. You a free man, and in two months all the black folks in this state be free."

Still, don't matter what he say. Don't matter what anybody say. Standin' here lookin' down the lane goin' ta Belmont, where I worked from sun-up ta sun-down every day far back as I can remember, where Old Taylor usta whip me, I feel scared.

The lane got a lot of deep ruts in it like nobody work on it last fall. And a whole lot of dead branches and leaves layin' under the trees. Weeds bin growin' in the drive in front of the house. Bushes long the porch need trimmin'. Shutters need paintin'. Whole place look sorry and run-down.

Lieutenant knock on the front door. I'm real surprised time Rose the cook open it.

"I'm Lieutenant Charles McCormick, United States Army. I'd like to speak to Mr. Hammond Dorsey."

"He ain't here," Rose say.

"Mrs. Dorsey, then."

Rose look the lieutenant up and down. She look us two up and down. Then, she study ma face for a couple minutes and ask, "Don't I know you?"

"Ma name's Lijah, I usta be a field hand here."

"Well, Lijah," she say kinda friendly, "you look real good in that uniform."

"What's going on out there, Rose?"

She stop smilin'. "Some soldiers here, Miss Dorsey, askin' for you or the master."

"What do they want?"

"I don't know. They didn't say."

"Oh, for heavens sakes." The door jerk all the way open and Miss Dorsey standin' there, givin' us all real hard looks.

Funny, she ain't tall like I remember her. And she ain't pretty no more either. She got dark circles under her eyes and a lotta wrinkles. Her dress got dry mud on it and don't look like it bin washed in a long time.

"Well, what do you want?" she ask the lieutenant.

"I'm Lieutenant Charles McCormick, ma'am, and I've brought this wounded soldier home to visit his mother. He was a slave here before he...."

Miss Dorsey, she move where she can see me better. "Before he ran off or you took him for the army."

I can see her face gettin' red. "Like you took all the good able-bodied men and left us with nothin' but the old and the sick and the women with young children."

She grab hold of the door. "And now you bring me one that's wounded. And you expect me to take him in and feed him like he's one of the family. Well, I've got news for you--we don't have food for ourselves. And if Mr. Dorsey can't sell the family plate in Baltimore, I don't know what we'll do. So, you just take that nigger down to Washington and let Mr. Lincoln take care of him."

She slam the door in our face.

"She always have a bad temper," I tell the lieutenant. "One time I hear she whip a maid almost ta death cause she spill soup on her new carpet."

"Well, bad temper or not, she made it clear you can't stay here."

"Lieutenant, I got ta stay. I'm feelin' too tired ta go back ta Balmore t'night."

"But, Mrs. Dorsey said...."

"That don't matter. She don't ever know wha's goin' on down in the quarters. She never bin there the whole time I lived on this plantation.

"Well...if you're really sure."

"Course I'm sure. Just leave me a horse so I can get back ta Ellicott Mills time I'm ready."

Even in the dark, I don't have no trouble findin' the path leadin' down ta the quarters. I can walk it with ma eyes shut, even leadin' a horse. About half the way, I think it's funny I don't smell much smoke. At the turn, I see why. No light in most a the cabins. And I get this funny feelin'. Like maybe Momma ain't here either. Like maybe I ain't never goin' ta see her again. I start walkin' fast as I can. Down past the rows of empty cabins. Turn right on the cross "street," and right away, I see smoke comin' out the chimney of the second cabin. See light comin' through the curtains Momma made a long time ago. And I know she's inside.

I don't wait till I get ta the door. I start callin' out just like in ma dreams, "Momma, Momma, it's Lijah. I come home."

The door swing open. Momma stand there, tryin' ta see out in the dark. And all of a sudden, I can't move. Can't say anythin'. Can hardly see her.

"Lijah, that really you?"

I whisper, "Yes, Momma," and she's down the two steps and throwin' her arms round me. Then, she hug me till ma ribs hurt. And she keep sayin' over and over, "Lijah, you're safe; Lijah, you're safe."

And I can't do nothin' but hold her and say, "Momma...Momma...."

After a long time, she let go and step back. "We best go inside before we both ketch a chill."

Like a chile, I folla her up the steps and inside the cabin. Maybe the fire make the cabin too warm, or maybe it's bin too long since I et. But, soon as I step inside, I start feelin' dizzy and hafta set down.

Momma rush over, study me real close. "You look real bad, son, real bad."

"I bin wounded." I open ma overcoat so she can see the bandages on ma shoulder and arm. "And the doctor he say maybe I die if I stay in the hospital at City Point. So, he send me home on a convalescent leave."

Then, I feel real cold and start shakin'. Momma put her arms round me again. Kiss me on the head. "You best get in the bed," she say. You ketched a chill."

I don't know how long I sleep. But I dream I'm back in Camp Stanton, and I just got ma new Enfield. And I'm settin' in the tent cleanin' it and runnin' ma fingers long the smooth wood stock and feelin' like I'm good as any white man. Then,

I'm back in Florida, and Mrs. Clinch laughin' and laughin' and laughin'. So I got ta shoot her ta shut her up, but I can't find ma Enfield. The door open, and Old Taylor come in with it and tell me no nigger can have a weapon. And he start beatin' me with it. Mrs. Clinch she keep on laughin'. Then, Mr. Arnow come in and start laughin'. And the man from Camlin's Slave Pen...and the captain down in Hilton Head. And the whole room fill up with white folks laughin' and pointin' they fingers, and callin' me a dumb nigger. I break away from Old Taylor and curse 'em all so loud I wake maself up.

Momma's settin' on the bed. She put her hand on ma head. "Your fever broke. I think you're goin' ta be all right, now."

"Can I have some water? I'm so thirsty."

She go to the bucket and dip some. It taste real cool slidin' down ma dry throat. After two or three dippers, I lay back on the pillow. "Momma, sing ta me like you usta time I was a chile."

She set down on the bed and start singin' real soft-like. In a couple minutes, I'm asleep again.

This time I wake up real hungry. Like she already know what I'm goin' ta ask for, Momma bring over a big plate of greens swimmin' in gravy, and a big piece of corn bread.

I start eatin' real fast, and she say, "Slow down or you'll bring on the fever again."

I don't pay her no mind. I keep eatin' and she keep bringin'. Time I finish the last helpin', I feel real good.

"Thank you, Momma. That was great. Especially after all the hardtack and dry army beef I bin eatin'."

She kinda smile, like a mother do sometime, and take ma plate away. I lay back and watch her for a few minutes.

"I was real surprised ta see Rose come ta the door. What happen ta Henry, the butler?"

"He run off like most a the other black folks."

"So, Miss Dorsey tell the truth. I think she just bein' her mean old self."

Momma put down the rag she use ta dry off ma plate. "No, she was tellin' the truth. Times hard for 'em up at the big house. Most a the field hands go last summer, and the house servants bin goin' one by one since. Now, her and Mr. Dorsey ain't got hardly nobody ta fetch and carry for 'em"

"She say they ain't got no food. But, you got plenty down here."

Momma set down next ta me. "I'm goin' ta tell you somethin', Lijah. Black folks on plantations usta just gettin' by. White folks ain't. We know how ta scratch round for food like barnyard hens do. White folks who bin livin' high and mighty all they lives, with us ta do all they work, can't do a damn thing for themselfs. So, bad times come, we know what ta do. They don't."

She drop her voice real low. "And 'tween you and me, serve 'em right if they all starve."

"If everybody else run off, why you stayin' here?"

"Where I can go? I was born on this plantation. I bin workin' here in the hot summer sun and freezin' in this drafty cabin more winters 'an I can count. I birth ten chil'ren here. Bury four of 'em before they were a year old. Seen all the rest, except you sold off. Seen two husbands sold off. Seen ma own mother sold off. And like I told you a long time ago, I never bin off this plantation. I don't know no place but here."

"But what if you was free, and the Dorseys don't want you stayin' here?"

"Free? me? why're you talkin' like a crazy man?"

"Nothin' crazy about it. Soldier I come ta Ellicott Mills with tell me the state govmint abolishin' slavery in March of this year."

"You lyin' ta me?" she ask and study ma face real close like she do time I was a little boy.

"No, Momma, I ain't lyin'."

She throw her head back. "Praise Jesus," she shout. "Praise Jesus. I'm goin' ta be free."

She start dancin' round the cabin, shoutin', "Praise Jesus," and shakin' her body like I never seen her do. Then, she stop and come over by the bed. And she don't look old no more. Her face shinin' like a black sun.

"Soon as you better, we leavin' here."

"But, Momma, didn't you just tell me how you never bin off this plantation? And how your dead chil'ren buried here? The way it sound, you expect ta be buried here yourself."

She throw her head back again and laugh. And the laugh seem like it come up from her soul. It seem like it fill up the whole cabin and then seep out through the cracks in the walls cause the cabin too small ta hold that much happiness.

"That was the slave me talkin'. Now the free me's tellin' you I ain't stayin' here one more day than I got ta."

I don't want ta spoil things, but I got ta ask her, "Where you plan on goin' time you leave here?"

"With you."

"You can't do that. The army ain't no place for a woman."

A lotta the light go outta her face. "Then, you hafta find me a place ta wait till the war's over and you come back and fetch me."

Long after she's in the bed and the fire gone out, I lay awake and think on wha's goin' ta happen after the war. I seen the runaways comin' inta City Point from all over Virginia and North Carolina. They dirty and sick and hungry. And the army feed 'em and give 'em a place ta rest and then send 'em on to govmint camps up near Washington City. And I wonder if the army and the govmint goin' ta keep doin' that after the war. Or if they goin' ta say it ain't they problem. Then what--who's goin' ta help all the free black folks in the North and the South?

I get so tired out from worryin', I fall asleep, but I have bad dreams. Dreams about me and Momma walkin' on a road somewheres. And we're both hungry. But every time we see a house, the folks inside act like they ain't home. Or, they slam the door in our face when we ask for food. So, we keep walkin' and walkin'. But it don't seem like we get anywhere. And it don't seem like the dreams ever end.

MAJOR AUGUSTUS T. ALEXANDER

Washington City,
December 15th, 1864

Dear Major Alexander,

I so enjoyed reading your letter of December 12th instant. I especially enjoyed learning the good news that, at long last, you have been transferred to an army hospital. I can tell, by the tone of your letter, that you are much happier doing the important work of taking care of our wounded soldiers than you were sitting in that office in Baltimore.

On Thanksgiving, I went with the Freedman's Relief Association to take food and clothing to the camps outside Alexandria, Virginia. Goodness knows, the free black folks in Washington City have little enough, but they gave generously to help their brothers and sisters who have escaped from slavery. Our gifts were warmly appreciated because there is so much need in the camps. The folks there have little more than the clothes on their backs. Though they seem in good spirits, one can tell how much they worry about what will become of them once the war is over.

Speaking of the war, Bishop Payne went to President Lincoln's New Year's Reception and was told, by Mr. Lincoln himself, that the war must be finished this year. With all my heart, I hope he is right. It seems as if the fighting has been going on since the beginning of time.

Bishop Payne also said that both Senator Sumner and Representative Stevens have introduced bills in Congress to establish a Bureau of Freedmen's Affairs to administer relief and to protect our brothers and sisters when the Rebellion is over. The bishop has no doubt that, even in defeat, the former masters will be a powerful threat to their one-time slaves.

In a few minutes, I have to attend a choir rehearsal, so, with great reluctance, I must now close this letter. But I end it with the hope that you will have the time to write to me soon.

Yours most sincere friend,
Sallie King

I read the letter once, twice, three times. And each time, I feel the same excitement when I reach soon. "There can't be any mistake," I say to myself after the third reading. "She definitely meant it as a sign that my attentions are welcome." And I do a little waltz turn around my bare little room with an imaginary Sallie King in my arms.

Bumping against the table suddenly jerks me back to the real world. "You silly old fool, she probably writes to a dozen young men and ends all her letters that same way." The picture of her writing a dozen letters at the same time flashes through my mind. Rubbing my thigh, I make my way over to the bed and ease down on it. I lie there some time, plotting the destruction of young men I have never met, one minute, and feeling foolish the next.

Finally to settle my mind, I get up, walk over to the table, pick up her letter, and read it again. The phrases--"with reluctance," "I hope," and "Your most sincere friend"--take on added significance. "There," I announce proudly to the bare walls, "what more proof do you need?"

With an enthusiasm that surprises me, I write a reply. Reading it after I'm finished, I decide it sounds too much like a love letter and tear it up. "Take it easy, Augustus; you don't want to appear too impulsive. It might frighten her."

The next one is filled with the news of my day-to-day activities and the various opinions I've heard regarding whether the war will end this year or not. When I'm finished, I think a long time of how I should close. Finally, with a flourish, I write, "Your affectionate friend."

Now, I think, let's see how Miss Sallie responds to that.

FLETCHER HOWARD
Fortress Monroe, Virginia

Today's a sad day for the 39th and the other colored regiments here. General Butler bin dismissed as commander of the

Army of the James. We hear President Lincoln himself did it cause General Grant gave Butler a direct order not ta withdraw from Fort Fisher, and he did. White soldiers say Butler's a coward, and they're glad he's gone. We ain't so glad cause he always treated us fair. And he was the one what first called the runaway slaves "contraband of war," so the army could take 'em in and help 'em. Don't like ta think what woulda happened ta the brothers and sisters if he didn't do that.

Before General Butler hand over command ta General Terry, the Army have this big parade and ceremony. All the white soldiers in the 2nd Division pass the reviewin' stand. Now, the turn of us in the 3rd Division. The 39th fall in behind the 4th, 6th and 30th. Colonel Stearns call out, "Eyes right," and we hope General Butler can see we're sorry he's goin'.

After the parade, General Butler make a speech. He's a short, heavy man, bald on top. Soon as he start talkin', we can tell he's not happy at bein' replaced. He say he's proud he didn't order the useless sacrifice of our lives. "The wasted blood of my men does not stain my garments. For my action I am responsible to God and my country." He say that us black troops, "Have unlocked the iron-barred gates of prejudice, opening new fields of freedom, liberty and equality of right to yourselves and your race forever."

At the end, he raise up both his arms and call out, "Comrades of the Army of the James, I bid you farewell! Farewell!"

If we weren't in formation, I think we all would cheer him.

After everythin's over, I think on General Butler who lose his command for not attackin'. And I think on General Burnside last summer who lose his command <u>for</u> attackin'. It seem funny they both get punished the same way for doin' opposite things. Of the two, I think Butler made the best decision. He saved the whole 2nd and 3rd Division, so they can go somewheres else and fight. Burnside can't say that.

The next day, we board the <u>Montauk</u> and head south again. Officers claim they don't know where we goin', but everybody else pretty sure it's either ta Savannah or...back ta Fort Fisher. We hafta anchor off Beaufort, South Carolina cause of a storm. I spend another day and a night sea-sick as hell. Jesus, I hate bein' on a ship.

Storm finally end, and on the mornin' of January 12th, the Montauk take its place with other transports. A long line of warships form on each side of the transports, and the whole fleet turn north.

"Lieutenant, you can tell me now. We're goin' back ta Fort Fisher, ain't we?"

"No doubt in ma mind," he say.

At half-past eight on the mornin' of January 13th, the navy start bombardin' Fort Fisher again. Half a hour later, the launches startin' carryin' troops ashore. Course the white ones go first. But, they don't have such a easy time of it. The sea kinda rough and a lot of 'em get a good soakin'. Time it's our turn, somebody have the idea ta tie a rope from the Montauk to a launch on the beach. We're suppose ta jump in the water, grab holda the rope, and pull ourselfs along till we're on the beach. It work all right for me till I step in a sink hole and fall. I'm kinda scared when the cold ocean water cover ma head.

I crawl up on the sand and hunt for a black man with a fire goin'. Don't take long ta find one.

"Say brother, can I share your fire?"

Christian Bradley the man I ask. He's a corporal like me. I seen him around the regiment, but never had a reason ta talk ta him before.

"Sure and after you dry up some, I got a nice piece of fatback ta make us some skillygalee. You interested?"

"What the hell's skillygalee?"

"Before I come ta the 39th, I was a orderly in a white regiment. That's what they called hardtack fried in fatback."

"You got any coffee?"

"Enough ta drive the chill outta the devil's bones."

In a little while, everythin's ready and we sit down ta eat.

"We got ta say a grace first," he tell me.

I look at him real funny.

He start laughin'. "It ain't that kind. This one I learned from the white soldiers in the old regiment."

"I hope it's short cause I'm awful hungry."

"Oh, it's short all right. Just bow your head."

I do and he start.

> "Oh! Lord of Love,
> Look down from above,
> Upon we hungry sinners:
> Of what we ask 'tis not in vain,
> For what has been done can be
> Done again. So please turn
> Our water into wine, and give us strength
> Ta break these <u>crackers</u>."

Time he finish, I'm laughin' so hard, I don't think I can eat.

Christian like ta talk a lot. While we eatin', he tell me his life story. How his father work all his life for the rector of St. Paul's Church in Balmore. How every Sunday, the whole family stand up in the back of the church so they can be at the service. How his father give all his chil'ren names out of Scripture.

"See, ma father give ma older brothers names like Matthew, Mark, Luke and John. Time I was born, he's not sure what ta call me, so he ask the rector. Rector say just give him a good Christian name like your other chil'ren. So, Daddy think and think, and he say he can't come up with a better Christian name than <u>Christian</u>."

By the time we finish eatin', I think Christian's a good man. Somebody I want ta be friends with. And I ain't wanted that since Jeremiah was killed. Maybe it's time ta let Jeremiah go.

"Build those campfires real big. We want the rebels to think the whole Army of the James is here."

We folla General Terry's order to a T. It take a couple hours ta get all the wood he want, but we do it. When the fires blazin', we slip off in the woods leavin' only a few companies from different colored regiments ta keep 'em goin'. The rest of us, white and black, suppose ta cross over ta the river side of the peninsula we landed on and head down ta the fort.

It's real slow goin' through the woods cause the underbrush's heavy and the ground's swampy in a lotta places. Sometimes, we got ta cut our way usin' bayonets and trenchin' tools. We make the paths only wide enough for one man at a time. If the secesh attack us, I don't think we have a chance.

Finally, I hear somebody say, "The river...I see the river," and we come outta the woods.

"Sure, look pretty in the moonlight," Christian say.

I tell him, "It'd look a lot prettier if it didn't belong ta the rebels."

About a hour later, we come up on some high ground real near the fort. I hear Captain Daniels tell Lieutenant Wrightson we're goin' ta dig a trench from here down ta the river. The lieutenant form us in two details. One get spades ta dig with. Other get axes ta chop down trees.

"No matter, where we go in this man's army, I seem ta always end up diggin'," I tell Christian.

"Amen ta that, brother."

Almost daylight time we finish. Lookin' at the trench and the logs piled up on both sides, I ask the lieutenant, "Sir, we expectin' visitors from Wilmington?"

"General Terry thinks General Hoke's North Carolinians will pay us a call as soon as we attack the fort."

I look at the trench we just dug. Tired as I feel, I want ta dig it deeper.

Half a hour later, though, I throw down ma spade. "I can't dig no more," I tell Christian. "I'm too damn tired."

"You better get un-tired real fast. A whole lotta brass headin' this way."

I pick up the spade just as three generals I never seen before; Colonel John Ames, our brigade commander; Colonel Elia Wright, the commander of the Third Brigade; and our own

Colonel Stearns come by inspectin' the trench. They don't pay me no mind, but I hear one of 'em tell Colonel Stearns he better keep his "darkies outta the way when the fightin' starts."

If he weren't a high-rankin' officer, I think I woulda hit him with the spade.

After they're gone, Lieutenant Wrightson say it's OK ta eat. Me and Christian have a fire goin' and some hardtack fryin' in no time. No sooner we set down ta eat and the Navy open fire again. He look at me, and I look at him. We both know this time, the army ain't pullin' out.

"Sometime this afternoon," Captain Daniels say, "the naval bombardment will cease, and the 2nd Division, led by the 117th and 142nd New York, is going to attack the fort's landside near a gate that's about a mile south of here. Their aim will be to capture the battery the Wilmington Road so that other regiments will be able to gain entry."

He point kinda south-east. "At the same time, a boarding force from the navy and marines will attack the oceanside."

"Sailors--attackin' the fort?" A lotta men start laughin'. The captain kinda half-smile. "It may sound odd, but my guess is that it's intended to divert the rebels' attention away from the river side, where the main thrust will be."

Men stop smilin' and start noddin' their heads. What he say make sense.

"And us," somebody ask, "what're we doin'?"

"We are going to be right here, waiting for the secesh forces that General Terry, Admiral Porter, and every other high-ranking officer feel sure are on their way down the peninsula to keep us from capturing Fort Fisher."

I look at the trench we dug last night, then at the woods on the north side, then at all the black faces round me. And I wish the trench was even deeper.

Waitin's always the hardest part. Time drag on and on till you think you go crazy if somethin' don't happen. Round noon, me and Christian soak some hardtack in coffee and eat it real fast. We don't want ta be foolin' with food time the rebels attack.

A hour later and the navy's still shellin' the fort. Me and Christian clean our Enfields again, mostly cause we so bored.

"Time?" I ask Christian.

"Nearly two o'clock."

"You sure that watch didn't stop?"

He hold it up ta ma ear so I can hear the tickin'.

"Then, it must be slow."

"Never bin slow since ma father give it ta me."

Round half-past two, a company of sharpshooters come through carryin' Spencer repeatin' rifles.

"Wish I had me one of them."

"So do I, Christian, so do I."

Three o'clock and still nothin' happenin'. Some fellahs so tired of waitin', they ketchin' a nap. Some others playin' cards. A bad habit they pick up from the white troops in the 47th New York. Course the black men losin'.

At half-past three, we hear the Navy shellin' get real loud, then stop. In front of us, the Spencers open fire.

"Sound like the battle's startin'," Christian say.

For just a minute, I wonder how the navy boys doin' down on the beach.

We bin listenin' ta the firin' in front of us for maybe half a hour. Then we hear the first pop-pops behind us.

"Here they come," Lieutenant Wrightson say.

Everybody turn round and get ready for General Hoke's brigade.

"You scared?" Christian ask.

"I'm always scared."

He let loose a little sigh, "Me too."

"Steady," lieutenant say, "wait for my command."

Our pickets come runnin' like hell for the trench. And we can hear the rebels yellin' as they move through the trees. Then, I see the flag of the 17th North Carolina in the clearin' and behind it more rebels 'n I seen since the Crater.

"Fire," lieutenant shout.

We open up, and the first rank kinda crumple up and hit the ground. We drop down and re-load. Time we back up, ain't so many of 'em in the clearin'. But they ain't stoppin'.

"Fire," lieutenant call out again.

More rebels drop. Others stop runnin' like they ain't sure this such a good idea.

We give 'em one more good volley; then, lieutenant say ta fire at will. I take real careful aim at a rebel with a red beard. He look like one of them Micks who beat up on me back in Balmore. I hate him so much it's easy ta squeeze off the shot. He stop, look down at his belly, look back at me with the saddest eyes I ever seen, then fall face down in the dirt. For a long time, I watch him layin' there, bleedin' and moanin'. And I don't hate him anymore.

A shell explode right in the middle of 'em. A piece of some rebel's arm hit me in the face, and I forget about the one I killed and re-load ma Enfield. When I look out again, I see one, two, three, four shells hit in a line from the middle of the clearin' straight back inta the scrub pines. That take the fight outta the 17th North Carolina. They turn and head back ta the woods.

"God bless the navy," Christian say, "they sure can shoot straight." He stand up and start dancin' round like a crazy man. Others do the same till a shell hit close enough ta throw sand on 'em, and they drop down in the trench.

"Our boys goin' ta kill us," somebody yell out, and some climb outta the trench and start runnin'.

Lieutenant Wrightson aim his pistol at the closest one. "Stop or I'll shoot."

The runner don't pay him any mind, so the lieutenant fire a shot just over his head. He stop dead in his tracks. Others stop too. They come back ta the trench and Wrightson say, "Keep your heads low and get ready for the next attack."

Two more shells hit near us and then start hittin' the woods again. So ain't nothin' for us ta do, but re-load and wait.

Dark now, and we're still waitin' for the rebels ta come back. Behind us in the fort, we hear some fearsome fightin'. Over on the east, we see the sky light up every time our ships fire. But no more North Carolinians come outta the woods.

We hear that Colonel Abbott's white brigade retreated when the rebels attack. Now I think whoever say ta keep us outta his way kinda glad we back here. Course, I ain't willin' ta bet money on it.

"You think they attack again?" Christian ask.

"Soon as they get reinforcements."

He quiet for a minute.

"Think we can hold 'em off again?"

"We gotta."

Funny what you can think about when you're waitin' and waitin'. I keep seein' that rebel's eyes and how they were tellin' me he didn't want ta die. I think prolly he have a wife and some red-headed chil'ren somewheres, and now he never goin' ta see 'em again. And how his chil'ren goin' ta cry when he don't come home after the war. I feel real bad for him, layin' out there, and I feel real bad for his chil'ren. Cause the young ones ain't never goin' ta know their daddy.

For a long time, I think like that; then, I ask maself, "What about all the black chil'ren that never know their daddies?" Maybe, he didn't have slaves, but he was fightin' so rich planters could. So they could sell black mommas and daddies and chil'ren cause they was property. That's why he come runnin' outta the woods. And that's why I had ta kill him.

Now, I don't feel so bad.

"Ain't you hungry?" Christian ask.

"You be surprised how much noise ma empty belly bin makin'." "Yeah, almost nine hours since we et. And you know, even a hardtack cracker taste good right about now."

"Maybe so, but I'd settle for a piss," I say, and he laugh.

Round ten o'clock, somebody say, "Lookit that."

I see the sky light up like Fourth of July fireworks. Can only mean one thing. "The fort's ours," I tell Christian. "We won."

In a couple minutes, we get the official word passed on from Captain Daniels. "Fort Fisher has surrendered."

Now the cheerin' and dancin' round and poundin' on the back and huggin' start. Now, nobody's thinkin' about his belly or his bladder. Now everybody's thinkin' how we come ta capture this fort and we did.

After the cheerin' and celebratin' stop, we ordered ta move inside the fort and help flush out the rebels hidin' in bombproofs. We cross over the bridge the Pioneers replanked and see the palisade almost smashed ta splinters by many shells.

The open area inside the high dirt wall so tore up by shells, it feel like we walkin' over a plowed field. It's so dark after the fireworks stop, we can't see nothin'. But we hear 'em all round us--moanin', callin' for water or cryin' out, "Help me; for the love of God, please help me."

"We'd better see what we can do," the lieutenant say.

We spread out in the dark, keepin' real quiet so we can find the live ones and give 'em a drink of water, maybe say a last prayer with 'em ta try and make 'em feel better. And in the dark, don't really matter if they rebels or Union. Sometimes, the only way I find one is when I step on him and he moan.

Just before dawn, I'm ready ta lay down with the dead. I roll maself in a shelter half close ma eyes for maybe a hour.

"Sweet Jesus, Fletcher, look at that."

I open 'em and for the first time see what Fort Fisher look like. Through the cold, gray drizzle, I see heavy artillery pieces blowed apart. Their gun carriages lookin' like piles a kindlin'. And bodies. Without heads, without arms, without legs. Bodies split in two. Bodies split up in so many pieces, they look like butchered hogs. Bodies with heads smashed open and brains showin'. Legs and arms stickin' outta the sand just like at the

Crater. And the smell of all that death hangin' heavy in the damp air make me glad I ain't et since yesteday. There ain't nothin' in me ta puke up.

I'm ready ta close ma eyes again, but a voice behind me say. "Fall in for burial detail."

"Two arms, two legs and a head--doesn't matter if they match or not. Just so we got a complete body for each grave. That's all that matters. One more thing, try and separate the rebs so they don't get buried with our boys."

For hours, we do what General Terry's aide say. First, we tie bandannas soaked in camphor cross our faces. Then, we drag bodies outta bombproofs. Dig 'em out from under fallen timbers. I pick up what must be a hunnert heads and arms and legs. Lay 'em out and put 'em t'gether the way he said: one head, or parts of heads, two arms, two legs. Our troops in one line; the rebels in another. The pieces that ain't big enough ta say what part they are all go in a pile. Later, coal oil poured on it, and the whole thing set on fire.

Round noon, we take a little break for coffee and hardtack.

Then, we climb up on the seaface wall and look down on the beach. More bodies--they was Admiral Porter's sailors and marines that landed 'tween the Pulpit and Armstrong batteries. Most of 'em never made it off the beach. Their bodies blowed apart just like the ones inside the fort. Some of 'em lay half-buried in the sand on the steep slope of the wall. A few got almost ta the top. Their heads are smashed in, and their bodies got big gashes from rebel bayonets.

It's hard work draggin' the remains down the slope, then climbin' up again. The sand's deep and shift under ma feet. Sometimes, I slide down two steps for every one I take up. In spite of the cold, I'm hot and sweaty before we finally get 'em all laid out on the beach.

Almost dark time we finish. Lieutenant say we can eat and then get some sleep. Me and Christian climb up the slope, find us a quiet spot inside the seaface palisade and go ta sleep. We too tired and sore ta fix anythin' ta eat.

. . .

From somewhere inside or outside a dream, I hear a explosion, feel the ground under me shake just like at the Crater. I open ma eyes and see dirt, sand and chunks of heavy timber fallin' round me. Men pickin' themselfs off the ground. And over where the fort's main magazine was...a flame shootin' straight up in the air, smoke pourin' out in every direction.

"What the hell's goin' on?" Christian holler.

"I don't know."

I stand up, not sure if I should stay or join the men runnin' for the south end of the fort.

Sergeant Cooper spot us. "The rebels blowed up the magazine and prolly goin' ta attack. Grab your weapons."

We folla him t'ward the landface palisade. When we get 'tween the inside earthworks and the magazine, the smoke startin' ta clear and it look like yesteday. Bodies and parts of bodies everywhere. In places, only a hand or a foot stickin' outta the sand. Some movin' ta show somebody buried alive. And where the magazine usta be...nothin' but a big hole.

We start through the area, but a officer from the 169th New York stop us. He order us ta help dig up the men buried under the sand. "The whole regiment was sleeping here. Who knows how many are still alive under all that."

For the rest of the day, we move timbers and dig. The major was wrong, though. Weren't many alive. The ones we find we carry back ta a field hospital set up in the Pulpit Battery. The rest we lay out on the sand near the riverside gate with the bodies we collected yesteday.

The rebel attack never come. But a lotta men think they blowed up the magazine anyway. They say a detonation wire was hooked up ta a torpedo inside it. They swear the wire bin found. Another story say Union looters went in with torches, and they accidentally set off the gunpowder. Either way, a lotta men who survived the fightin' died.

What a damn waste.

CHAPTER 19
FEBRUARY 1865

FLETCHER HOWARD
Fort Fisher, North Carolina

Special Orders 2144

WAR DEPARTMENT,
ADJUTANT GENERAL'S OFFICE,
Washington, February 5th, 1865

(Extract)

36. Corporal Fletcher Howard, 39th U.S. Colored Troops, to be awarded a Congressional Medal of Honor.... Ceremony to take place when circumstances permit.

Citation will read: He planted his colors on the Confederate works in advance of his regiment, and when the regiment was driven back to the Union works he carried the colors there and bravely rallied the men.

I read the copy Captain Daniels give me once, twice, three times. I even read the end ta make sure it say,

"By order of the Secretary of War;
E.D. TOWNSEND,
Assistant Adjutant General."

Then, I ask him, "You sure they got the right man? I didn't do anythin' special that day. I just did what I was suppose ta."

"Colonel Stearns thinks you did. He recommended you for a Congressional Medal of Honor because he thought your bravery and quick-thinking helped save the regiment."

"Sir, when I first read the orders, I feel proud, but then I think on Jeremiah and all them men that died. And I think, You ain't no hero, Fletcher Howard. You're just lucky."

He put his hand on ma shoulder. "I suppose, in the final analysis, every hero is also lucky, but that doesn't take anything away from them or from you."

"I don't deserve any medal," I say, "and I think maybe I ought not accept it."

He look at me kinda a long time.

"Yes you should. If not for yourself, then for the regiment. Because without your courage, a lot more of them would have died that day."

Even after what he say, I ain't sure I oughta accept the medal. Then, I see Christian, and I tell him what's botherin' me.

He look me straight in the eye. "Take the medal cause like the captain say they ain't just honorin' you, they're honorin' all the fightin' men in this regiment. And when they pin it on you, all us, livin' and dead, goin' ta feel proud."

Later just before I go in the tent, I look up at the stars. Say ta the brightest one I see, "Jeremiah, the medal's really yours."

Soon as the dead are buried and the last prisoners are loaded on transports, we get ready ta march on Wilmington. The rebels blowed up Fort Caswell, so our ships are in the Cape Fear River. They can support us time we attack the secesh holed up in Sugar Loaf, on this side of the river, and in Fort Anderson on the other.

In the mornin' on the 18th of January, we see white soldiers headin' north on the Wilmington Road. A lot of 'em braggin' how they goin' ta "kick the shit" outta the rebels in Sugar Loaf. But the next day, they come back draggin' their asses and cryin' how they was stopped cold.

. . .

Finally, the order we bin waitin' on come down, "Advance on Wilmington." Seem like General Schofield tired of gettin' no where on this side of the river so his division cross over. Us in General Paine's suppose ta stay on this side and move up the road ta Wilmington.

Soon as it's light enough ta see, we eat a quick breakfast and strike the tents. Time the Quartermaster's wagons arrive, we're ready ta start loadin'. Then, we just got ta roll up shelter halves and get our mess gear t'gether.

In a couple hours, everythin's loaded and we fall in by companies. The regimental colors are in their place and everybody's ready ta move out. Colonel Stearns tell us we're goin' ta attack Sugar Loaf same time as General Schofield's attackin' Fort Anderson on the other side of the river. "Together the 2nd and 3rd Divisions should be able to capture the last obstacles keeping us from Wilmington."

We all cheer cause we all got the feelin' he right.

Course we don't go nowhere when he finish. The army don't work that way. It never move when you're ready. No, you got ta stand round and wait and wait. Wait till your belly start rumblin' cause it's empty again. And your bowels and bladder fill up, and you got ta wander off and relieve yourself.

Then, just when you think you're goin' ta desert if somethin' don't happen, the order come ta "Fall in." Men what snuk off come runnin' back, some tryin' ta pull their pants up. Rest of us tighten up cartridge belts and packs cause we don't want nothin' comin' loose on the way.

"Move out," and the long blue lines start on the march we hope takin' us ta Wilmington and victory.

Seems like we ain't gone a mile before the rain start. Ain't a real rain, just a cold drizzle. The kind that make the wool in ma long coat stink. That soak ma kepi so water run down ma neck and pretty soon ma union suit wet and ma pack start rubbin' a raw spot in the middle of ma back. That wet down the sand in the road just enough ta make it stick ta ma boots and they get heavier every step I take.

Then the wind pick up and blow the drizzle in ma face no matter which way I turn ma head. And ma Enfield startin' ta feel like it weigh a ton. No sir, it ain't long before I'm a wet, cold sonofabitch, who don't care nothin' about Wilmington or any place. I just want ta go home, and lay down in a soft, warm bed with ma Rebeccah and not get out till spring.

The fort called Sugar Loaf in front of us. Takin' it ain't goin' ta be easy cause we got ta charge cross a swamp, then up a steep slope. Our gunboats bin shellin' it and Fort Anderson cross the river all day. Lieutenant Wrightson say we're attackin' early in the mornin' at the same time the 2nd Division attack Fort Anderson.

Me and Christian set up talkin' till we so cold we go ta bed just ta get warm. But, I can't sleep. The gunboats keep up the shellin' all night long. That ain't enough, I can't stop thinkin' about Rebeccah. Think about her soft and warm body. How much I like kissin' her titties. How good it feel bein' inside her. "Got ta stop this," I say ta maself. "Ain't no good thinkin' on them things just before a battle."

It's hardly light, and we're up and havin' breakfast. Drink ma coffee real hot ta get the early mornin' river chill outta ma bones.

"You think they'll put up a big fight this time?" Christian ask.

"Even if they do, they ain't stoppin' us."

"Amen ta that, brother."

"The rebels had four years to build these fortifications. Now let's show them they didn't do a good enough job to keep out the 39th," Colonel Stearns say.

We cheer. This's what we bin waitin' for since we came ta North Carolina. We didn't do much fightin' in Fort Fisher, but we're goin' ta make up for it now. We're goin' ta show these rebels just how good black men can fight.

Colonel yell, "Charge," and we wade till we waist-deep in the cold swamp water. It's like somebody hit me in the belly, and ma balls shrink up till they feel small as peanuts.

"I love you, Rebeccah," I say when the rebels start firin' on us. "I love you, and I hope I see you again."

Climbin' outta the swamp, I don't feel nothin'--no fear, no worry, nothin'. I just keep thinkin' one thing--<u>live through this, live through this</u>. And pretty soon, me and the whole regiment movin' up the slope ta the parapet.

The firin' ain't heavy. And there ain't much smoke. I wonder if the rebels are runnin' outta ammunition, or they just waitin' for us ta get close ta the top.

I feel a hot fire cross ma face. "Jesus," I yell and touch where it burn. Lookin' at ma fingers, I see blood. I stop runnin' and stare at ma hand. Touch ma face again. See more blood. <u>I bin shot</u>.

"You O.K.?" Christian ask.

I turn ma head his way. Hold up ma bloody hand.

He study me real close. "A lotta blood, but look like a minie ball just graze your cheek."

"That's all?"

He start laughin'. "Why, did you think you wounded bad?"

"That's just what I think."

"Fraid not, but we keep standin' here and I guarantee we both be dead soon."

At the first abatis, the tree trunks packed t'gether so tight half the regiment hafta open paths so the rest can get through. I ain't got time ta think about anythin' else when I'm hackin' at dead limbs, and somebody's shootin' at me. If I did, I might just lay down and hide maself till the war's over.

After what feel like a couple hours, we get through and start runnin' for the next one.

This one worse'n the first. Pointed stakes bin pounded in the ground we got ta cut down before we can go through. And bein' at the base of the parapet, the rebels got good, clear shots at us. Ma legs are cold and wet, but the rest of me's sweatin'. If I don't get shot, I'm prolly goin' ta ketch pneumonia.

Somehow we get through, and start up the slope. Hunnerts of sweatin', pantin', cussin' black men. All of us got one idea--take Sugar Loaf and kill the rebels inside.

About halfway up, the shootin' stop. The lieutenant say, "Keep moving. It's just a rebel trick."

But it ain't. Time we get ta the top of the parapet, we can see they're gone. Well, most of 'em anyway. A few tired-lookin' old men and some scared boys are left. One of 'em hand Colonel Stearns a sword and say, "As an officer in the North Carolina Senior Reserves, it's ma unpleasant duty ta officially surrender ta y'all."

Next day, most of us in the 2nd and 3rd Divisions head up the road ta Wilmington. Only the 10th U.S. Colored stay back ta guard the prisoners. We fight a few skirmishes with the rebels, but it's clear they ain't really tryin' ta stop us. They know they can't. We just keep gettin' closer and closer ta Wilmington.

Round supper-time on the 21st, we make camp right outside the city. We can even see church steeples. Soon as it's dark, we see somethin' else.

"The whole damn town on fire."

"Guess they don't want ta leave us anythin'," Christian say.

"What they got we want anyway?"

All that night, smoke's the only thing you can smell.

On the mornin' of the 22nd, Captain Daniels tell us, "General Bragg has pulled out of the city. It's ours."

In spite of bein' in formation. In spite of nobody givin' us, "At ease," we start cheerin'. Ain't loud as back at Fort Fisher, but it's loud enough.

When we quiet down, captain say, "General Schofield wants the entire 2nd and 3rd Divisions to march into Wilmington. He wants to discourage any further resistance on the part of the general population."

Somewheres up in the front, a band start playin'. The command, "For-ward mar-ch," come and we step off, just like we learned back in trainin'. The music make everybody feel good. We stick out our chest a little extra. Swing our arms a little more. Hold up our head a little higher. We're marchin' inta Wilmington and we feel damn proud.

Time we first come in the town, I don't see nobody--not even a dead dog in the streets. But I know rebels in every house I pass. I can feel their eyes watchin' me. I can almost hear 'em whisperin,' "Look at that. Nigrahs, right here in Wilmington." I like ta tell every damn one of 'em their day's over and mine's just beginnin'.

We turn a corner, and I see somethin' I never seen before. Black folks line up on both sides of the street. They see us, and chil'ren start jumpin' up and down, and some older folks start rockin', and a most of 'em call out, "Bless you, brothers, for freein' us." Some of the young women even run out in the street and try and kiss and hug us.

We turn right on Market Street and halt in front of a buildin' with a lot of steps and big white columns. General Terry already standin' on the top step facin' a group of men not wearin' uniforms. I'm pretty sure they're rebels waitin' ta surrender the city.

One of 'em take a step toward the general and tell him. Then, the general say somethin' back and stick out his hand. The man shake it, and they talk for a few minutes before he walk back ta his group. He say somethin' ta them, and they kinda nod their heads and act real pleased.

General Terry hold up his hand, and the regimental commanders go up ta him. After a few minutes, they walk back down the steps.

When the ceremony's over, Colonel Stearns tell us, "General Terry has ordered that there will be no looting and no destruction of any civilian property. He does not want Wilmington to be another Atlanta or Columbia."

Sunday evenin', half the companies in the 4th and 39th allowed ta attend church. This's a very special day cause the first sermon ever preached by a black man in Wilmington's goin' ta be delivered by Reverend William Hunter, Chaplain of the 4th, in Bethel A.M.E. Church.

When I first see the church, I'm impressed. It's large, made outta bricks and have big white doors in front. I'm even more impressed time we file inside. All the walls painted white and look like 1,500 maybe 1,600 people can set in here with no trouble. T'day, the pews are full of soldiers, and the gallery full of black folks from the congregation.

The pulpit's in the front. Over top it, the words, "For my house shall be called a house of prayer for all people," written. Chairs are set up on both sides.

At eight o'clock sharp, the choir stand up and the words, "Sing unto the Lord a new song," fill the whole inside of the church. It's the best choir I ever hear sing. When they finish, General Terry, General Schofield, General Hawley, General Abbott and the regimental commanders file in and stand next ta the seats on both sides of the pulpit. Then the Reverend Hunter and the Reverend Jeremiah Asher, Chaplain of the 6th, come in. Reverend Asher lead us in a openin' prayer. After, we all set down.

Reverend Hunter climb up ta the pulpit. He look at us soldiers. He look up at the folks in the gallery. He look at the flag hangin' behind the pulpit. He look back at us and say, "My text for today is...sing unto the Lord a new song, for he hath done marvelous things; with his right arm he hath gotten him a victory."

He start back in Africa. Tell how black folks was captured and brought ta this country in chains on filthy, over-crowded slave ships. How we was sold time we got here. He tell about workin' in the fields, bein' beaten, families broken, men, women, chil'ren bein' sold off.

"Brothers and sisters, you might have been a king or a queen in Africa; but, in this country, you were just a nigger."

Folks in the gallery, soldiers in the pews say, "Amen."

Then, he tell the history of Old Bethel Church. He tell how the Reverend William Meredith give black folks the land on Zion Hill for the church back in 1799, and they build it. But white Methodists take over runnin' it. They make black folks set in the gallery and say the pastor always hafta be white, or they goin' ta burn the church down.

He tell us he was born a slave right here in Wilmington, and he run away 16 years ago. He tell about escapin' ta Philadelphia and goin' ta school there and becomin' a preacher. And when the war start, he join with Frederick Douglass and Bishop Payne in callin' for black soldiers ta fight in it. And when the 4th was recruited, he became its chaplain.

He talk about the war. Then, he look up in the gallery and say, "Everyone of you sitting up there owes more than you can ever repay to the men sitting down here."

And they stand up and say, "You're right," and "Thank you, brothers," and "Amen."

"But they couldn't have done it without the Lord. For it was His Arm that made them strong. It was His Arm who won the victory."

He stop.

"Praise the Lord," "Praise the Lord," we all say.

I never heard a sermon like I heard t'day. And I don't think anybody else did either.

ELIJAH DORSEY
Belmont Plantation, near Ellicott Mills

"Ain't so cold t'day, Momma, I think I take me a walk."

"You bin awful sick, Lijah; maybe, you oughta just stay here by the fire."

"Now, Momma, you done such a good job nursin' me I feel like I can take a short walk."

She come up real close and study ma face. "You don't look that strong ta me."

"I am, Momma; I swear it."

She walk over ta the fireplace mutterin' about how I never listen ta her when I was a chile, and she don't know why she expect anythin' different now. I go over and give her a little hug, tell her I be back in a hour.

Outside, I got ta squint a minute till I used ta the light again. But when, I feel the sun on ma face and a little touch of cold in the wind, I think this the best idea I have in a long time.

For the last week, I'm real tired bein' cooped up in the cabin. I bin waitin' for this break in the weather, so I can go outside. Without thinkin', I start headin' for where I seen that hawk summer before last.

Take longer gettin' there than I think cause I'm so stiff. Course ain't no hawk out this time of year, but still I can picture him circlin' round in the sky. And I think back on how I want ta know wha's on the other side of the trees. And how I make up ma mind ta run away. Funny thing...now that day seem a long time ago.

So I stand thinkin' and rememberin' for a long time. When I start back for the cabin, it's dark so I ain't sure which way ta go. And I feel so tired, I want ta set down and rest.

"Don't do it, fool," I say ta maself. "You set down and maybe you never get back up."

I keep walkin' till ma legs shakin' so much I think I'm goin' ta fall down. Then, I hear the water, and curse maself for walkin' to the river instead of away. Now, I wish I listened ta Momma.

I lean up against a tree a few minutes ta ketch ma breath. Then, I start back the way I come, hopin' I can get back ta Momma's cabin before I freeze.

Don't know how long I bin walkin', but finally, I see a cabin up ahead. From the look of it, I know it ain't Momma's, but I smell smoke, so I know somebody livin' in it. I bang on the door and hope they let me in.

"What you want?" a soft voice ask.

"Ma name Lijah. I used ta be a field hand here. Now I'm in the army, and I come back ta visit with ma Momma."

No sound on the other side of the door.

"Please let me in. I bin wounded and this ma first time out. I can't make it back ta ma Momma's cabin I'm so cold and tired."

The door open a little, a eye peer at me, then the door open all the way. "Come in, Mr. Lijah, come in where it's warm."

Before I can, ma knees give out. Fallin' in the room's, the last thing I remember.

Openin' ma eyes, I see the purtiest girl I ever seen. "You a angel?" I ask.

Hear a laugh so sweet give me goose bumps. "No, I'm real as you, Mr. Lijah."

I pull maself up a little bit. Look her over real close, and I still think she's a angel. I never seen eyes as big and brown, or teeth so white and straight before. Not even Florence Crittenden was this pretty.

"You ready for some soup? I made some fresh yesteday."

For the first time, I see the sun comin' in the window. "It's mornin'?"

She laugh again. "Mornin'? No sir, Mr. lijah, it's almost three o'clock in the afternoon."

"Sweet Jesus, I got ta go and tell Momma I'm O.K. She prolly worry herself sick."

I lift maself up ta try and get outta the bed.

She come over and put her hand on ma shoulder. "You eat your soup, Mr. Lijah. I'll go tell your Momma she got no cause ta worry."

I look deep down in her eyes, and I feel somethin' for her I never felt before.

"Be back soon as I can," she say and give me a little kiss on the forehead, and the warm feelin' it give me spread all the way ta ma toes.

She go, and I eat the whole bowl she give me. Good soup too, Momma can't make no better. After I finish, I lay back and think about her. And the more I think, the more they somethin' familiar about her. But, I can't say what.

. . .

"Ain't you somethin'?" The voice sound like Momma. I open ma eyes and see her. But the room behind her ain't right. The fireplace's on the wrong wall, and I never seen the table and chairs before. <u>Maybe I'm dreamin' again</u>, I think. I close ma eyes and open 'em again. But nothin' change. It ain't no dream.

"Let you outta ma sight for five minutes, and you wander off so nobody can find you. And I worry maself sick all night afraid you layin' cold and helpless someplace, and I can't do nothin' ta help you." She start cryin'.

"Momma, please don't. I'm sorry I worry you. I stay out in the field too long thinkin'. Then it got dark, and I got mixed up, and time I straighten maself out, I was too tired ta walk back home. So, I come here. And this young woman." I look round the room. "Her," I point to the young woman standin' by the table, "she take me in. And I go ta sleep and wake up and think she's a angel."

Momma start laughin' even though she still cryin'. "A angel--Lijah, you don't know how right you be. Don't you recognize Sam Butler's little girl?"

Sam Butler? Sam Butler? I almost ask who the hell's Sam Butler. Then I remember. He was a free black man who lived on a piece of land he own right next ta Belmont. He do carpenter work sometimes for Mister Dorsey.

"Wha's he got ta do with anythin'?"

Momma's laughin' so hard she hafta set on a chair. "Lijah, don't you remember Sam Butler have a daughter?"

It come back ta me. "Yeah, a little girl name Angel. But she's just a chile." I look over at Momma. "You ain't tellin' me tha's...tha's...."

Momma look at the young woman, then look over at me. "Lijah, meet Angel Butler."

The young woman do a little curtesy and smile. I live ta be a hunnert and fifty I'll never forget that smile. And I want ta be with this Angel for the resta ma life, so I can see that smile every day.

"A pleasure meetin' you again, Miss Angel," I say. And she give me a look that say somethin' happenin' inside her too.

Two weeks now since I take ma walk and end up in Sam Butler's cabin. And I can say it's bin the happiest time of ma life. Angel and me are t'gether almost the whole day. She feed me, shave me, read ta me. She do everythin' she can ta help me get better. Sometimes, after her daddy in the bed, she come and set with me. Lay her head on ma shoulder. We don't say nothin', just look in the fire. But I know we're thinkin' the same thing.

And her daddy he can't do enough for me either. He see that the fire always goin' and sometimes give me a little sip of whisky, "ta build up the blood."

Course Momma come every day. I see her lookin' at me and Angel and smilin' like she know a big secret.

I almost forget about the army and the war till one day Mr. Butler come back from Ellicott Mills. He's real excited sayin' he hear the army capture Wilmington, North Carolina, and the war may be over soon. I tell him I'm glad ta hear such good news, but inside I feel rotten. I know I'm strong enough ta go back ta the 7th, but I'm too happy bein' here with Angel.

Late that evenin', she come and set with me like she always do. Soon as her daddy get in the bed, she ask me, "Why're you so quiet?"

"Thinkin'."

"About what?"

"Nothin'."

She look me in the eye. "Lijah, don't tell me that. You're thinkin' about somethin' important, like maybe you oughtta be back in the fightin'."

"How you know?"

"Ain't hard ta figger out after I seen the look on your face when Daddy tell us the news he hear."

She put her face next ta ma ear. "Every mornin' for the last week, I bin wakin' up and prayin' you won't tell me, 'Angel, I got ta go back ta the army t'day.' And every night, I thank the Lord you're stayin' one more night under this roof with me."

Then, she kiss me. Not like a sister. Not like I ever bin kissed before.

"Don't you know I love you, Lijah? And don't you know I can't live if you go away?"

I put ma arms round her and kiss her like I never kissed no woman. I try and tell her in ma kiss I ain't never goin' ta love another woman like I love her.

I don't know how long we kiss, but time it's over she pull back her head a little and whisper, "You're tellin' me good bye, ain't you?"

"Yes, but I'm also tellin' you I love you. And I'm askin' you ta wait for me till the war's over. Then, I'm comin' back and marryin' you."

She kiss me again. This time ma parts get hard, and I want her under the covers with me, so I can love her. I reach ma hand down and feel her titty. It's soft and warm, and ma blood feel on fire. I got ta have her right now.

I start movin' ma other hand up her leg. She pull away from me. "Lijah, much as I love you, I can't give maself to you. Not till I'm your wife."

I grab her real tight. "You don't understand, Angel, I'm burnin' up inside with love for you." I try and pull her on top of me.

"Lijah, stop. Don't make me call Daddy."

I let go, and she get off the bed. "I think it's time ta say good-night, Lijah." Then she walk over by the fireplace.

I lean over till I almost fall outta the bed. "I'm sorry, Angel."

She turn back and look at me. "It ain't cause I don't love you, but this ain't the right time or the right place." She blow me a kiss and go through the door inta the other room.

I lay back on the pillow and think about her till I'm half-crazy. Ain't never gettin' ta sleep long as I feel this way, I think. I reach ma hand down under the quilt. Best I take care of this situation right now.

MAJOR AUGUSTUS T. ALEXANDER

City Point, Va.
February 21st, 1865

Dear Sallie,

I read and re-read your letter of February 2nd instant so many times I'm afraid it has deep creases from being folded and unfolded so much. I hope your mother's cold is better. Be sure to keep her warm at all times.

I share your joy at the good news from the South. General Sherman's victories in Georgia and South Carolina are glorious indeed. However, I fear that the Confederate hound is far from dead. The head--of course I mean General Lee--continues to hold on to Petersburg and Richmond with a tenacity that is beyond belief. The combined armies under General Grant's command must exceed 300,000 men versus no more than 50,000 in Lee's force. In addition, the Rebels are half-starved, bare-footed and lack even the simplest medicines. Yet, they fight on with a ferocity that daily sends a steady stream of wounded and dying to this hospital. And daily, the feeling that we may not be able to defeat Lee seems to grow.

You asked me if my situation has improved. I am sorry to say it has not. The white surgeons will have nothing to do with me. For the most part, they pretend that I am not even here, although one will occasionally comment favorably on my surgery or treatment of a particular case. In some ways, I think I was better off back at Birney Barracks in Baltimore. There was nothing for me to do, but at least I had friends to talk to. Here, there is no one.

I am sorry this letter has such a melancholy tone, but the dreary weather and the seemingly endless stalemate here have me feeling low. If only Spring would come, then perhaps this gloom will be lifted from my soul.

Your affectionate friend,
Augustus

CHAPTER 20
MARCH 1865

ELIJAH DORSEY
Belmont Plantation Ellicott Mills, Maryland

Momma and Angel know well as I do time I be goin' back. Still they don't say anythin'. I don't say nothin' neither. Guess we all hopin' news come the war over, and I don't hafta go anywhere.

Sun finally come out after rainin' almost a week. I take me a walk back ta that same field. Don't really know why. Maybe I'm lookin' for that hawk. Maybe I just need ta be by maself so I can think.

Lookin' down ta the trees by the river, I see somethin' comin' straight at me. "Sweet Jesus, tell me it ain't that hawk."

I watch him from way down by the trees till he right over ma head. And I got a feelin' he's that same hawk.

He make a couple big, lazy circles in the air, right over me, then fly straight south. Long time after, I stand thinkin' cause I got the feelin' he's tellin' me somethin'. That it's time ta go. The war and the 7th waitin' on me.

But, it ain't so easy now. I go back, maybe I get wounded again. This time maybe they cut off a arm or a leg. Angel goin' ta love me if I come home a cripple? Or suppose I get killed. Then, I never see her sweet face again.

That make me feel so sad, and I holler out ta the empty sky, "Ta hell with the army. I'm stayin' here."

But then, I think about the hawk, and bein' free, and all the brothers fightin' so all black folks can be free. "Ain't right for me ta desert now. I got ta go back and help finish what we start."

"Why I can't come with you ta Ellicott Mills?"

I look down at Angel, at the purtiest face I ever seen, and I can't say, "Cause I love you so much I don't know I can get on the cars if you're there." I just stand like some kind of big dummy.

She play with a button on ma shirt. "Sayin' good-bye be the hardest thing I ever done. But I want ta do it at the car shed, so I can watch till the train gone. Maybe that way, I'll feel like I'm goin' with you--least part of the way."

What can I do? I bend ma head down till our lips touchin'. Then, I pull her against me tight as I can, and I kiss her till I feel we ain't two people no more. Time we finish, I move back just a little and whisper, "You can come with me."

They're only two colors in Ellicott Mills. The houses and buildin's all gray cause they made outta the same kinda stone, and the road all brown cause it nothin' but mud. Especially t'day--the day we ride in so I can get the cars ta Balmore.

Bin rainin' since early in the mornin'. Not a hard rain, just a cold drizzle that soak our clothes and chill our souls as we ride over from Sam Butler's place.

Momma didn't want me ta go this mornin'. She put her arms round me and say, "Lijah, I'm goin' ta pray for you every night you away." Then, she kiss me and hold me a long time. Finally, I got ta pull maself loose.

Mr. Butler, he shake ma hand and say, "Come back ta us, son." Then, me and Angel get on the horses he lend us and head on down the lane.

For a spell, Angel talk a lot and act like we goin' in town ta buy supplies. But it ain't no use. The sadness inside her's too strong, and soon she stop. Then, we ride on the rest of the way without talkin'. From time ta time, we look over at each other.

The train's already there time we get ta town. It's settin' on the track hissin' out steam like it's mad at havin' ta wait on me and in a big hurry ta get movin'. "I wish the damn thing was long gone," Angel say.

But it ain't, so we get down off the horses and tie 'em up. I take ma carpet bag and we walk over by the only passenger car. Suddenly, standin' there, facin' each other, we got nothin' ta say.

Two sharp blasts on the engine's whistle. Black smoke and sparks come pourin' outta the smoke stack. Two white men get outta a carriage and rush past us ta get on the train. One of 'em mutter, "Damn niggers, all over the place now."

I start ta go after him. Show him who's a nigger, but one more blast on the whistle tell me I ain't got time.

I throw ma arms round Angel, hug her harder'n I ever done before. Tryin' ta make her part of me so I can take her with me anywhere I go.

"I love you, Lijah. More'n I love anybody...ever. And I'm goin' ta miss you every minute you're away."

"Angel, I can't tell you how much I'm goin' ta miss you."

"Then, don't try; just kiss me."

I do. And the second our lips touch, don't seem like there's any train, any army, any war. Just us holdin' each other...lovin' each other.

"Hey brother, your train's leavin'."

I look over her shoulder and see it pullin' outta the shed.

"Jesus, Angel, I gotta go."

I break away and start after it. I swing up the steps; then, I look back...see her standin', wavin', lookin' too young and purty ta be so sad. For a second, I think about jumpin' off and runnin' back. For a second, they don't seem ta be anythin' more important than makin' her happy.

But I can't. I just call out, "I love you, Angel, and I'm comin' back. I swear it."

She wave till the train go round the big bend by the Ellicott Brothers Mill and I can't see her no more.

MAJOR AUGUSTUS T. ALEXANDER
Depot Field Hospital City Point, Virginia

Washington City
March 6th, 1865

Dear Augustus,

It truly distresses me that you are in such low spirits. I know the war seems endless--it does to me as well--but, I beg you do not lose heart now. Surely, our armies have subdued so much of the body that even the head, which you say so stubbornly clings today, must surrender soon. What is left to support it?

Mother was almost over her cold when her sister, my Aunt Martha, arrived from Boston. Mother insisted on cleaning the house from top to bottom and on cooking all the meals. Needless to say, she has a fever again and is back in bed.

Speaking of Aunt Martha, she had the most incredible news. Mrs. Frances Harper...maybe you remember her as Miss Frances Watkins, the poetess and anti-slavery advocate...has begun lecturing again. Aunt Martha heard her address, "The Mission of the War," and said it was one of the most moving speeches she has ever heard.

I have taken the liberty, dear Augustus, of enclosing a copy of a poem Mrs. Harper read that night in Boston. I hope that it will inspire you as Aunt Martha said it did the audience in Boston.

"Bury Me in a Free Land"

Make me a grave where'er you will,
In a lowly plain, or a lofty hill;
Make it among earth's humblest graves,
But not in a land where men are slaves.

I could not rest if around my grave
I heard the steps of a trembling slave;

His shadow above my silent tomb
Would make it a place of fearful gloom.

I could not rest if I heard the tread
Of a coffle gang to the shambles led,
And the mother's shriek of wild despair
Rise like a curse on the trembling air.

I could not sleep if I saw the lash
Drinking her blood at each fearful gash,
And I saw her babes torn from her breast,
Like trembling doves torn from their parent nest.

I'd shudder and start if I heard the bay
Of bloodhounds seizing their human prey,
And I heard the captive plead in vain
As they bound afresh his galling chain.

If I saw young girls from their mother's arms
Bartered and sold for their youthful charms,
My eye would flash with a mournful flame,
My death-paled cheek grow red with shame.

I would sleep, dear friends, where bloated might
Can rob no man of his dearest right;
My rest shall be calm in any grave
Where none can call his brother a slave.

I ask no monument, proud and high,
To arrest the gaze of passers-by;
All that my yearning spirit craves,
Is bury me not in a land of slaves.

Dear Augustus, please do not think I am criticizing, in any way, your commitment to our cause. I know in my heart that you are as dedicated as you were when you first volunteered for the army. You would not be in Petersburg treating the wounded and caring for the dying if you were not. And I know I am not the only one who admires you and appreciates your efforts in behalf of our people. Instead, I hoped, in my own small way, to lift your spirits with Mrs. Watkins thrilling words which so eloquently remind us all that we cannot rest until the scourge of slavery is driven from this land. If I did otherwise, I am deeply sorry.

With great affection,
Sallie

"All the eloquence is not Mrs. Watkins," I say softly after I have read the letter several times. "You have lifted my spirits, dearest Sallie, more than you can imagine."

I read and re-read, "With great affection," "Dear Augustus," "I am not the only one who admires you," and cherish the hand that wrote them.

I look over at the face smiling at me from my shaving mirror. "Augustus," I say to the face, "I think you're in love with Miss King."

I wave the letter in front of the mirror, "And this gives me some reason to think she returns the feeling."

Special Order
No. 767

WAR DEPARTMENT,
ADJUTANT GENERAL'S OFFICE
Washington, March 13th, 1865

(Extract)

7. Effective this date, Major Augustus T. Alexander, Chief Surgeon, 7th U.S. Colored Infantry, promoted to Lieutenant Colonel, Brevet.

By order of the Secretary of War;

E.D. TOWNSEND,
Assistant Adjutant General.

"Well...I suppose congratulations are in order." General Sibley rises slowly and extends his hand. I shake it, and he quickly sits down.

"And...it looks like Secretary Stanton has a transfer in mind for you sometime soon."

He hands me a piece of paper that, in effect, says I am to proceed to Hilton Head, South Carolina, to await orders.

"Whatever he has in mind, though, will have to wait. I can't let you go now. You're too important to me."

Every muscle, every fibre inside me stiffens. "Request permission to speak frankly, sir."

He looks at me for some time. Finally, he nods, "Granted."

"When I first reported to this hospital, I sensed that no one particularly wanted me here. And since that time, nothing has happened to prove those impressions wrong. I work alone with only a few colored nurses and orderlies. None of the white surgeons will assist me or, for that matter, so much as say 'Good morning.' When I'm not on duty, I keep to myself because that's better than being snubbed by my fellow officers."

I pause to let my words sink in. "So I ask you, sir, why not just let me go? Wouldn't that solve both our problems?"

He picks up a letter opener, examines it for several very long moments, then puts it down. "You're right. When you first came here, I was not pleased. As you yourself know, white officers will not serve under a colored one, and I did not want a repeat of that business at Camp Stanton. I asked that you be assigned elsewhere and was told, by the Secretary of War himself, that it was out of the question. But after watching you work, and seeing how the men respond to you, I think you're a fine surgeon. The kind I want on my staff when the big push comes. You have my word: after our army breaks through into Petersburg and Richmond, you can go anywhere you want to. But until then, you're staying right here."

Outside the general's headquarters, I stand for a long time thinking. And the truth is...I don't know how to feel about what he just said. Should I be happy that he thinks enough of my skills to want me here, or should I be angry at him for forcing me to stay in this damn situation?

"Coming through," a voice behind me says.

Without thinking, I step off the plank sidewalk into the mud.

"Well, I'll be damn. It's the nigger surgeon."

The voice--I'd know it anywhere. I swing around and stare up at Lieutenant Joel Morgan.

"I've been promoted to surgeon and reassigned--to the 117th Ohio," he says grinning.

I want to hit him. I hate him more than any white man I ever knew. I want to pay him back for all the trouble he caused me. Going behind my back to Stanton...the President. Keeping me tied up doing nothing in Birney Barracks when I should have been with the 7th. I feel my hand squeeze in a fist.

"I hear you been promoted too. Lieutenant Colonel. Ain't that a kick in the pants." He steps out of the way of a captain hurrying on some important errand.

"You know, I've hated you for years cause, long as you was chief surgeon of the 7th, I couldn't get promoted or reassigned. So every day, first thing in the mornin' and last thing at night, I cursed you. Then yesterday, I got these orders."

He holds up a sheet of paper. "This finally gets me out from under you. So now, I got what I want...and you got what you want. Guess everything's worked out for the best, then. Well, be seeing ya." He turns and walks away.

I stand watching until he's out of sight, and I know I'm smiling. Then, I look down at my fist. Slowly, I open it, then shove it deep in a pocket. Happy for the first time in months, I carefully make my way through the mud back to my hut.

Moments later, I start a letter to Sallie. I want her to know about my promotion. And even more important, about Morgan.

FLETCHER HOWARD

Outside Goldsborough, North Carolina

In March, it ain't so cold, but it rain almost every day. We left Wilmington on the 3rd of March, and it was rainin'. We headed for Goldsborough where we're suppose ta meet up with General Sherman. After that, on ta Petersburg ta smash through and ketch Old Bobby Lee--that's what the white soldiers call him--and end this damn war. At least, that's what everybody keep sayin'. The only thing I know for sure, I ain't bin dry since we left Wilmington.

T'day, on the 21st of March, we're just outside Goldsborough, and there's bin a cold drizzle all mornin'.

"Lieutenant, take your company and see if you can move around behind them and find out how many they are."

We bin pinned down for almost a hour, and the colonel's gettin' tired playin' games with the rebels. He ain't the only one.

In a few minutes, A Company's wadin' up ta our chest in a creek that's swollen and runnin' fast from all the rain. The water's so cold ma nuts shrivel all up.

On the other side, we got ta climb up a steep clay bank. First one that try slide back in the water. "It's too slippery here, lieutenant."

"Let's go downstream a ways."

Holdin' our Enfields over our head, we make our way real careful down the creek till we come on a bend. Lieutenant's the first one round. He wave his pistol over his head for us ta come on. "We can get out here. The bank's a lot lower."

A minie ball go through his open mouth so clean I don't think he know what happen till he see blood pourin' out in the water. He make kinda a croakin' sound before two more ketch him in the head makin' it jerk ta one side, then the other.

Now, they're rebels everywhere on the bank. "Lookie here," one say, "niggers," and open fire. The ball splash 'tween me and Christian.

"Get down," I yell and duck ma head under the water, pullin' the useless Enfield with me.

I don't think Christian hear me, or either he don't have time ta do anythin'. When I come up, he's still standin' there.

"Come on, Christian, we got ta get outta here."

He turn his head, and I see he ain't got a eye. Just a big red hole where it usta be.

I let go ma Enfield and grab a hold of his arm. "Come on," I yell and pull him, but I ain't fast enough. Another ball hit his shoulder. I hear the bone crack.

"Go on and save yourself," Christian whisper. "I'm done for."

"No way I'm leavin' you here." I pull on him hard as I can and start movin' back the way we come.

I only gone a couple steps when I see a reb raise up his long rifle. I see him aim, and I know he got me in his sights.
I duck under the water draggin' Christian with me. Stay there till I think ma lungs bust. Up I come.

For a second, I can't see nothin' so much water pourin' off ma head. Then, I see the rebel still aimin' at me. I hear a pop. Somethin' sting ma neck, like a yellow jacket, and it feel kinda warm under ma collar. I know it's blood.

"Yahoo, I think I got me one." The reb with the long rifle drop down on his knee and reload.

<u>We ain't dyin' here, not like no fish in a barrel</u>, I think.
I put ma arms round Christian's chest, lock ma hands t'gether, lay back in the water, and push off for the bank we come from, leavin' a trail of blood behind us.

<u>Got ta make, got ta make it</u>, I keep thinkin'. And we almost ta the bank when that rebel stand back up, aim and fire again. This one burn inta ma cheek like all the fire of hell. "Jesus Christ," I holler, lettin' go of Christian so I can cover ma face. Like ma hands goin' ta pertect me. Like they're goin' ta stop the pain.

I hear more pops and drop ma hands. Christian's body hit a couple more times and start floatin' away. I reach for it, and a ball smash in ma arm. Somehow it don't hurt. I grab hold a Christian and start for the bank again.

All of a sudden, I feel ma head jerk back; then, there ain't nothin' but a real bright white light and no more pain, no more cold. From somewheres on the other side of the light, I hear a voice say, "Good-bye, Rebeccah, I love you."

ELIJAH DORSEY
Outside Petersburg, Virginia

For better'n a week I bin travelin'. First, on the cars ta Balmore, then on the steamer, Prometheus, ta Fortress Monroe. All that time, I think about Angel and how much I love her and miss her. Now standin' on the dock at City Point, Belmont, Momma, Angel...they seem like some kinda dream I had. And right here, in front a me's, the real world. The tents and sheds, mules and wagons, crates and barrels, cussin' teamsters, and more soldiers in blue 'n even God can shake a stick at. For a minute, I don't know what ta do.

"You lost, soldier?"

I turn round and see a captain. He's got kinda a pointy face and big, brown teeth. He look like a weasel ta me.

"I...I just got back off convalescent leave, sir. And I... ain't exactly sure where ma regiment is."

He spit out a wad of tabacca juice. "Lemme see your orders."

Quick as I can, I hand 'em ta him.

He study 'em for a minute. "Seventh U.S. Colored, huh?" He hand 'em back. "You missed the big review for General Grant on the 19th. All the colored regiments were in it."

He spit some more tabacca juice. "Best damn show I seen round here since last summer."

"You know where the 7th be now?"

"Down by Fort Burnham." He point over the northwest.

"Come ta think of it--didn't I hear somethin' about the whole brigade movin' out this afternoon?"

I grab ma bag and head up the bank the way he point. If the 7th's goin' ta battle, I'm goin' too.

Turns out the captain weren't much help. I got ta stop and ask in four or five places before I find the 7th. It's rainin' and almost dark time I get there. First thing, I see a long line of wagons bein' loaded. Ain't goin' ta be easy findin' the adjutant ta report in, I think.

Two hours later, I'm in the ranks and we're headin', near as I can figger, t'ward the James River. "What you bin doin' since I left," I ask.

"Nothin' that make any sense," Solomon Greene, ma old friend say. "One day they march us up ta the lines. The next, we march back again. We done that so many times I can't count."

I try thinkin' about Angel and the last night we spend t'gether. How soft and warm her body is when she love me. But it make me miss her so much, I start hurtin' inside. So, I stare down at ma boots sinkin' in the mud and don't think no more.

"Sure good ta be back," I say real quiet.

"Glad ta have you back," Solomon answer, and I know he mean it.

Some time near dawn, we halt in a big muddy field. The baggage wagons waitin' on us.

"This here place sure look familiar. Lijah, I got the idea we back ta City Point."

Before I have a chance ta ask how he know, Lieutenant Califf snap, "Start unloading the wagons, we're setting up camp here."

We unload the wagons and set up the tents. Then, they let us get some rest. I roll up in ma shelter half, but I can't sleep. I keep hatin' maself for comin' back.

Later in the mornin', tired as hell, we line up. Roll call just finish when Colonel Shaw hisself come out and address us. "A lot of you are probably wondering why we came back here to City Point. Well, the answer is that President Lincoln is going to review the Army of the James this afternoon...and you're going to be part of it."

President Lincoln--I can't be no more surprised if he say "Jesus Christ comin'."

I ain't the only one. The excitement go right through the regiment and everybody start talkin' like we ain't in formation. Like the colonel ain't standin' there waitin' on us.

"Atten-huh," the company commanders finally call out. We all snap to.

"You have only three hours to get ready. So, when you fall out, don't waste any time."

Three hours later, we're ready. Our boots shine the best we can make 'em. Our uniforms brushed hard so they look blue again. We line up in columns of fours and wait.

It's hard standin' and waitin'. Knowin' any minute you're goin' ta march in front of the President. You're goin' ta see, just for a second, the man you bin hearin' about since this war started. The man who signed the Emancipation Proclamation. The man you ain't even sure till now is real.

The band start playin'. The clouds open up. The sun shine down on the parade field. At the command, "Forward march," we step off sharp as we know how. Cause we're proud of bein' fightin' men. And we want President Lincoln ta know we're proud.

"E-y-e-s right." Every head in the 7th turn t'ward the reviewin' stand.

I see him. I see him. Tall and straight. Wearin' a long black coat and a big black hat on his head. And I know I ain't never goin' ta forget this day long as I live. Some day I be tellin' ma grandchil'ren how I fight in the war for freedom. And how one day, President Abraham Lincoln hisself come down and review the army. And I seen him.

"E-y-e-s front," the command, but I'm a little slow. And I see him standin' in shaft of sunlight, and I think he's what all white men oughta be like. Then, the whole country be better off.

We don't have much time ta think on seein' the President. By five o'clock, we're movin' out. As usual nobody tell us anythin'. Everybody think we're headin' back ta the lines near Petersburg.

Just before midnight, the rain start. Ain't too hard at first, but time we move away from the Appomattox River, it's comin' down so hard you can't hardly see the man in front a you. The road get so slippery, some fall down when we come on a big dip nobody see. Solomon's one of 'em. I give him a hand up and he mutter, "Just once, I'd like ta go on a march down here when it ain't rainin'."

About a hour later, we halt. Wet, tired and hungry we stand in the pourin' rain and wait. And wait--five minutes, ten minutes, fifteen, half a hour--hard ta say how long.

Finally the commands, "A-b-o-u-t face," then "Forward march" come, and we head back down the road we just come up.

Maybe, a half hour later, we halt again. Same kinda long wait. Then, we turn round and head right back up the same road. "You gettin' the feelin' we're lost?" I ask Solomon.

"Uh-huh, and if we don't get found soon, we're all goin' ta have pneumonia."

This time, we take a fork we passed right by before. This road's so narrow, wet branches keep hittin' us. Pretty soon, it ain't nothin' but a path.

"It appears we're lost again, Solomon."

But I'm wrong. Ten, maybe fifteen minutes later, we come on some railroad tracks. They must be what we're lookin' for cause we follow 'em till we're back behind our lines outside Petersburg.

"You think these the tracks goin' ta City Point?" Solomon ask.

"I do."

"Then, why in the hell didn't we just follow 'em last night, instead of marchin' round in all that rain?"

"Cause, brother...this's the army."

We both laugh.

Just past noon, we're on the move again. We camp that night near the Weldon Railroad tracks, so we're south of Petersburg. Next mornin', we head west till we get ta Hatcher's Run and stay there the resta the day. Bin rainin' so long, it's hard ta find any dry wood. Me and Solomon get a small fire goin', just enough ta make some coffee ta soak our hardtack in.

Next mornin' we're on the move by six o'clock. In no time, we hear firin' and halt near our old lines.

"A Company's going to deploy as skirmishers," Lieutenant Califf say. We get ourselfs ready and wait for the order we think comin' any minute.

Only it don't come. Only thing happen, it start rainin' again.

Couple hours later, we don't hear no more firin', and we told ta "Stand down."

Again, we try and find some dry wood ta make a fire and fry up some bacon ta mix with the hardtack.

We start eatin' and the clouds open up and we can see the sun for the first time in days. "Lookit that rainbow," I say.

"Maybe, it's a sign things go better for us tomarra."

CHAPTER 21
APRIL 1865

LIEUTENANT COLONEL AUGUSTUS T. ALEXANDER

Special Orders
No. 323

HEADQUARTERS
ARMY OF THE JAMES,
Outside Petersburg, March 25th 1865

2. Special leave of absence, on account of private business, is hereby granted Surgeon A.T. Alexander, 7th U.S.C.T. for a period not to exceed five days, commencing April 2nd, 1865.

By Command of Major General George G. Meade:
S.W. Williams,
Assistant Adjutant General.

The brief shower has just stopped. The clouds are starting to move eastward, and the sun is trying hard to shine. A horse car has just pulled up in front of the shed, and I step out to board it. Since March 31st, anyone who pays the fare is entitled to ride the horse cars here in Washington City. So, this time, the conductor can't refuse to let me on. I hand him my nickel and do my best to ignore his dirty look.

There are several empty seats, but I prefer to stand. It isn't the contempt of the white passengers that stops me. It's just that I'm too excited and nervous to sit still. In a few minutes, I will see Miss Sallie; and, if my courage doesn't fail me, I will ask her to marry me.

Although Pennsylvania Avenue is "paved," there are large holes which the cars' wheels seem to have no trouble finding. To keep from breaking an axle, it moves so slowly that by the time we finally reach the corner of 13th Street, I can no longer control my impatience. When the car stops, I jump off.

Ten minutes of brisk walking helps me feel a little less nervous. Just as I reach the alley off 13th Street where Miss Sallie's family lives, the last cloud hurries away, and it is suddenly a nice day. "A good omen," I say quietly as I knock on the door.

"Miss Sallie, what a great pleasure it is seeing you again." I remove my hat and bow, I hope, not too stiffly at the waist.

"It's an even greater pleasure seeing you again, Augustus." She smiles so sweetly that I want to grab her and kiss her.

"Who is it, Sallie?"

"It's Major, excuse me Lieutenant Colonel Alexander, Momma. I think he's come to pay a call."

"Where are your manners, child? Show him in."

"You heard Momma; please come in."

I step over the threshold, and my heart is beating so hard I'm sure everyone in the room will hear it. Worse, I feel light-headed as I follow her into the parlor.

"Sit down, Colonel, please." Mrs. King motions me toward the horsehair sofa. "Sallie will get us some tea."

"Momma, Colonel Alexander may prefer something stronger."

Both pairs of eyes fasten on me. Although a whisky or brandy would certainly help at this point, I quickly say, "no." I'm fully aware Mrs. King's brother, Bishop Payne, is a leading temperance advocate. It just makes sense not to take any chances.

During the small eternity Sallie is out of the room, Mrs. King and I don't have much to say to each other. After she congratulates me on my promotion...and I say the expected modest things...we lapse into an awkward silence. Next, she asks me how the war is going.

"Everyone at City Point thinks we will break through Lee's lines any day now." I'm surprised how strained my voice sounds. Worse, my palms feel so wet that I may never be able to dry them.

Several times, I catch her studying me, and I wonder if she suspects why I'm here. And each time, I can't help wondering if she's laughing at me behind that beautiful smile so much like her daughter's.

Just when I'm about to say, "Look, it was a terrible mistake for me to come here," Sallie appears with a tray.

"Have you come to see Secretary Stanton about your next post?" she asks.

"I intend to pay Mr. Stanton a visit tomorrow. With Lee's surrender fairly imminent, I think this is the time to discuss my future with him." I try not to look at Sallie. "But that's not my only reason for coming."

"Mr. King heard that the Freedmen's Bureau is going to operate hospitals in the South, after the war. Perhaps, you'll be assigned to one of them."

"I have heard the same thing, and you can be assured, Mrs. King, I shall mention it to the secretary." I would like to say more, but I feel sharp pain in my lower back. If I don't get off this damned stiff horsehair sofa, in a few minutes I'll be in agony. But how can I do move without offending Mrs. King? This sofa is obviously her pride and joy.

"Are you all right, Augustus? You have the oddest look on your face?"

"Actually, Sallie, I'm having a little trouble with my back. I have a touch of rheumatism in it. Probably from those first nights at Camp Stanton when I had to sleep on the cold damp ground."

"Well then, don't sit there, Colonel. That old horsehair sofa is the most uncomfortable piece of furniture I've ever owned."

As I settle down on a chair, I want to kiss Mrs. King for her kindness. After another cup of tea and some more polite conversation, I start worrying that it's getting late--already I can see the shadows deepening in the room--and I won't have any time alone with Sallie. To ask her....

A clock in another room chimes four o'clock. "Mercy, is that the time? Mr. King will be home soon and want his dinner. Please excuse me, Colonel, but I must get busy in the kitchen."

For some minutes, the only sounds in the house are those coming from the kitchen--the snap and crackle of burning kindling, the banging of pots and pans, the soft rhythm of ingredients being mixed, and finally, the hiss of hot grease. Meanwhile, Sallie and I sit absolutely frozen, not even looking at each other, as if afraid any word or movement might break the silence and have unforeseen consequences.

"Sallie, I...."

"Yes, Augustus?"

I lose my courage. "Nothing...nothing at all."

More silence.

From the kitchen, there are no sounds now except Mrs. King's soft humming, but the first faint aromas warn me Mr. King's supper will soon be ready. Then, I'll have to go. And if I don't speak my mind first, I may never get another chance.

"Sallie,there-is-another-reason-why-I-came-to-Washington," I blurt out. The suddenness makes her jump just a little.

"I'm...I'm terribly sorry. I didn't mean to startle you." But, no sooner are the words out of my mouth, than I'm sorry I said them. I'm making such a mess out of this visit that I'm beginning to wonder if I shouldn't just rush out the door before I make a complete ass out of myself.

She looks at me with her big brown eyes, and I make up my mind. "The other reason is...is...well, personal and involves you."

"Personal and involves me? Whatever is it, Augustus?"

I can't quite make out the look on her face. Is it tender, or is it playful? Either way, I have her full attention. So, I look her straight in the eye, clear my throat, open my mouth, and hope the speech I rehearsed over and over, during all the long hours traveling from City Point will come out.

To my immense surprise, it does.

"Miss Sallie, in the few months since we first met, I...I have come to have a...uh...high regard for you."

I'm sweating. I know I'm sweating. I can feel the beads running down my forehead, my cheeks, under my collar. And I'm starting to feel chilled. The muscles in my jaws are beginning to quiver, and it's all I can do to keep my teeth from chattering.

"Augustus, are you sure you're all right?"

"Yes...yes, perfectly all right. I'm just a little nervous."

"About seeing Secretary Stanton?"

"No, about asking you to marry me."

There is a moment or two of absolute silence in the room. From the kitchen comes the sound of something hitting the floor. But neither of us takes our eyes off the other. And I know, before she says a word, what her answer will be.

Feeling stronger and braver than I ever have in my whole life, I stand up and walk over to her. She smiles up at me, and I know I will never forget the look of love I see in her eyes. I touch her hands, and she rises off the chair. I put my arm around her. "I'm not a young man. And I certainly do not have the figure a young man has, nor the hair. But no man could love you more than I do."

She smiles warmly and picks a small piece of lint off my lapel. "Since we're engaged now, Augustus, please stop calling me Miss Sallie."

I pull her closer, "Sallie, you've just made me the happiest man in the whole world."

"Then, stop talking and kiss me. Or I might just change my mind."

Our lips are barely touching when a deep voice behind us demands, "Daughter, what are you doing?"

I jerk my head away so quickly I feel light-headed for a moment. When the dizziness stops, I see Mr. King standing in the doorway, scowling at us.

"I repeat, daughter, what are you doing?"

"I...that is, Colonel Alexander...he...he...."

"I asked Sallie to marry me, sir. And I'm pleased to say she has accepted." I turn to her. "You did mean yes, didn't you?"

She pokes me playfully in the ribs. "You know that's exactly what I meant."

As he closes the door behind him, Mr. King's scowl is already changing to a pleased smile. "Did you hear that, Mrs. King; our daughter is going to marry this fine Christian gentleman?"

"Of course, I did. So, don't just stand there--give them your blessing; then, all of you come in and sit down to dinner."

ELIJAH DORSEY

Outside Petersburg, Virginia

For the last two days, we bin movin' from place ta place like nobody know what ta do with us. T'day, April 1st, half past nine in the mornin', we're back where we started from.

Now, the order come down for us ta line up for a charge. We take our good old time cause we ain't really expectin' nothin' ta happen.

Then, it start. A long, low rumble over by the South Side Railroad on our left. Gettin' louder minute by minute, till it sound like every artillery piece in the Union army must be firin'. Makin' the ground shake like I never feel it shake before. And I know...and every man in the 7th, 109th, 116th, in every black and white regiment know--this what we bin waitin' on. This's the big one--the attack tha's goin' ta take us inta Petersburg and Richmond. The attack tha's goin' ta end this war.

The order come ta stand down. We get in little groups and try and talk, but we got ta holler so loud we soon give it up. Lieutenant Califf say we can make fires, but we don't. Nobody feel much like eatin'.

All afternoon the firin' go on. Then, round four o'clock it get real quiet. Over on the right, near the VIth Corps, we hear rifle fire. Little bit, then more and more till it almost loud as the cannons. Any minute now, I think.

But no order come. And I feel madder'n hell. "Look like we bein' left out again."

"Yeah, the white boys always get the glory," Solomon Greene say. "But we only get ta work and clean up."

"Amen, brother," the rest say.

"Lieutenant, can we make some fires? It's almost dark, and we're hungry."

"My orders are that this company is to be ready to move out on a minute's notice. That means--no fires."

I pull a hardtack package outta ma pack. Look at the almost three-inch square crackers and decide I ain't hungry enough ta eat one without some coffee ta soak it in. So, I lay down on the grass and listen ta the bombardment tha's startin' up again.

It's bin dark for a hour or more. I'm feelin' cold and hungry. And I close ma eyes and make out I back home with Angel. The two of us settin' in front of the fire, talkin' and laughin' and bein' happy t'gether. The picture in ma head seem so real I start ta smile.

Then, I hear Lieutenant Califf say, "This is it, we're movin' out."

He don't hafta say it twice. Every man in A Company jump ta his feet. We line up in columns of fours, and don't move a muscle till we hear, "Seventh regiment...f-o-r-w-a-r-d." In a couple minutes, we line up in front of the rebel abatis. "Fix bayonets," the order.

"Charge," the lieutenant yell loud as he can. And we hit the abatis like it ain't even there. Smashin' through the piles of dry brush. Breakin' off the dead limbs. Jumpin' over the trunks. Everybody runnin' hard as he can. Every man wantin' ta be the first one through. The first one ta climb up the parapet and see the rebels who bin keepin' us back so long.

Me and Solomon reach the base of the parapet before anybody else. "Up and over?" I ask.

"Amen, brother."

We start up, runnin' hard as we can. Rest of A Company right behind us. Maybe Lieutenant Califf yell for us ta wait on him, but I don't pay him no mind.

A couple feet from the top, I start wonderin', Why ain't they firin' on us? I look over Solomon, and I think he got the same question in his head.

We reach the top and look down the other side. Empty.

"The VIth Corps beat us," I say and I never felt more like I bin cheated than right now. And I don't know if I'm madder at the rebels for retreatin' or at the VIth Corps for beatin' us.

"Shit," Solomon say. "Shit, shit, shit."

Rest a A Company reach us, look down and start cussin'. I hear more cussin' in the couple minutes it take the lieutenant ta join us. If a rebel come and try ta surrender right now, we prolly tear him apart we all so mad.

Lieutenant look down and don't say nothin'. He wait till most of us done swearin'; then, he make us form a line. "The war isn't over yet. We've still got to take Petersburg and Richmond. So let's move out."

We drop down in the trench and out the back side. Then, we march along behind the works. The artillery's in new positions and they layin' down a terrible barrage on Petersburg itself. Look like the whole sky light up every time they fire. And the lieutenant start singin', "We look like men, we march like men," but nobody join in. We want ta get ta the fightin' before it's all over.

Light enough ta see now and up on top a little hill, I glance back. "Solomon, lookit that."

Behind us and on the left, far as we can see, long lines of Union soldiers. In front, big columns of smoke comin' up outta Petersburg. And the cannons and mortars still firin' round after round on the city.

"I almost feel sorry for 'em," Solomon say.

I start ta say, "Because you never bin a slave," but I don't. Maybe he's right. Maybe women and chil'ren bein' killed in Petersburg who have nothin' ta do with this war. Maybe they....

"Move on you two," lieutenant snap. "You're holding up the war."

I don't like the way he talk ta us. And I think, White folks's white folks. Don't matter where--Balmore, the army, Petersburg--they all the same. They all think they better'n us.

I don't feel sorry for none of 'em, especially the rebels.

Round one o'clock we halt, and me and Solomon make us a fire. Then, we fry some fatback and break up hardtack in it. It ain't Momma's or even Angel's cookin'; but hell, when a man ain't et for a whole day, it gets the wrinkles outta his belly.

After we finish, we get some bad news. "The regiment's been ordered to Ream's station to guard the trains," Lieutenant Califf say. "So, put out the fires and fall in."

"Guard the trains--why they need guardin'?" Solomon ask.

"They don't," I say. "That ain't nothin' but a way ta keep us outta the fightin'."

"Then, I guess this war's over for us."

I don't hafta tell him I agree.

Marchin' away from the fightin' and everybody else headin' for it give me the worse feelin' I have in a long time. I try and think on Angel, hopin' that make me feel better...but it don't. Then, seem like we only march a mile and we stop. Now what? I ask maself.

After a long time standin' in the road waitin', we turn round and head for Petersburg again. I shake ma head, "This army don't ever know what it want us ta do."

"Maybe so, Lijah, but least we headin' the right way now."

"A Company, take up your positions on the right."

We get down behind anythin' that give us cover. The rebels here don't seem ta know they lost the war. They're keepin' up such a steady fire they got everybody stopped.

We trade fire with 'em the rest of the afternoon. Little by little, we push 'em back till they got only one line of works left. Then, the lieutenant say we're goin' ta charge. "But wait for my signal," he say. "This attack's being coordinated so that everybody in this sector goes at the same time. If it succeeds, there's nothing to stop us from entering Petersburg."

I make sure ma bayonet clean and ma Enfield loaded. And I try not ta think about gettin' killed here. Bein' one of the last ta die in the war ain't a honor I want. I got too much ta live for.

"Ready, A Company?"

We stand up and form a line.

"C-h-a-r-g-e."

I head for the low rebel parapet fast as I can go. On ma left and right, I hear yellin'. Turn ma head and see everybody in the regiment got his mouth open. Even with the minie balls fallin' on us and kickin' up dust everywhere, don't look like anybody's scared. What the hell, I think. I open mine and start yellin' too. And I feel good, like I ain't felt in a battle before.

Don't take no time ta reach the parapet. In minutes, we're up and over. But the rebels behind it don't seem ta have any idea about surrenderin'. They get in little bunches and keep firin' at us. So, we surround 'em and wait till they run outta ammunition. By ten o'clock, the last of 'em give up.

From over Petersburg, we hear explosions; then, so many fires light up the sky it look like sunset all over again.

"They're pullin' out," I tell Solomon. We stand and watch till Lieutenant Califf say we hafta help escort prisoners back ta our lines.

"These the sorriest lookin' white men I ever seen," Solomon say.

And he's right. They're mostly old men and boys. And it look like it's bin a long time since they have a decent meal. So, I pull some hardtack crackers outta ma pack and offer one ta a old man who's havin' trouble walkin'. Damn rebel spit right in ma eye. In a second ma Enfield's up in the air, and I hit 'im upside the head. He fall on the ground, holdin' his bleedin' ear and hollerin', "Y'all see what that goddamn nigger done ta me."

"I show you what this goddamn nigger can do...you piece of white trash." And I kick him hard as I can.

He double up, moanin', and the other rebels start comin' for me. I point ma Enfield at the one on the ground. "Come on. Make me happy ta kill this spittin' white sonofabitch."

Lieutenant Califf put his hand on ma shoulder, say real calm-like, "Corporal Dorsey, lower that weapon and give it to me."

"But, lieutenant, you seen what he done. And I can't let nobody, white or black do that ta me."

"I saw it, but he's a prisoner of war and unarmed. If you shoot him, the colonel will have you in front of firing squad tomorrow morning. Mark my words."

What can I do? If I kill 'im, maybe I feel good for a minute, but I never see Angel again.

Don't take me long ta decide he ain't worth it. I kick 'im again, then give the lieutenant ma Enfield.

For the next couple hours, we round up little batches of rebels and march 'em back ta the collection area. Some of 'em give up without firin' a shot; some of 'em put up a damn good fight. But finally, they ain't none left. It's real quiet--no artillery, no musket fire--for the first time since we got here.

Solomon and me climb up a little rise so we can see the fires burnin' in Petersburg.

"Wha's the time?" he ask.

"Round three o'clock in the mornin'," I say, "Why?"

"Just wonderin' how soon the first troops goin' in."

"You ain't gotta worry. Won't be us."

Half a hour later, I find out how wrong I was.

"Fall in," Lieutenant Califf say, "the last rebels have pulled out of Petersburg. And General Grant wants us and the 8th to be the first Union troops in the city,"

We're so ready for this he don't hafta tell us again. When the order come ta move out, we start off so fast up the Halifax Road lieutenant yell at us ta "Slow down."

Passin' through the last line of works, I get this funny feelin'. All the hair on ma arm, the back of ma neck start standin' up.

Even feel a little chill, thinkin' <u>This's what we bin waitin' for since last summer</u>.

We come on a fork in the road, and they're waitin' for us. Black folks line the road far as we can see. "Bless you, brothers," they say. "Praise Jesus, you come at last." Lots of the women and old folks cryin'. Mommas hold up they young chil'ren and even babies, tellin' 'em we the ones who free 'em from slavery. Purty gals run up and try and kiss us. As soon as we pass, the black folks fall in behind and folla us cross the Boydton Plank Road, and onta Harrison Street.

We halt in front of the city hall where the Confederate flag's still flyin' from the clock tower. A small group from the 1st Michigan ran in the buildin' and tear it down, puttin' up the Union flag in it's place. Time I first see it, I feel ma eyes gettin' wet and a big lump comin' up ma throat. I thank the Lord I live ta see this.

General Ord step forward. "By the grace of God, Petersburg is ours," he say, and the cheerin' start. Solomon and me grab each other and hug and pound our backs and cheer...and do it again and again till we can't do it no more. I feel tired, but I don't think I ever bin happier in ma life.

We bin stretched out on our shelter halfs a while, not really sleepin', just kinda restin' and talkin'. Then, the news come, "Lee and his army slipped out of Richmond and are heading west." Lieutenant Califf so excited he gotta ketch his breath before he go on. "And if they reach the Blue Ridge Mountains and Joe Johnston can join 'em, this war could last ten more years."

"No, it ain't either, lieutenant. We ready ta go after 'em."

And about a hour later, we're marchin' west outta Petersburg on the Cox Road. Late in the afternoon, we reach Sutherland Station and the colonel call a halt. Nobody want ta stop. We all think ten miles ain't very far when you chasin' Lee.

I tell the lieutenant that. But he just say, "The colonel thinks this is a good place to rest and that's what we're going to do." Then he walk away, and I start ta go after 'im ta argue.

Solomon grab ma arm. "What you think you're doin'?"

"Don't make no sense for us ta rest if Lee keep movin'."

"Maybe it don't, but what you think arguin' with the lieutenant get you except arrested?"

I look at Califf's back, then down at Solomon's hand. "They really have us by the balls, don't they?"

"All the time we wearin' these uniforms, brother. But time this war over, things goin' ta be different."

I look him straight in the eye and say, "I hope so. I really hope so."

We spread our shelter halfs and lay down without talkin' any more. I must be real tired cause I feel maself driftin' off right away.

Seem like I just close ma eyes and some fool blow reveille. Still dark, and ma head full of sleep. So, take me a minute or two ta remember, <u>Lee and his rebel army headin' west. We got ta stop 'em</u>. And I ain't sleepy no more.

But, it's a good two hours before the whole division ready ta move. Finally, round four in the mornin', we start headin' west. Least we think we're headin' that way. When daylight come, we find out we ain't on the Cox Road. We're on the Namozine Road, and we hafta keep stoppin' ta let wagon trains of the Quarter Master Corps go by. Seem they got the right-of-way.

Round noon, we've gone only seven miles and we're sure Lee must be in North Carolina by now. And we et so much dust from passin' wagons we got ta stop and get water. Nobody have a chance ta fill his canteen since day before yesteday.

The command, "Fall out for a two-hour rest," come and we all make for a creek just off the road. The cold water feel real good goin' down ma hot and dusty throat.

In no time, me and Solomon got a fire goin' and fryin' up some bacon ta mix with crumbled up hardtack. This's one of them times when even hardtack taste good cause it's bin so long since we et. After we finish it and drink a pot of coffee, we're feelin' ready ta go again.

At the order, "Fall in," we set off at a purty fast pace, and it don't take long ta reach the Cox Road. Then, somethin' funny happen. We turn the wrong way. Everybody know we ain't headin' west cause the sun settin' behind us, but none of the officers do anythin'. In a hour, we're back ta Sutherland Station.

"How come we're back here, sir," I ask the lieutenant.

"Soon as I find out, I'll let you know," he snap.

Later, he tell me we got ta wait for General Willcox's Ist Division cause we run outta rations. I look down at the bacon Solomon fryin' and think maybe we oughta save some for mornin'.

"Too late now," he say.

T'day, April 4th, we hafta wait till four o'clock in the afternoon for General Willcox's division. And they can't give us more'n a day's ration of hardtack, some coffee and a couple cows. With just that little bit, we start movin' again. This time, Colonel Shaw or somebody decide we better off stayin' close ta the South Side Rail Road tracks.

Twenty miles later, we camp at a farm, about five miles short of Nottoway Court House, belongin' ta a family name of Epps. Me and Solomon real hungry, but we only got two hardtack crackers and some dry beef. We think about helpin' ourselfs over at the farm, but orders come down not ta take anythin'. Lieutenant say we get full rations tomarra when we reach Burkeville.

Tomarra start round four o'clock in the mornin' when reveille blow. A little past noon, it start rainin' real hard. "Just what we need," I tell Solomon. "Now we can be wet and hungry."

Round half-past two we reach Burkeville, and the rain stop, leavin' us all smellin' like soaked hound dogs. But for once, the lieutenant was right about somethin'. The supply wagons are waitin' on us.

After me and Solomon draw rations, we cook us a real dinner.

Then, we kinda lay back on the grass lettin' the food settle and we see men runnin' over the road. "What you think's goin' on?" Solomon ask.

"Only one way ta find out," I say and we both folla after the others.

We reach the road in time ta see important rebel prisoners bein' escorted by a cavalry detachment. And I mean important, we spot General Ewell and General Custis Lee, a nephew of Robert E. Lee hisself. Surprise me the rebels don't look that unhappy. Maybe they kinda glad the war almost over too.

Half-past four in the mornin' and we're on the march again. This time General Ord ain't takin' no chances, the division stay close ta the railroad tracks. Round ten, we stop for a short rest and who you think we see ridin' east and not lookin' too happy? Our old commander, General Birney. He's on his way ta Fort Powhatan. He give a little wave with his hand, but he don't say nothin' ta nobody. I kinda feel sorry for him, but I still glad he ain't commander no more.

We reach Farmville about four o'clock, but we don't stop. Just west of the town, we start hearin' heavy firin'. We try and pick up the pace, so for a time, seem like the firin' and the Blue Ridge Mountains gettin' closer every step we take. But we can't keep it up, so nobody's really sorry when the order come down ta halt and make camp. Twenty-five miles about the most we can do in a day. Anyway, time we get our fires goin' the shootin' stop.

Me and Solomon don't bother fryin' no bacon. Just boil some water for coffee and soak the hardtack in it. Then, we roll ourselfs up in shelter halfs and go ta sleep.

Half-past four the next mornin', we're on the march again. "What day you think this is?" Solomon ask.

"Prolly Sataday the 8th."

"We bin chasin' after Lee almost five days now, ain't we?"

"Yeh, but from the look of the smokin' wagons and cartridge boxes we keep passin', I'd say we're gettin' real close."

We go on about a mile and Solomon suddenly ask me, "What're you goin' ta do when this war's over?"

"Go back home and marry Angel."

"No, I mean what kinda work you goin' ta do?"

I don't answer right away cause I ain't really thought about it. Finally, I say, "Farmin' I guess--only job I know how ta do."

"Where you gettin' the land?"

"I figger they give us some same as they talkin' about givin' black folks in the South."

He look me in the eye. "Suppose they don't. Then, what're you goin' ta do?"

I shake ma head. "I don't know. I really don't know." And I don't say nothin' the rest of the afternoon. Even after we make camp a couple miles east of Appomattox Court House, I still ain't figgered anythin' out.

Headquarters, Army of Northern Virginia
April 9th, 1865

U.S. Grant,
Lieutenant General U.S. Army

General:

I received your note this morning on the picket line, whither I had come to meet you and ascertain definitely what terms were embraced in your proposition of yesterday with reference to the surrender of this army. I now request an interview in accordance with the offer contained in your letter of yesterday for that purpose.

Very respectfully,
Your obt. servant
R.E. Lee

Sunday mornin' we reach Appomattox Court House round noon. Ain't much ta see: couple big houses, a store and the court house. Farms so close in I can't tell where the village end and they begin. Goin' past other regiments, we hear a lot of talk about how the rebels are camped on the other side of town, and how they're waitin' ta surrender.

"Solomon, sounds like we might be seein' the end of the war t'day."

Headquarters, Armies of the U.S.
April 9th, 1865

General R. E. Lee,
Commander, Army of Northern Virginia

General:

In accordance with the substance of my letter to you of the 8th instant, I propose to receive the surrender of the Army of Northern Virginia on the following terms, to wit: Rolls of all the officers and men to be made in duplicate. The officers to give their individual paroles not to take up arms against the Government of the United States until properly exchanged, and each company or regimental commander to sign a like parole for the men of their commands. The arms, artillery, and public property to be parked, and stacked, and turned over to the officers appointed by me to receive them. This done, each officer and man will be allowed to return to his home, not to be disturbed by the U.S. authorities so long as they observe their paroles, and the laws in force where they may reside.

Very respectfully,
U.S. Grant, Lieut. General

In the afternoon, we line up on both sides of the road leadin' outta the village. From where I'm standin', I can see a big brick farmhouse with a white front porch. Lieutenant Califf say the house belong ta Mr. Wilmer McLean who ustta live outside Manassas where the Union army lost so bad back in the first big battle of the war.

"Then, I guess it's fittin' the war end in his house."

"I think so too, Elijah."

We wait and wait. Finally, round half-past three, a big buzz go down both sides of the road, "General Lee's come in from the west side of town." I stare hard as I can, and I just make out two men wearin' gray standin' on the porch. I guess the one with the gray hair's Lee. They go on in the house.

Just before four o'clock, a cheer start up. I bin squattin' on ma heels cause I'm so tired of standin'. I straighten up in time ta see a bunch of officers comin' in from the east. Solomon say the short, thin one General Sheridan. I recanize General Grant from the review last month. T'day he past by so close I can see his rumpled uniform, the black circles under his eyes and the stump of a cigar stickin' outta his mouth.

Grant hold up his hand, and the cheerin' stop. Him and Sheridan ride up ta the house, dismount and go inside.

Maybe a half hour later, the word come down the line ta us what ain't close enough ta see that General Lee come back out on the porch. Then we hear, "He's pullin' on his gauntlets. He's walkin' down the steps. He's takin' the reins from a sergeant. He's up in the saddle."

Now, they say General Grant and a group of our officers come outta the house. And General Grant start ta walk down the steps, but seein' Lee on his horse, Grant stop and salute 'im. Then, Lee do the same ta Grant. I can't see Lee ride off and turn west on the road, but them who can say he just ride past lookin' straight ahead so they can't tell what happen inside the McLean house.

Up and down both sides of the road, the same questions bein' asked over and over: "What happen?" "The war over or not?"

"General Sheridan just come out on the porch," somebody say. We all hush up and he hold up a piece of paper. Surprisin' such a small man got so big a voice. When he say, "General Grant wants the following telegram sent to the Secretary of War," I have no trouble hearin'. And when he read the telegram, he sound like he standin' right in front of me.

"Headquarters, Appomattox Court House, Va.
April 9th, 1865, 4:30 p.m.

Hon. E. M. Stanton, Secretary of War
Washington City.

GENERAL LEE SURRENDERED THE ARMY OF NORTHERN VIRGINIA THIS AFTERNOON ON TERMS PROPOSED BY MYSELF (STOP) THE ACCOMPANYING ADDITIONAL CORRESPONDENCE WILL SHOW THE CONDITIONS FULLY (STOP)

U. S. Grant,
Lieutenant General"

There's a long pause. Sheridan put down the piece of paper and look at us. Then, cannons in the fields behind us start firin'. I throw back ma head and yell, "Hal-le-lu-jah, the war's over," and throw ma kepi in the air. Solomon drop down on his knees and keep sayin', "Thank you, Jesus," till I pull him up on his feet. Then, we grab each other and dance round in a circle, hollerin', "We're free, we're free. Praise Jesus, we're free."

Everybody's out in the road now. Black and white soldiers throwin' kepies up in the air, cheerin' General Grant and President Lincoln and anybody else they can think of, poundin' each others' backs and dancin' round like me and Solomon doin', firin' Enfields and Springfields up in the air. I don't think they're any happier men in the world than us.

All of a sudden, the artillery stop firin'. The road's full of lieutenants, captains and colonels wavin' they arms in the air. The dancin' and firin' and cheerin' stop. We get in line and wait till it's quiet enough ta hear Colonel Shaw. "General Grant thinks this demonstration has gone on long enough. He says we should not exult too much at the Confederates' defeat. He wants all units not on guard duty here to go back to their camps."

"Damn," Solomon say so only I hear. "We waited a long time for t'day. Why we can't celebrate some more? We earned it."

"With our blood," I say, "with our blood."

But the officers don't pay us no mind. They get us in formation and head us back ta camp.

On the way, I'm still mad, and I keep mutterin' ta maself, "Damnit, we earned the right. We earned it with our blood." And I think about desertin' and goin' back ta Angel--t'night.

Then comin' round a bend, I look up in the sky. I don't believe what I see. Comin' right at me, outta the north--a hawk.

I grab Solomon's arm. "Lookit that," and I point ta the bird.

"So what," he say. "Ain't you never seen a hawk before?"

"That ain't just any hawk; tha's my hawk. The one that come ta me back at Belmont and tell me ta run away so I can be free."

"You're crazy."

"No I ain't. Watch."

The hawk act like it see me cause it hover in the air right over ma head for a couple minutes, then make three big circles, and fly off the way it came--straight north.

Solomon shake his head. "I never seen nothin' like that before."

I just smile. "You know, brother; it don't matter if we celebrate a long time or a short time. The war's over, and us and black folks everywhere are free. Tha's what's really important.

"Lijah, you never bin more right in your life."

Down the road a piece, I look up at the sky. And I say a little prayer ta Jesus that the days ahead be good ones for us.

"Now, I just want ta go home and be with ma Angel."

THE END

EPILOGUE

ELIJAH DORSEY

It took Elijah Dorsey a lot longer to get home to his Angel than he thought. First, the 7th had to spend a few days in camp outside Appomattox Court House guarding relief supplies distributed to the defeated Confederates. Then, the regiment was ordered to Richmond to guard supplies. On April 15th, he and the others heard the news of President Lincoln's assassination on reaching Sutherland Station. They formed and stood bare-headed in a heavy rain while Chaplain Gregg said a prayer for the dead President. When the march resumed, many cried openly, struggling with grief and forebodings about the future.

On May 24th, the regiment boarded steamers for the long journey to Indianola, Texas. The 7th patrolled the border with Mexico until October 1866 when it returned to Baltimore.

Elijah Dorsey was promoted to sergeant while in Texas and was discharged from the army on November 15, 1866. He and Angel were married soon afterward. The following spring, they bought 60 acres near a new African-American community in Howard County, Maryland, called Freetown, and built a house. Momma Dorsey came to live with them and to help them farm the land. In October 1890, Elijah suffered a severe stroke and died the following spring. Angel filed for, and was awarded, a war widow's pension. She died in August 1915.

After Angel's death, her eldest son, Elijah, gave the farm to his brother, Solomon, and moved to Baltimore, where he worked at various jobs until he died in 1922. Solomon maintained the family farm, passing it on to his son who bequeath it to his son. In 1967, the farm was sold to a group of investors and became part of the new town of Columbia, Maryland.

LIEUTENANT COLONEL AUGUSTUS T. ALEXANDER

The Reverend Henry M. Turner married Lieutenant Colonel (LTC) Augustus T. Alexander and Miss Sallie King at Israel Bethel Church early in May of 1865. Less than a week later, Colonel Alexander was on his way to Beaufort, South Carolina, where he awaited orders until late June. From July until November 1866, he was stationed in Savannah, Georgia, first at the Camp for Freedmen at Ogechee, Georgia, then at the

Lincoln Refugees and Freedmen's General Hospital. In September of 1866, he was appointed superintendent of the Lincoln hospital, a post which he held until mustered out of the army on November 13th of that year. He returned to the hospital a week later as a contract surgeon in the Freedmen's Bureau and was re-appointed superintendent shortly thereafter.

At the end of March 1867, Dr. Alexander resigned from the Bureau and returned to Washington, D.C. He established a practice there and later served on the faculty of the Howard University School of Medicine. Dr. Alexander also established a free clinic which treated any poor person, regardless of race.

Miss Sallie, as she was always known, taught Sunday School at Israel Bethel Church for many years. She was also an instructor at the Miner Normal School, where she helped prepare a generation of African-Americans to teach in the District of Columbia's public schools.

When Lieutenant Califf wrote the Record of the Service of the Seventh Regiment U.S. Colored Troops from September 1863 to November 1866, he sent a complimentary copy to all but one of the regiment's officers. Therefore, Dr. Alexander never knew how openly Califf sided with Lieutenants Morgan and Grange in their conflict with him at Camp Stanton.

Dr. Alexander died of penumonia on January 3, 1891. Miss Sallie's widow's pension was denied in 1895 by the War Department due to a clerical error. She re-applied, but suffered a fatal heart attack before the process was completed. In 1905, her claim was stamped "Abandoned" and the filed closed.

The Alexanders had five children. Their two sons, Daniel Augustus and Henry Jerome, received medical degrees from Howard University in 1894 and 1898, respectively. Daniel joined his father in practice that same year and continued the free clinic until he went to France with the American Expeditionary Force in July 1917. After the war, he settled in Harlem and practiced medicine until his death in an automobile accident in 1926. Henry Jerome went to the Philippines at the end of the Spanish-American War. At his brother's urging, he returned to Washington, D.C., and joined him in the family practice.

Henry continued the practice until he retired in 1946. Sallie Ann and Elizabeth, the eldest daughters became teachers like their mother. Both taught in the District of Columbia public schools until the late 1930s. Their sister, Rachel, married Henry M. Turner, Jr., in June 1905 and moved to Philadelphia where he was pastor of the Zion AME church. She died of influenza in December 1919 after giving birth to their third child.

FLETCHER HOWARD

Fletcher Howard's body was recovered from the creek near New Bern, North Carolina, and was buried at the National Cemetery outside Wilmington, North Carolina. Rebeccah Howard finally received his Medal of Honor in a brief ceremony when the 39th was mustered out at Birney Barracks in November 1866. She remarked afterward that she was proud of her late husband and pleased that the government had honored him. "But," she said, "no medal can ever make up for my loss." As a war widow, she received a small pension from the government which she supplemented with work as an oyster shucker and house maid. In spite of her meager resources, she managed to educate her daughter Rachel and send her to the Coppin Normal School to become a teacher in the Baltimore public schools. Rachel's granddaughter was one of the first African-American woman to be admitted to the University of Maryland School of Nursing. In 1963, one of Rachel's great-grandsons was the first African-American to be elected president of a senior class at Baltimore Polytechnic Institute.

AFTERWORD

Of the three main characters in the novel, only LTC Augustus T. Alexander is based on a real person. Lieutenant-Colonel Alexander T. Augusta was the chief surgeon of the 7th USCT and also the highest ranking African-American officer during the Civil War. The only significant departures from the known facts of his life in the body of the novel were that I transferred him to the army depot field hospital at City Point, Virginia, and married him to a young woman from Washington,

D.C. And, although Dr. Augusta did practice medicine in Washington for 29 years, he did not have any children.

With the exception of his actions at the Battle of the Crater, described in chapter 13, Fletcher Howard is a completely fictitious character. Sergeant Decatur Dorsey was the real African-American soldier who planted the 39th's regimental colors on the Confederate works and later rallied scattered remnants of that regiment. For his bravery, he was awarded a Congressional Medal of Honor on November 8, 1865.

Elijah Dorsey's military experiences are based largely on the events Lieutenant John Mark Califf described in his history entitled Record of the Seventh Regiment U.S. Colored Troops from September 1863 to November 1866, published in 1878. Elijah's personal life in the novel is entirely fictitious.

Generals George Meade, Ambrose Burnside, Edward Ferrero, James H. Ledlie and Colonel Henry Pleasants and Sergeant Harry Reese were actively involved in either the Mine Explosion or the Battle at the Crater. Their testimony in chapter 14, although not word-for-word, is accurate and based on material in Record of the Court of Inquiry on the Mine Explosion, the proceedings of the army's official investigation.

Colonel, later General, William Birney and Colonel James Shaw were the actual commanders of the 7th USCT. Colonel Ozora Stearns was the 39th's commander for its entire time of service. With only a few exceptions, the names of junior officers of both regiments are fictitious.

Finally, I want to mention a few of the sources I used for the information contained in this novel. In addition to the ones mentioned above, I also consulted the War of the Rebellion--Official Records, Series I, Dyer's Compendium of the War of the Rebellion, and the service records of Lieutenant-Colonel Alexander T. Augusta and Sergeant Decatur Dorsey. Other sources included, but were not limited to: Freedom: Series II, the Black Military Experience, edited by Ira Berlin, A Stillness at Appomattox by Bruce Catton, The Last Citadel by Noah Andre Trudeau, and Confederate Goliath: The Battle of Fort Fisher by Ron Gragg.

Soldiers of Company E, 4th USCT (courtesy of the Massachusetts Commandery Order of the Loyal Legion and the US Army Military History Institute).

Soldiers of the 107th USCT (courtesy of the Massachusetts Commandery Military Order of the Loyal Legion and the US Army Military History Institute).

BOOKS OF MILITARY INTEREST

ACE!--Autobiography of a Fighter Pilot in World War II by Melvin Paisley is the extensive autobiography of one of the great aerial fighters of the big war. Cloth, ill., ISBN 0-8283-1943-X, $22.95.

THE DANCE OF THE TWELVE APOSTLES by P. J. Carisella deals with the most daring plan on the part of Hitler to annihilate Rome with its Vatican. Cloth, ill., ISBN 0-8283-1935-9, $17.95.

FIGHTING MEN--A Chronicle of Three Black Civil War Soldiers by John Zubritsky tells the story of three soldiers who, from disparate backgrounds, come together in that war. Cloth, ill., ISBN 0-8283-1963-4, $21.95.

FIRST FLIGHT by John Williams Andrews is a narrative rendition of the world's first flight by Orville and Wilbur Wright. Cloth, limited edition numbered and signed, ISBN 0-8283-1228-1, $25.95.

THE FORTIES--When We Were Dreamers of Dreams by Ray Barron is the autobiographical odyssey of Ray's war days--full of nostalgia about London, Paris and Boston. Cloth, ill., ISBN 0-8283-1915-4, $19.95.

FROGMEN--First Battles by William Schofield and P. J. Carisella recounts the historical facts of a group of frogmen who, singly or in teams of two, captured the Mediterranean from the Allies. Cloth, ill., ISBN 0-8283-1998-7, $19.95.

MATTER OF SURVIVAL--The 'War' Jane Never Saw by Chris Noel develops the contrast between Jane Fonda and Chris Noel and their roles in Vietnam. Cloth, ill., ISBN 0-8283-1903-0, $19.95.

ODE TO AMERICA'S INDEPENDENCE by Vittorio Alfieri recounts the fight of the colonists against the British. Paper, ISBN 0-8283-1667-8, $11.95.

THE SAVING RAIN by Elsie Weber tells how the Khmer Rouge heartlessly destroyed the lives of millions while the world stood still. Paper, ill., ISBN 0-8283-1911-1, $17.95.

TO AMERICA AND AROUND THE WORLD edited with and introduction by Adolph Caso contains the logs of Christopher Columbus and of Antonio Pigafetta first to America and then around the world. Cloth, ill., ISBN 0-8283-1992-8, $25.95.

THE TUSKEGEE AIRMEN--The Men Who Changed A Nation by Charles Francis recounts the history of those who fought in the great war and brought about the integration of our armed forces. Cloth, ill., ISBN 0-8283-1955-3, $24.95.

YOUNG ROCKY--Biography of Rocky Castellani by Kinney-Caso tells the story of a Marine in the battles of Iwo Jima and Guam, his boxing tour to China, and then his memorable battles in the ring of Madison Square Garden. Paper, ill., ISBN 0-8283-1802-2, $11.95.